The Opera Fanatic

Anna Blajoc

THE

OPERA

FANATIC

Ethnography of an Obsession

CLAUDIO E. BENZECRY

The University of Chicago Press   Chicago and London

CLAUDIO E. BENZECRY is assistant professor of
sociology at the University of Connecticut.

The University of Chicago Press, Chicago 60637
The University of Chicago Press, Ltd., London
© 2011 by The University of Chicago
All rights reserved. Published 2011
Printed in the United States of America

20 19 18 17   16 15 14 13 12 11   1 2 3 4 5

ISBN-13: 978-0-226-04340-1 (cloth)
ISBN-13: 978-0-226-04342-5 (paper)
ISBN-10: 0-226-04340-1 (cloth)
ISBN-10: 0-226-04342-8 (paper)

Library of Congress Cataloging-in-Publication Data
Benzecry, Claudio E.
The opera fanatic : ethnography of an
obsession / Claudio E. Benzecry.
p. cm.
Includes bibliographical references and index.
ISBN-13: 978-0-226-04340-1 (cloth : alk. paper)
ISBN-10: 0-226-04340-1 (cloth : alk. paper)
ISBN-13: 978-0-226-04342-5 (pbk. : alk. paper)
ISBN-10: 0-226-04342-8 (pbk. : alk. paper)
1. Opera. 2. Opera audiences. 3. Music fans. I. Title.
ML1700.B326 2011
306.4'848—dc22
2010034632

♾ The paper used in this publication meets the minimum
requirements of the American National Standard for Information
Sciences—Permanence of Paper for Printed Library Materials,
ANSI Z39.48-1992.

For Monique, who feels the music like no one else

CONTENTS

ILLUSTRATIONS

PREFACE

I was traveling in 2002 with a group of opera enthusiasts to La Plata—the capital of Buenos Aires State—to see a new production of *La bohème*. We were all going on a bus provided by the provincial government in its efforts to reacquaint people with the Argentino Opera House, which had recently been reinaugurated after a twenty-five-year hiatus (a monstrous fire consumed the previous incarnation in 1977). The new building is a modernist cement construction, really uninviting and, more important, with capacity for 2,200 people, too large for a city full of university students that at best has 100,000 inhabitants. Because of this, and because of the importance of the Colón Opera House in Buenos Aires, the buses picked you up for free at the parking lot of that "rival" opera house downtown. It was a way to get people used to the forty-five-mile trip to the Argentino Opera House, not to mention a way of competing with the older house on many other levels. The government of the city, which administered the Colón, was part of the alliance between the traditional Radical Party and left-of-center forces; the Argentino Opera was administered by the Peronist party, then in opposition. Confrontations between the artistic directors of the two houses were even more virulent since one wanted to replace the other (at the Colón) and one decided to stage operas with charged political meanings, as his rival had been doing for some time. The competition was personal, political, and also geographic (rich city vs. poor province), but the terrain was artistic, and the booty was prestige and audience.

The people on the bus—which, despite the aim of the trip, had a radio playing *cumbia*[1] for most of the way—were mostly middle-class "opera people" who took advantage of every available opportunity to attend live opera. Between one and three hundred people travel regularly by this kind of bus to La Plata[2]—some others make the trip by regular bus lines or carpools—to attend performances at the Argentino. During that trip, a woman asked immediately who I was. "We all know each other, and I haven't seen you. Are you an opera person?" When I admitted that my trip had a sociological purpose, she replied, "You are doing the smartest thing by coming here. This is where you learn everything you need to learn about opera. You came to the right place. You should also go to the lines to buy cheap tickets and to the standing room of the house; that's where you'll get schooled. The people who attend there really love opera and know all about it. They will talk to you, tell you the difference between a coloratura and a dramatic soprano, and you will slowly start to learn." I took note of her advice but remained focused on the most obvious traits of the Argentinean opera world that had emerged at the beginning of my trip—the public and subsidized character of its funding, the political character of its organization, and the middle-class character of its consumption, which also included elements of the lower class—as I was trying to combine them into what I thought would be a case against *Distinction*.

For years, ideas from that seminal book by Pierre Bourdieu had haunted my understanding of cultural practices, and, whenever someone would talk to me about the things they enjoyed, I would try to reduce them to a place—albeit highly microdifferentiated—in the social structure. Trips like this one provided a chance to elaborate on these ideas by asking people about their personal trajectory, their education, and their personal history. I was also interested in developing an instrument that would help me classify taste and attach it to positions in a social space. I was hoping that most of these people would like other high-culture practices, as the American literature on arts consumption presumed.

I was not sociologically prepared to manage what I started to learn on that trip and soon after, whenever I entered into conversation with opera people. I was surprised by the intensity of their engagement. I was mesmerized when, on the way back from La Plata, a woman my age told me that she had probably seen *Bohème* some fifteen times, and heard it many more, but could not stop crying at the end, when Mimi dies, even though she knew what was coming. She had actually coined a name for this experience—*the Bohème effect*.

On that trip, I started seriously considering other questions: What kinds of emotion can be produced by art? What exactly does music do to people?

Philosophers like Plato had pointed to the civilizing characteristics of certain kinds of music; Theodor Adorno had tried to achieve a better understanding—through homologies between social structure, forms of consciousness, and music structure—of the ways music mediates social relationships. For me, up to that point, all this had been, paradoxically, just noise.

Soon after, I discovered that the opera house is a place where people feel compelled to talk with strangers about what they have just heard (I explicitly exclude *seen* here) and compare it to previous experiences with the same work, seemingly adding to their never-ending conversation about a particular opera. These spontaneous conversations would not happen at just any point; they would always be after very specific fragments of music, ones that were well-known and eagerly anticipated. This preparation would not stop the enjoyment; rather, it would increase it. Names of arias and references to music fragments spilled out every time an opera fan opened his or her mouth. Much as the mouth starts to salivate right before a candy is tasted, the aural experience seems to prepare the body for a whole series of reactions, reactions that are mediated through discourse as much as through embodiment. All this led me to consider how a particular work of art could be a locus for personal and emotional engagement, a place for investment that resulted in an accumulative series of effects that could be picked up through conversation but were best understood through observation.

Contra the sociological literature that made artworks equal to their condition of production, with every aesthetic choice a search for distinction, I felt that there was something more to it: the belief that only through the love of opera—the sung drama—can emotions be expressed, the belief that sometimes spoken words are not enough. Or as one of my interviewees told me: "Opera is really visceral. You have to think of it like this: Men don't sing, but when emotion taints the spoken word you immediately start singing. It's like if I told you your mother just died. You start: *No, No, Nooooooo* [high pitched and sustained]. You are already singing. It's like Brünnhilde screaming." It was at this point that my research came to a stop for a while; I could not make sense of it with the sociological tool kit I then carried. There were some things I could learn about class, status, and politics—and many others that did not sound sociological at all. I was still trying to transcend some of the mesmerizing experiences I had witnessed (people mimicking the soprano at a Verdi recital, some others on their knees for hours with their hands pressed against a handrail while listening to Wagner, people crying not only when listening to an aria but again when talking to me about why they like opera, people who smiled and gained poise when recalling the first opera they ever heard) and things I had been told (stories of personal and family sacrifices made just to attend a performance, the conviction that a child died because she had the name of the main character of a "jinxed" opera). I sought a way to link individual stories to a more collective level of analysis and to some of the questions I thought were easier (or more sociological?) to answer. I was also trying to figure out how to frame opera as high culture, how to do justice to the discursive prowess of the interviewees, with their detail-oriented and highly esoteric knowledge, while including my observations of all those bodies running around to get a better view of the stage, or standing for hours on a summer afternoon, or crying after the end of an aria. I was working hard to link the distinction literature—and its emphasis on class, status, and morality—with a more personalized, microunderstanding of practices that would emphasize the many techniques of engagement and the lash-up of the social and the personal until the individual got dissolved into a "sociotechnical disposition of passion." I was also trying to solve some puzzles that were specific to Argentina. For example, what is the relation between high culture and the enjoyment it offers in a country where an art form was popularized early on? How did people from the middle class relate to high culture in an extended period of social, economic, and political decay? I was interested in illuminating the limits of dominant sociological models, explaining the relation between art, status, and class in peripheral countries. It was then that I saw Alain Resnais's film *On connaît la chanson* (Same old song). The last song in it was Claude François's "Chanson populaire":

> It comes and goes.
> It's made out of nothing,
> You dance to it and sing to it and come back to it,
> You remember it like a popular song.
> Love is like a chorus.
> It escapes between your fingers,
> You dance to it and sing to it and come back to it,
> You remember it like a popular song.

While at first glance the song presents a theory of emotion (as exemplified by love) and music and the mnemonic quality that produces the link from one to the other, there was something more to it that helped relieve some of my sociological worries. This presentation of French chanson brought me closer to something that the British literary critic Richard Hoggart (1957) had discussed when talking about the popular culture of England in the early postwar years: finding "a home for meaning." On the one hand, it approached one of the most central and melodramatic ideas of opera: the belief that, when words are not enough to name your suffering, the *dramma per musica* takes the slug. On the other, it established the frame of reference or tradition through which people can elaborate some of their personal conundrums. Resnais's work utilizes chanson as a possible means of expression, if not resolution, for some of the characters' personal issues. Whenever a problem rears up, music suddenly comes out of the main character's mouth. What we hear in the movie are the "precise" fragments—for those who "know" and want to express their personal issues—of an anthology of well-known popular songs. Édith Piaf, Charles Aznavour, Johnny Hallyday, Serge Gains-bourg, Jane Birkin, Gilbert Bécaud, Josephine Baker, and Eddy Mitchell are called on to be the protective mantra that helps express publicly what the characters suffer in private.

Understanding how people attach themselves to opera—an extremely for-mally complex cultural product, historically considered a signifier for class, nation, and status—and make it their own private song is the emotional, biographical, cognitive, and music lesson gleaned from the many opera trips I took during the last four years. I unravel the results of this journey in the pages that follow. I hope that by the last one, I can emerge as victorious as the character at the end of the movie and wonder out loud: "Is there anybody who knows this song?"

ACKNOWLEDGMENTS

Dorothy Parker used to say that she hated to write but she loved to have written. I would like to make her words mine and forget, at least for these few pages, the intense anxiety that I felt before writing every section of this book. During this process, friends, colleagues, and family made my life easier.

Fist and foremost I would like to thank Craig Calhoun. I have only words of gratitude for him. His intellectual rigor, combined with a rich sociological imagination and a profound knowledge of social theory, improved this book—I hope—and made my work in general better, even if just by osmosis! Tom Ertman has been a champion of my work and a tireless companion in conversations regarding opera, Argentinean movies, and Max Weber. He generously opened the doors of his home, introduced me to his family, and guided me through the many transitions of the American academic life. Eric Klinenberg pushed me to focus on my work, to think what is interesting about it, and to finish—articles, comps, the dissertation, the book!

I was also blessed to receive guidance and encouragement from two real Renaissance men who have served as role models in academic activities and in life: Juan Corradi and Richard Sennett. Many thanks to Neil Brenner, Harvey Molotch, Doug Guthrie, Florencia Torche, and Ruth Horowitz at NYU and Patricia Clough, Michael Blim, Mitch Duneier, and the late Bob Alford at the CUNY Grad Center for the generosity of their warmth, intellectual stimulation, and magnificent analytical skills.

Javier Auyero is in a league of his own. Since the beginning of my life in New York he has taken on the role of big brother and, with his *compañera*

Gabi Polit, made every effort, intellectually and otherwise, to make me feel at home. *Gracias, O'sheer!*

I wrote the final version of the manuscript at the University of Connecticut, where colleagues in the Department of Sociology offered fresh perspectives that allowed me to see beyond the frames I had initially employed. My deepest gratitude goes to Gaye Tuchman and Andrew Deener, who have read the book in many of its incarnations. Andrew has become an academic collaborator and friend; sometimes I have a hard time knowing which of us first suggested or came up with an idea. I'd also like to thank Davita Glasberg, Bandana Purkayastha, Maya Beasley, and Clint Sanders for the many intellectual exchanges as well as the collegial atmosphere that has allowed me to focus on finishing the book. The university provided support for the book by giving me a Junior Faculty Small Grant to finish the revisions.

I presented parts of this research in many venues and have benefited from the feedback of colleagues outside my immediate surroundings. Thanks to Tia DeNora, Howie Becker, Paul DiMaggio, Vera Zolberg, Randall Collins, Marco Santoro, Lisa McCormick, Rene Almeling, Ryan Centner, Shamus Khan, Colin Jerolmack, Tom Kemple, Nancy Hanrahan, Sunwoong Park, Andy Lakoff, David Halle, Diane Barthel, and Rob Jansen.

For the last several years I have been part of the weekly workshop at the Yale Center for Cultural Sociology. Many thanks to Ron Eyerman for inviting me, to Jeff Alexander for commenting on parts of this project, to Isaac Reed for inviting me to the JTS and putting me in touch with the group, and to the colloquium participants for keeping my intellectual muscles working.

Phil Smith has gone beyond his duties as reviewer of the book, providing advice, criticism, and encouragement at every step of the way, challenging me when necessary, pushing me to think things through and to own my sociological voice. I've been very lucky to have Victoria Johnson as the other reviewer. Her work on historical sociology, opera, and organizations has been a source of inspiration, and her detailed comments and generosity with writing advice have gone far beyond her professional obligations. Thanks.

It has been a pleasure to work with the University of Chicago Press. Doug Mitchell has matched the myth that preceded him. He has pushed the project forward, found the best possible reviewers for it, and made of it an intellectual adventure. Thanks to Ruth Goring, Tim McGovern, Rob Hunt, and Joe Brown for taking care of the book in the various stages of publication.

Moving to New York meant the choice of an active intellectual life, cultivated not only at school but in bars, movie theaters, restaurants, bookstores, art galleries, concert halls, opera houses, clubs, and public squares. I've never had a doubt of its worth, regardless of the many things one loses by leaving home (even the definition of home). I shared a few of my favorite things with a group of people I've learned to call my friends, regardless of where we all are now. To all of them my deepest gratitude: Juan Vaggione, Mariano Siskind, Mark Healey, Analía Ivanier, Laura Fantone, Santiago Deymonnaz, Fermín Rodríguez, Ernesto Semán, Javier Uriarte, Grace Mitchell, Marion Wrenn, Jon Wynn, and Erin O'connor. Cecilia Palmeiro, Cesar Boggiano, Nerea Pozos Huerta, Daniel Fridman, Marcelo Guidoli and the MANY, Christian Gerzso, Sebastian Bania, and Gabi Abend have all taught me over the past few years that the reserve of warm, smart, inventive Spanish-speaking friends in New York is never-ending.

At NYU I had the honor and pleasure of being surrounded by a group of smart, accomplished academics and intellectuals: Noah McClain, Michael McQuarrie, Monika Krause, Dorith Geva, Owen Whooley, Alton Phillips, and Aaron Passell. I want to add to this list three remarkably generous people who put up with my work in a very special way, editing a manuscript that was written at first in broken sentences: Melissa Aronczyk, Jane Jones, and Ashley Mears. Marion Wren and Christian Gerzso also went out of their way to make the manuscript look as good as possible. When friends were not enough, Rebecca Winzenried edited it with professional zeal. With her editorial skills and musical knowledge, Rebecca was a big help in getting it into top shape for publication. The usual disclaimers apply.

In Buenos Aires I must thank Lucas Rubinich, who mentored me in the doing of cultural research; Gastón Burucúa, who convinced me of the worth of doing a project about music; and the late Eduardo Archetti, whose work is a source of inspiration. I also want to mention the intellectual camaraderie of the workshop and journal I've been a part of for the last fifteen years, regardless of my geographical location. My understanding that doing research is a craft and that intellectual dialogue is always a stimulant even when the exchanges are heated comes from this group, which always has time for lunch together after engaging in discussing someone's project for three hours. *Grande*, CECYP! Many thanks especially to Daniela Soldano, Pablo Semán, Paula Miguel, and Pablo Palomino.

During all these years a few people have kept track of me regardless of the distance, through e-mails, chats, and phone cards: Daniel Sazbón, Eugenio Medina, Sebastián Arismendi, Sebastián Corti, and Alejandro Costabile. Thanks to them all.

This book would have never been completed without the help of a group of opera scholars, critics, enthusiasts, and producers in Argentina. Thanks to Néstor Echevarria, Boris Laurenz, Gustavo Otero, Victor Hugo Morales, Patricia Casañas, María Jaunarena, Daniel Suárez Marzal, Eduardo Cogorno,

Julio Raggio, José Luis Sáenz, Claudio Rattier, Andrés Tolcachir, Eduardo Casullo, Héctor Coda, and Daniel Varacalli Costa.

There would never have been an impetus for this research without my parents. My dad, Mario, has been an avid reader for as long as I can remember; my mom, Titina, was the first musical passionate I've ever met. I've tried to combine these paths in my life and work. *Gracias* to them and to my brother, Esteban, for being such a supportive family. Thanks are also in order to my aunt Susana, who is always waiting patiently for my news from abroad.

This book is dedicated to Monique Rivera. The last six years have been an absolute delight, and I would have never finished this text without the joy she has brought to my life. To many more pages, shoes, trips, and beats together.

INTRODUCTION

Da Capo with Opera, Sociology, and Ethnography

In the second half of the twentieth century, an axiom began to travel through music and intellectual circles around the world: opera is in crisis. The cries ranged from extreme positions—such as the contemporary composer and conductor Pierre Boulez's remark "We must blow up all opera houses!"—to more moderate ones. On the one hand, the *dramma per musica* had lost its ability to gather elites at the opera house for social interplay and mutual recognition. On the other, forms of opera reproduction—CDs, television, videos, movies—had gained preeminence over production. These factors combined with the tendencies of contemporary music toward structural autonomy—as described by the German philosopher and sociologist Theodor W. Adorno in *Quasi una Fantasia* (1963/1992) and *Philosophy of Modern Music* (1949)— and with omnipresent competition from the culture industry, which can offer multimedia heirs apparent to the "total work of art."[1] All these elements combined leave us trapped within a peculiar effect.

Let us imagine that the film industry stops producing new films, that our screens no longer feature sugary romantic fables from Elizabethan times, pretentious epic dramas about the life of the average U.S. soldier, or ironic police movies in which the main character exchanges gratuitous acts of violence with his costars. Let us imagine that this week we have, not four or five releases with different casts and directors, but only scene-by-scene remakes of movies made, not five, but thirty or forty years ago or even during the earliest days of film. Opera is in this situation today. The repertoire has stopped growing; it has become an unfashionable art. The aforementioned causes and their consequences should have put an end to a medium that lost its taste for novelty after the first decades of the twentieth century and then abandoned the agenda of formal reformation. The problems and shortcomings of opera become even more poignant if we look at them through a sociological lens.[2] If we followed the sociological dictum, opera should have disappeared by now as it stopped being the stage for elaborated social drama, the meeting point for the conformation of the local bourgeoisie, or the popular culture of the time.[3]

Eppur si muove. Despite the death certificate neatly signed by critics, intellectuals, sociologists, and vanguards, audiences keep filling galleries and standing rooms; they keep ecstatically contemplating the white deaths that afflict Violetta and Mimi; listen with naïveté and horror to Iago's "Credo"; accept fat old women portraying fragile and helpless creatures. We all know that filmmaking has adopted some of the innovations, narratives, and formats of the verismo movement of opera or the Wagnerian tetralogy.[4] Film has established itself as an art and entertainment form while employing the naturalistic formulas of realism in opera, its taste for everyday drama, for dignifying the quotidian life, its sugarcoated passions, and its contained excesses. The film world understands the corporeal and institutional mechanisms that guarantee the silent, nonparticipant (see Sennett 1977; Levine 1988; Johnson 1995; and Ahlquist 1997) enjoyment of the audience, the divided seating arrangements, the naturalism of the actors, and the obscuration of the music source. We also know that cinematic realism has conspired against the traditional modes under which opera has been represented, undermining the suspension of disbelief that was the foundation of audience expectations, making the presence of fat sopranos or artificial styles of acting unacceptable.

In this discussion about the simultaneous loss of the elite, novel, and popular character of opera lies the opening point of this inquiry: How does a modern audience perceive and experience opera when the art form has lost both its popular and its distinguishing characteristics? How and why do audience members feel compelled to participate in this social game? What explains their intensive and extensive investment when status, ideology, and popularity are not enough?

In response, this book focuses on the affectionate character of the attachment to opera—a particularly complex cultural product—and on how it is used as a meaningful activity, allowing passionate fans to fabricate meaning in and of their own lives and to craft themselves as worthy individuals. The aim is to build a sociology of the attachment to cultural forms that centers on the affective and embodied character of such engagement, looking to issues of self-formation and self-transcendence for clues.

This book studies a specific social universe built around high-culture practices, yet its focus is on, not questions of cultural domination, but affective regimes of evaluation or, more explicitly, love.[5] As the Argentinean art historian José Emilio Burucúa (2002) has recently noted, the topos of war—the faces under which power and domination have appeared throughout human history—has been excruciatingly explored (as ideology, hegemony, *dispositif*, apparatus, symbolic violence) by social theorists as diverse as Antonio Gramsci, Michel Foucault, Louis Althusser, and Pierre Bourdieu. The result has been an agonistic idea of cultural production based on the building or maintaining of power relationships after conflict among groups. Once we explain the dynamics of domination, the cultural realm is just a legitimating epiphenomenon accompanying a more real level of explanation: the subjugation of one group by another. However, there has not been the same impetus to trace a history of the topos of eros,[6] a history of the diverse regimes of affective evaluation, how they are produced, which people partake of them, the formal and informal mechanisms through which social actors affiliate, how they get reproduced over time, the meanings they adopt, and their relationships to other realms of society and other social taxonomies, including questions about class and status. This means, not to ignore how culture and power relate to each other as intimate bedfellows, but to bracket them and look beyond them into a comprehensive understanding of value-charged classifications.

Entering the Opera House through the Backstage Door

One of the many paradoxes of the Buenos Aires opera house is that its public face is not the main entrance but the secondary one for artists and in-house workers. The Colón's main entrance is in front of a small square close to the courthouse, several elite public schools, and what used to be the stock exchange. Yet, despite its close proximity to these symbols of power, the best-known entrance is the one in the back. In the 1950s, the small street that led to the backstage door was torn out and merged with four other streets in the construction of what, with modernizing frenzy, was proclaimed to be the widest avenue in the world. So perhaps a good way to enter the house and think about some of its more common representations and practices is through the backstage door and the side entrances where those who make the house from below (as workers) and the audience enter the theater (see figure 1).

FIGURE 1. The Teatro Colón as seen from its back entrance. Photograph by the author.

Because I am the son of a musician, my early memories of the art form are not related to public acclaim, generous applause, or a breathtaking performance. One of my first memories is hanging around the little kitchen backstage at the Colón Opera House, listening to a tango on the radio while looking at the pictures of all the famous (but then unknown to me) singers of the world. My idea of fun at the time was not related to seeing my father conduct the Stable Ballet or the Buenos Aires Philharmonic Orchestra, watching the dancers flying around the stage or admiring the quality of the soloist or the musicians. My idea of fun at the opera house consisted basically of greeting the performers, resting in my father's dressing room, or talking to the kitchen attendant. However, for most other members of the audience, the music world was filled with magic and authority. It was difficult for me to understand why people I had known for years still referred to my father as *Maestro*. After a performance, many people approached him or my mother, to talk about how mature his interpretation of Brahms was, or the soloist, to mention that they had seen him or her debut as the concertmaster of the National Youth Orchestra. I was used to clapping after performances because I knew when I had to, but it was difficult, if not impossible, to understand why people went crazy at the end of an aria, a soloist's concerto finale, or an acrobatic solo by a ballet dancer. I had met most of the soloists and musicians and always remembered them better for their soccer anecdotes than for their public presentations. Those who approached the musicians to praise their performance were rarely dressed for the part. While their comments made them appear to be high-culture mandarins, their frayed jackets and worn shoes gave me a different impression.

That is why, years later, I was surprised to read about the relation between status, class, and cultural consumption. I never understood the charged words that hung around concepts like *status*, *social hierarchy*, and *cultural capital*. Moreover, the disjuncture between my understanding of the performers as regular everyday people and the devotion the audiences invested in them, the charisma attributed to them, usually contradicted most theories of both high-culture consumption and cultural hierarchy. Any study that can make sense of this disjuncture needs a powerful hermeneutic and phenomenological way in, rescuing the sensuality of the experience as a key to understanding why audiences become so passionate about opera.

The perspective I am interested in emphasizing here has to do with states of self-transcendence and self-formation,[7] with instances of discovery and revelation where the world around opera fails to attract the passionate lover's interest, an attachment that uproots the person from the mundane, takes her out of the boundaries of self, delivers her to self-surrender, and readies her for sacrifices. Nevertheless, following the work on romantic love by the British sociologist Anthony Giddens, I am also interested in the traits of freedom, regulation, and self-realization that the metaphor *to love* encompasses. Loving opera, in these definitions, means voluntarily committing oneself to it. It means as much to have felt love at first sight as to accept the series of duties, activities, and obligations that commitment involves. It means accepting that, along with idealization of the object of the attachment, there are a series of prescriptions and compromises to be conquered. It means understanding that, next to communion of the souls, there is an active quest for the validation of self-identity and an anticipated yet malleable horizon for the future, that the dissolution of the self is a paradoxical way of achieving autonomy.

Unfortunately, when sociology has dealt with music consumption, it has done so with theories that have, mostly, left us bereft of tools to understand the long-term, passionate commitment of the opera fan. It has centered mainly on issues of social distinction and class identity, focusing on a societal/class level of analysis in which the practice is merely the basis for a status-based value tournament that reproduces the legitimacy of the dominant class (see Bourdieu and Passeron 1977; DiMaggio 1982a, 1982b; and Bourdieu 1984). This has taken shape through three theories (Halle 1993): *art as status*, following the work of Max Weber on class and status and the work of Thor-

Similar to football
Fans with season tickets

reps. see pub.

(handwritten marginalia)

stein Veblen on conspicuous consumption, which states that culture is a confrontational space where art is monopolized as a restricted resource and used as a weapon of distinction and status; *art as ideological domination*, following the Frankfurt school (Adorno and Horkheimer 1972; Adorno 1985) reelaboration of Karl Marx's thesis from *The German Ideology* that "the ideas of the ruling class are in every epoch the ruling ideas" (Marx 1846/1978, 174); and *art as cultural capital*, developed by Pierre Bourdieu in France and Paul DiMaggio in the United States, according to which the definition of what constitutes high culture works as a symbolic exclusion and subordination mechanism.[8] *see also Lamont & Lareau 988*

The American school of the production of culture has focused on the organizational context of production, distribution and evaluation, and consumption[9] but has not inquired much about the relationship that people establish with the content of music—the work itself, as Becker (1999) calls it.[10] The main contribution of this school to an understanding of consumption practices is the *omnivorous thesis*, which demonstrates how in recent decades the patterns of distinction have moved from a strict homology between high class and high culture into an omnivorous phase, distinguished by a degree of openness to and inclusion of diverse genres. Since its theoretical orientation stresses production systems that are more or less transposable across domains of production, rather than the ways emotional attachments of interpretative meanings are established, this school has lacked a serious engagement with the symbolic dimension of music consumption, aside from pointing out how networks and organizations have constrained meaning.

Cultural studies have, after a start where music was ethnographically presented as an enabler of lifestyles and forms of consciousness (Willis 1978; Hebdige 1979), slowly moved into a combination of first-person testimonies, analysis of literary texts as representative of larger social groups, and content analysis of the works themselves, instead of interrogating consumers about what different works mean to them and how they have built a relationship with them. If works like Paul Willis's *Profane Culture* (1978) were based on research that showed music in action and had the subjects "themselves establish the connection between music and social life" (DeNora 2000, 6), texts like those by Koestenbaum (1993), Abel (1996), Clement, Hutcheon, and Hutcheon (2000), and Evans (2005) have inquired about the gendered and sexualized character of opera consumption. Thus, they have opened the door to the exploration of the bodily character of the experience but have forgotten that what they are describing mostly resembles the author's own experience and, thus, lacks both a sociological and a historical understanding of how that experience came to be.[11]

Each of these approaches has provided a sociological framework for some excellent scholarship. Because of them, we know a lot about the routine work involved in manufacturing extraordinary products; the relation between cultural consumption and class, race, and gender; the conversion of particular symbolic products into markers of status; and how networks and institutional arrangements organize meaning. Yet we should not be blind to the problems with all three. The weight of contemporary sociological analysis has been laid on the contextual conditions for the production of objective culture. The processes through which these forms are incorporated into subjective culture, the diverse styles of self-cultivation, have been relegated to the background.[12] While the research on popular music has addressed how variation within cultural consumption is produced, not only by exogenous factors (like race, class, and gender), but also endogenously (see Thornton 1996; Grazian 2003; Fonarow 2006), when studying opera and classical symphony and chamber music, this dimension has usually been obliterated by the class-status-power nexus.

A more satisfactory approach to explaining the production of passionate attachment does exist, however. It consists of scholarship informed by two kinds of contributions. On the one hand, there are scholars and journalists who have studied diverse forms of fandom, ranging from obsession with soccer to the almost religious character of attendance at *Star Trek* conventions.[13] On the other, there is what is now called *music sociology*, which has Antoine Hennion and Tia DeNora as its main contributors. Where other approaches explained attachment as dependent on larger social arrangements, scholars of attachment seek to uncover the relatively endogenous logics and dynamics that produce and shape commitment and the mechanisms and processes through which this happens.

The literature on fandom provides a richly textured description of the social world of the fans. It analyzes self-obsession and connects it with the personal biographies of those involved, and it underscores the intensive investment fans make, the trivial knowledge they mobilize, the affective identification with what they do, the sacred, almost religious character that their identification takes, the thresholds they cross in order to let themselves go, the distinction they make between everyday life and the magical world they enter thanks to the object of their affection, and the nostalgic shade that colors their appreciation. It has provided us with a detailed account of soap-opera aficionados, soccer ultras, baseball diehards, guitar lovers, marijuana users, and comic and mushroom collectors. Nevertheless, there is almost no account of high-culture attachment in the fandom literature.[14] Scholarship has partitioned cultural life in two definite arenas; high culture has been observed as the realm of exclusion, reproduction of inequality, and capital transmission, while the analysis of pop-culture consumption has focused on the excessive character of attachment, stigma management, and the construction of isolated subcultural worlds that produce identity strictly through mechanisms of group integration against the outside.[15]

Where the literature on fandom tends to fall short in giving a complete theoretical account of the mechanisms through which the relation between cultural products and the attachment they generate works, the body of literature on music in action has focused on the individual level and shown the many techniques by which people lose themselves in music and use it as a resource, medium, and material for agency building (Hennion 1993, 1997, 2001; Hennion and Gomart 1999; DeNora 2000, 2002, 2003; Hennion, Maisonneuve, and Gomart 2000; Bull 2001, 2004; Hennion and Fauquet 2001). It has shown how taste must be conceptualized as an activity, not as something that is "already there," but as something that is constituted and redefined in action by the many devices and practices implied in liking something (buying records, listening at home alone or with other people, attending live performances). Key here is the focus on how objects and interactions with objects lend themselves to or *afford* uses. Nevertheless, that does not mean that the cultural object per se anchors or organizes its interpretation. Rather, it is through the access to and use of particular cultural objects (an opera performance, e.g.) that they can be understood to enable particular uses and forbid others.

While this literature has embraced the move from music as socially shaped to music in action, it has avoided examining the role that class/moral undertones of attachment to music play in actively mediating the constitution of taste. This approach also has limitations in explaining long-term attachments. If fans are such only for the particular moments that allow them pleasure, how do we go about explaining the elaborate "moral careers" of those who report the deprivation and sacrifices they go through in order to follow what they love? How do we approach the ideas of self-transcendence that fans describe, perform, and enact? How do we go about explaining the conviction that opera is, not only something pleasurable and organized around so many activities, but also something that makes fans better people, that allows them to get out of who they think they are, that they need to defend from others? How do we go about the multiple classificatory battles they get into, the localized status tournaments they partake in?

The *love for* something is a particularly strong and productive metaphor. More than driving action, it allows for a particular organization of action and selfhood. It allows us to explain both the work on the self that literature on music in action focuses on and the extreme character of affiliations described by the fandom literature. The love-for narrative allows us to explore the intense moments of surprise, the eccentric attachments that get produced beyond the familiarity with already knowing what we like (love at first sight), as well as to make sense of the "mature" love that makes attachment work only through a series of duties and activities. It opens our eyes to the intense process of discovery and self-exploration through which the loved object and the lover coconstitute each other. It allows us to understand the disqualification of those who do not like things in the same way we do and against whom we compete and fight to prevent the distortion of our idealized love object (romantic love). Thinking of fans as having a concept of themselves authorizes us to understand how the experience of opera allows for figures of transcendence oriented toward the future. Loving opera becomes a particular way of crafting the self in the present, as something that completes us, and in the past, including ideas of precognition in which, despite never having heard opera live before, we have been waiting for something like it our whole lives. To incorporate this temporal dimension also allows us to see ways to get out of ourselves that go beyond the mere moment of intense pleasure described by the music-in-action literature.

Voices: Natives, Strangers and Sociologists

The French cultural historians Michel de Certeau and Roger Chartier have discussed the difficulties that statistical research has had in giving a proper account of consumption activity (de Certeau 1984; Chartier 1998). First, when we limit research to the quantification of consumed goods, we miss the subject's own manipulation. While we see the attachment to certain products by certain groups of people, we are left without an understanding of the range of ways in which those people engage with those products. This kind of research understands only the material of the practices, not its form. Second, it falls short because it centers on the correlation between social groups and objects of consumption rather than consumption practices and their typologies. To quote Antoine Hennion (2001, 3): "[Quantitative] measurement is possible only because music lovers have been reduced beforehand to nothing more than the vehicle of their socio-professional category, without that posing the slightest problem, and music being nothing but a passive consumer good, whose only feature worthy of interest is the differential degree of education it requires." Finally, the research fails because we are also left without an understanding of how the materials people work with—in this case, opera and the meanings previously attached to it—constrain the uses and even the distinctions that a practice can afford.

How do we identify, then, what it is that people actually do with opera and what opera does to people. Ethnography is the appropriate method to fully describe and analyze cultural consumption since it captures the shape of the attachment with the practice. It gives us a sense of the nuances and internal differentiation as much as an understanding of the pattern of regularities. While the latter can be achieved by quantitative methods, it is only on the qualitative level—be it through participant observation or interviews—that the variation and the actual relationship with the content can be observed, described, interpreted, and analyzed. Interviews are important, too, but not enough. If I would have limited my research only to the interviewees' answers or to a discursive analysis of the narratives of appreciation, I would have missed one of the key features of this project, namely, the bodily character of opera appreciation and how this relates to and puts in question the high-culture character of opera attachment.

I would like to highlight at this point my double involvement with this particular cultural space. In a way, I try to define myself in this research in relation to what James Clifford (1988) calls an *indigenous anthropologist*. I belong to a family of musicians and have worked for diverse music organizations in a variety of roles—from musician to archivist—gaining firsthand knowledge of the internal point of view, production, and organization of high-culture institutions. I have also worked on several projects about spaces of cultural production, circulation, and consumption as a sociology junior researcher in Argentina. As has been the case with sociologist-musicians like Howard Becker, Rob Faulkner, and Edward Arian, I am in a special place from which to approach sociological research about cultural institutions that, nevertheless, takes into account the specificity and semantic density of the study object (see Wolff 1983). I did not have to surmount endless difficulties in order to gain access to the community in question, I did not have to learn the native tongue, and my presence did not introduce significant alterations to the everyday life of the group. This could enable me to recognize more precisely local categories and ratios.[16]

On the other hand, a perspective like this demanded that I turn the domestic life that had surrounded me for over thirty years into something exotic, rather than the usual practice of domesticating the exotic (Bourdieu 1984, 289). I had to break away from the tendency to disregard my intimate relationship with that way of life and thought, simply because of its familiarity. My familiarity, however, opened some doors as much as it closed others.

For some people, because of my last name, I quickly became Montecchi to their Capuletti. I tried not to give away my last name when among audience members as this always elicited some reaction about my father's conducting career or my brother's compositions. In music-appreciation classes, I actually listened with curiosity to what people had to say about one of the main courses, organized by my mother. However, the worst possible relationship to have as an adult ethnographer was the one I established with some key players in the opera world (like a former director of the Argentino Opera House, an overactive stage director at both the Colón and the off-Colón circuit, and the director of a small chamber opera auditorium and workshop) because they remembered me as an eight-year-old, traveling with them on tours. It was difficult to establish ethnographic authority in field situations in which the person on the other side saw, not a thirty-something adult inquiring about the recent history of opera organizations in the country, but a kid drawing incessantly on tracing paper.

In order to break with my point of view and my structural position in the music world, I collected as much information as I could: I had informal chats—as I had done all my life—and interviews with audience members and key figures from the opera world, gathered statistics, and collected payrolls, rosters and season programs, and newspaper reviews and interviews. Far from an autoethnography, this book is a reflexive exercise in traveling back and forth between the production of data in the field and social theory, and, thus, the ethnographer's presence is felt only when necessary. Although I used to go to the Colón with my family, I seldom went to the standing-room section (musicians and their families usually sit in a box or at orchestra level). When I had gone to that section by myself years before I started conducting this fieldwork, I was a stranger,[17] thinking sociologically about the tricks of the audience members and their compulsion for sociability. Similar to Wacquant's (2005, 469) defense of his book *Body and Soul*, this is not an autobiographical piece organized around some character's life. If there is a central character in this work, it is the opera house "as a socio-emotional melting pot and pragmatic-cum-moral vessel."

Throughout the 2002–5 seasons, I conducted eighteen months of ethnographic research on opera practices, centered mostly on the upper-floor standing rooms of Buenos Aires's Colón Opera House, one of the most traditional houses in the world and a cornerstone of the international opera circuit (Rosselli 1984, 1990). I waited on all-night lines, attended some seventy performances, went to as many as six performances of the same title during a single month, and took bus trips to minor opera houses four hundred miles away from the city. I focused on both spoken and nonspoken behaviors.

I interviewed forty-four audience members as well as key music critics, producers, and organizers. From 2004 to 2005, I conducted semiformal, qualitative, in-depth, open-ended interviews that lasted between one and three-and-a-half hours and concerned questions of initiation into music activities, family history, personal trajectory, music knowledge, and patterns of attendance. I concluded most of the interviews by asking what information had been overlooked, which usually opened the door to a long, self-reflective narrative about the place of music in the subject's life. These interviews were specifically aimed at understanding and making explicit some of the links between personal life, social status, conceptions of transcendence and enjoyment, and engagement with music that were hard to formalize from observation alone. I conducted the majority of these interviews after six months of observation of different activities (opera parties, lectures, conferences, CD clubs, etc.).

I built opera fandom as a set of practices that is Colón-centric but includes many scales and media, from Walkman CD players, background radio, specialized shows, and home listening to public DVD viewings, conferences, classes with music examples, amateur recitals, minor opera houses in and outside the city, crossover shows at sports stadiums, and trips to Europe and the United States with the sole aim of attending live opera. As such, in order to appropriately "follow the thing" (Clifford 1992), I adopted what George Marcus (1988) calls a *multisited ethnography*; much like Mitch Duneier's (1999) sidewalk (a Greenwich Village block that extended into neighboring restaurants, offices of the Bryant Park Business Improvement District, the New York City Council, and Pennsylvania Station), the Colón extended to all these different sites, from the competing opera houses to the living rooms where people got together for DVD viewings. In addition to interviews and observation, I conducted archival research among both primary and secondary sources, which resulted in a better sense of the history of opera consumption in Buenos Aires generally and the Colón specifically.

This book focuses on the cheaper upper floors of the opera house and especially on inhabitants of the standing room—who constitute about 20 percent of the audience. The upper floors are a relatively self-enclosed world. Here, four to six hundred people get together for three to four hours at a time, three to four times a week. In this secluded space, people act as if they are protected from the outside, with an intense sociability that excludes external events. The isolated character of the experience makes for an in situ laboratory to observe social interaction, the fabrication of meaning, and the variations in intense engagement with the same practice by people from diverse locations

I had many good reasons for choosing Buenos Aires. For one thing, it has been historically one of the key sites for the extension of opera as a global genre. For another, it is a place where opera is detached from the traditional national culture (unlike such Western European countries as Germany or Italy). Also, it presents a scenario in which people from many backgrounds engage with opera in a situation of extended downward mobility, despite economic constraints and the lack of a status payoff (unlike the United States). To a certain extent, it is a purer case of attachment to opera than any other. And, of course, I have the advantage of knowing it well, though I also came to look at it with new eyes.

The first chapter makes this point thoroughly while providing a brief history of opera in Argentina and its relation to nonelite audiences. The chapter also has a second objective: to set the stage for a better understanding of the specific population this study is focused on, the passionate opera fans who occupy upper floors of the house. Chapter 2 completes the background, providing life stories of six opera fans, inquiring whether certain characteristics will make someone more apt to love opera. In part 2—chapters 3–5—I discuss the phenomenology of being an opera fan and how opera is lived and thought of by this particular set of opera fans. Chapter 3 gives an overview of the diverse instances through which people learn to love opera and shows how, through formal institutions (like opera-appreciation classes) or informal ones (like the ticket lines or bus trips), they learn how to listen to opera and what to listen to. Chapter 4 shows how passionate fans differ from other audience members and how, in doing so, they bind the object of their affection in a particular way, defending it against competing interpretations. They engage in a local tournament for status that is not transferred to the outside and results, in consequence, in a noninstrumental understanding of the use of cultural capital since the benefits they obtain from it have to do with how they craft themselves. Chapter 5 continues this point and shows how status is not the only basis for variation within the opera house as passionate fans differentiate according to diverse models to achieve transcendence through the music they affiliate with. This chapter shows how fans craft themselves, not according to outside roles, but rather as a result of their affective relationship with music and the effects it has on the self.

In part 3, I conclude by showing how what happens within the walls of the opera house relates to the outside world. Chapter 6 shows how one of the constitutive tenets of enjoying opera at the Colón relates to it being an island in time and space, apart from the general impoverishment of the country. The chapter highlights how the breach of this isolation unleashes a slew of strategies to restabilize it. The chapter concludes by showing how the combat surrounding the collapse of the boundaries of the opera house is related to maintaining its extraordinary character. Chapter 7 discusses the theoretical implication derived from this case in order to understand the emotional attachment to complex forms. It explores the sociological significance of opera (as an intersection of activity and passivity) and how that could inform and be transposed to other realms of practice, like politics or a more encompassing sociology of culture. It also invites the reader to think of the work of art as a locus for personal and emotional investment or as a medium for moral self-formation instead of as a tool for the maximization of capital.

PART I

BACKGROUND

CHAPTER ONE

An Opera House for the "Paris of South America"

A Taste of Buenos Aires

If you walk around downtown Buenos Aires or some of the city's nicest neighborhoods, you will see at least one newsstand per block. Newsstands are placed on the sidewalk and sell not only newspapers but also magazines, cheap books, collectibles, and postcards. Among the latter, we can observe many competing ideas about the city and its proper photographic representation: the picturesque and colorful houses of Caminito in La Boca; the old bodegas and *almacenes* where the tango flourishes once again; the Pink House, in the historical center of the city, where the president works. However, all pale in comparison to the image that most often appears on postcards and in brochures: the Colón Opera House, usually photographed at night, bathed in its exterior lights (see figure 2). The Colón, inaugurated in 1908, is a pop icon, not only in the city, but throughout Argentina. Tourists often take tours of the house, and the guided visits have become one of the Colón's main attractions. Books about the Colón, filled with glossy pictures of its most luxurious features and texts by writers and artists who have graced the house over a hundred years, are an industry in and of themselves. Texts are obligatorily bilingual, and, as their prices indicate, the books are aimed mostly at the city's foreign visitors. Attached to this status as a monument that represents the city and, often, the entire country is the conviction that

Teatro Colón

FIGURE 2. A Teatro Colón postcard. *Source*: Archivo Nacional de la Nación.

the Colón is one of the greatest opera houses in the world and that its acoustics are unmatched by both older and contemporary houses like that of the Metropolitan Opera in New York. Such beliefs are a means of integrating Argentina into the modern world, and they underscore the Argentinean attitude toward the Colón as a national symbol of high culture, despite the consumption of opera at various venues and by a heterogeneous population.[1] This chapter tells the story of how this representation came to be.

Opera and the Old City

In *Tristes tropiques*, Claude Lévi-Strauss describes an unexpected discovery: the women of the poorly organized Caduveo tribe—a tribe on the verge of extinction—adorned their faces with drawings imitating the spatial and kinship structures of the neighboring and better-faring Bororo tribe. The French anthropologist concluded that, unable to solve their issues with social reproduction and social and political differentiation and organization, the Caduveo began dreaming of the society they could not build, on the faces of their women. In a risky analogy, the Argentinean cultural critic Eduardo Rinesi (1994) hypothesizes that, unable to create their ideal society, the liberal founding fathers of modern Argentina attempted to project it in the construction of as many European-style monuments as possible. While he offers a list of theaters, squares, and monuments that he sees as key examples, he forgets, in his focus on spoken theater, perhaps the most important of them all: the Colón Opera House.

Despite the Colón's representation as the backbone of the liberal, cosmopolitan city, its history stretches back well beyond the modern period of the country's organization (1880–1910). Established in 1857, the old Teatro Colón's location alone—next to the Plaza de Mayo, considered the main square of, not just the city, but the country; the cathedral; the presidential house; and the old Cabildo, stage of the country's first efforts in 1810 to free itself from Spain—reveals its central place in the nation's conscience.

According to newspapers from that era (Echevarría 1979, 14), the inauguration of the opera house on April 25, 1908, marked Buenos Aires's graduation day: "Tonight Buenos Aires has grown. We say goodbye to the old village and welcome the city in an artistic spiritual revelry." The large stage was celebrated as "one of the biggest in the world, after Milano's La Scala or Napoli's San Carlo Theatre." Two Italian artists had painted the ceiling with classical motifs of nymphs and caryatids, and all the seats in the house were covered in rich, brown leather. The initial subscription series included 120 performances. When interest waned, the theater opened its doors to other shows, like circuses, and to a great carnival dance, which introduced the house to those who did not or could not attend the opera.

On September 13, 1888, the old Teatro Colón closed its doors for good. Its small size, the growing city population, and a series of several spectacular theater fires in Europe that revealed the Colón's danger as a firetrap made it no longer tolerable. However, that was far from the end of the Colón as the center of Buenos Aires opera activity. Angelo Ferrari, the Italian impresario who had run the opera seasons since 1868, allied with Mayor Torcuato de Alvear to find a more suitable location for the new opera house. Alvear had already secured permission from the newly formed Concejo Deliberante (the municipal legislative body) four years prior to sell the old property, a municipal building, to the national bank for 950,000 pesos.[2]

The building of a new opera house became a political affair that involved city-level and national authorities as well as private and public characters. Some members of the local *porteño* elite[3] played dual roles as private sponsors of the project and public and legislative voices for its completion (Hodge 1979). Under Law 1969, the national state and the House of Representatives authorized the municipality of the city of Buenos Aires to sell the Colón in order to build a new municipal opera house, also to be named Colón (de la Guardia and Herrera 1933). Angelo Ferrari won the right to manage the opera seasons, and the construction of the building was awarded to Francisco

Tamburini, then the national director of public buildings, after an international competition was conducted. The completion of the new opera house became a comedy of errors, involving unexpected deaths and crimes of passion spanning over twenty years.[4]

Bourgeois Sociability and the Liberal City

Historians usually characterize 1880–1910 as the epoch of national modernization and, on the local level, as the era that inscribed the body of the city with architectural monuments, established the basis for spatial circulation, delimited social circles, and prescribed the places for the elites.[5] In his classic essay "The Bourgeois City" (in Romero 1983), the Argentinean historian José Luis Romero outlines the building frenzy of the period and the consequences of its modernization. In 1882, a new port was built, four blocks from the old Colón location, in order to export cattle, wool, and grain to Europe and to import the many products that filled the windows of new department stores and small neighborhood businesses. Most of the infrastructure was completed under the rule of Torcuato de Alvear, who became the first mayor after the city was officially recognized as the capital in 1880. In 1882, the city got public lighting and electric service as well as cobblestone streets; tramways were developed in 1897. However, the most important development was the opening of the Plaza de Mayo, which involved demolishing some of the more traditional buildings and constructing a Paris-inspired boulevard: the Avenida de Mayo. This avenue is where the new Municipal Palace found its home (1892). The avenue starts at the opposite corner of the Casa Rosada and ends at the National Congress, which was also planned in the 1890s but not finished until 1906. The new avenue linked all the major monuments of political power. The Palace of Justice was finished one year later next to the square where the new Colón would finally be located.[6]

As Gorelik indicates (1998, 237), the consolidation of the bourgeois city was marked by two series of buildings: the French-style palaces in the northern corridor and a series of monumental buildings that tried to provide a respectable home for the overgrown municipal and national state governments. The local bourgeoisie tried to deepen their social distance, and opera occupied a central place in this effort (Pasolini 1999). Finishing the Colón was both a national and a municipal political affair, and the bourgeoisie threw all their weight behind the project. For instance, in 1899, the congress passed Law 3797, which expropriated the properties surrounding the location of the new Colón. The maneuvering behind this action required the power of the municipal authorities. It was they who put up most of the money and took over the task of completing the theater from the impresario Ferrari; the national state also contributed by providing the location, the former Plaza de Armas and site of the Western Train Station.[7] The project also involved the cream of the local elite, who contributed by buying bonds issued by the state to finance construction. The twenty-five families who did so had already bought ten-year subscription-series boxes from Ferrari in 1891.[8]

A summary of the locations and buildings that had some family resemblance to the Colón might give us an idea of the central place given by the elite to the civilizing cultural mission the theater would undertake. The architects who built the Colón were Julio Dormal, Francisco Tamburini, and Victor Meano. They worked on drawings for the Tres de Febrero Park in Palermo (the mandatory place to stroll for the bourgeoisie); helped plan the Buenos Aires State Provincial Government House in La Plata and the National Government House in Buenos Aires; built the mausoleum for General San Martín (one of the country's founding fathers), the clubhouse of the Rural Society, the Normal School, the central police station, the military hospital, and the National Congress Palace. All these buildings were intended to transform the heart of the city (its downtown area and historical center) into the heart of the nation.

Tamburini died unexpectedly in 1899, and Meano, who was his disciple, continued the Colón project. Meano was stabbed to death by his butler in 1904, and construction was finished by Dormal. Problems with construction were not, however, confined to the health of the architects. As Hodge (1979) has shown, the twenty years between the closure of the old Colón and the opening of the new building were plagued by location changes, funding shortages, transfers of deeds and exploitation rights, a kaleidoscope of lists for box owners and occupants, and congressional debates over how the money should be allocated and what the purpose, and specifically the municipal character, of the opera house should be. Two of these debates are of particular interest because they are telling of the preoccupations behind the making of an opera house. Despite what might be expected, few of the conversations referred to the class character of the opera house. In fact, one of the most important points seemed to be that, although it was located in Buenos Aires and under the jurisdiction of the municipal government, it had to represent the country as a whole. As Hodge (1979, 238) shows, the representatives of the inner provinces made it clear that the bill should spell out the name Teatro Colón without mention of the word *municipal* "since Argentina's reputation in the music world would have been associated with a theater by that name." The finalization of the opera house became such an urgent concern that, in 1899, when the construction process seemed to be stalled and more money was needed, House representative Francisco Bollini asked that the relevant bill be placed ahead of other matters under consideration as "the honor and prestige of the Nation and the capital were at stake" (Hodge 1979, 248, citing *Diputados*, September 4 1899, 784).

By mid-1907, the work was all but finished. After eighteen years of construction far exceeding the thirty months outlined in the original contract signed in 1890, the Colón was ready to open. Construction had cost over four times the original estimate.

Who Was on First?

So who filled the Colón in its first years? While it is impossible to reproduce a given night at the opera house, a combination of several primary sources (playbills with the list of subscribers from 1908–10, 1912, 1914, 1924–25, and 1927) and secondary sources (de la Guardia and Herrera 1933; Matamoro 1972; Hodge 1979; Rosselli 1990; Sforza 1990; Pasolini 1999; Sanguinetti 2002; and Buch 2003) allows us to attempt a reconstruction of the hierarchical architecture of a stratified audience. In the orchestra seats, especially the first and second levels of boxes, we find those who had bought the ten-year subscriptions and the municipal bond to subsidize construction. This population of wealthy landowners, merchant entrepreneurs, and successful members of the financial industries occupied the thirty-eight central boxes among the seventy-four lower- and upper-balcony boxes.[9] Sanguinetti (2002) adds to these names others repeated throughout the orchestra seating and remaining boxes: Roca, Alvear, Mitre, Pueyrredon, and a few others that remind us that the who's who included many of the last names that have shaped the country's history since 1810.[10]

The map of the remaining important boxes obeyed the logic of the marriage between a politico-bureaucratic organization and the original impresario who managed the seasons. Fifteen boxes (five in each of the three levels of balconies) were allocated to the heirs of Ferrari. The remaining boxes were allocated to the president of the Republic, the city mayor, members of the municipal commission and the commission that oversaw the activities of the Colón.[11] The president would attend at least twice a year to celebrate the two key national holidays, May 25 and July 9. While some presidents, like Marcelo T. de Alvear, who was married to a former opera singer, attended more often, those two occasions were almost mandatory.[12] That is true even in the case of Hipólito Yrigoyen, who, although from the same party as de Alvear, the popular Unión Cívica Radical,[13] would fall asleep during performances, much to the dismay of other audience members. The presidential galas, as they were called, were a central part of the subscription series, and all the subscription packages included at least one.

The most obvious display of the connection between opera and the modernizing elite came during the celebrations for El centenario, the hundredth anniversary of the country's independence. As the cultural historian Esteban Buch (2003, 32) states, the celebrations of May 25, 1910, attempted to transform Buenos Aires "into the capital of the world for a day." President Figueroa Alcorta received the prime minister of France, the president of Chile, the president of Peru, the German military chancellor, and the Spanish princess[14] as well as internationally prominent figures such as Ramón del Valle Inclán and Guglielmo Marconi. The pinnacle of the celebration was the gala performance at the Colón, where the president was flanked, not only by these and other special guests, but also by most of the foreign ambassadors, all his ministers, the judges of the Supreme Court, and key members from Congress. The presentation of *Rigoletto* at the Colón was designed to show the success of Argentina's civilizing project: Buenos Aires, and Argentina, had finally arrived.

A comparison of opera debuts in Buenos Aires with those at renowned opera houses like La Scala, the Met, or Paris demonstrates how well synched the Colón was to the international scene. For instance, *La traviata* opened in Buenos Aires in 1856, just three years after its world premiere. This synchronicity accelerated with time, as evidenced by the premiere of *Pagliacci*, which appeared in Buenos Aires on February 28, 1891, only a few months after the work won an award given by Ricordi in Italy. *La bohème* premiered in Torino just four months before its Argentinean debut, and *Madame Butterfly* opened in Buenos Aires less than two months after its final revision in Brescia, on May 28, 1904. *Turandot* premiered in Buenos Aires on June 25, 1926, exactly two months after its world premiere at La Scala. Even operas premiered in the United States, like *La fanciulla del West*, which opened in Buenos Aires in July 1911, appeared in Argentina within a short period. This trend led to some operas actually premiering in Buenos Aires, like *Isabeau*, which appeared in 1911—with music by Mascagni (famous for *Cavalleria rusticana* and *Iris*) and a libretto by Luigi Illica (Puccini's main librettist)— but did not have its American premiere until 1927.

Isabeau was the second opera Illica wrote that premiered in Buenos Aires.[15] The first one, *Aurora*, while never included in the international canon, is the embodiment of how opera became a tool for nation building in Argentina. It premiered during the inaugural season of the Colón in 1908. Its story takes place during the wars of independence in 1810 and narrates the affair between the daughter of a Spaniard officer and a young Argentinean patriot. Aurora is the name of the female character, an allusion to the dawning (the Spanish meaning of *aurora*) of the Argentinean nation and the sun that occupies the center of the nation's flag. On the night of the premiere, the audience was so impressed with the "Song for the Flag" that it forced the tenor, Amadeo Bassi, to repeat the aria, an occurrence seldom repeated throughout the history of the Colón.[16] The fact that the text was in Italian made it difficult for the "Song for the Flag" to become widely known, which is why it was translated into Spanish in 1945. That same year, a decree from the executive power included it among the national anthems. Since then, the "Song for the Flag," or simply "Aurora," has been sung in schools and whenever the flag is raised.[17]

While opera aligned Buenos Aires with other global metropolises, erasing its distance from Europe and attempting to accelerate its modernization and development to match Western progress, the music genre also spread throughout Argentina, linking local elites and modernizing the inner country.[18] After the opening of the first Colón, opera houses of diverse sizes, artistic levels, and audiences started appearing in Buenos Aires and other cities and towns.[19] Seven operated in Buenos Aires, and their activity was so competitive and agitated that, on May 28, 1910, now known as the "Night of the Three Rigolettos," all the major opera houses staged a version of the Verdi opera.[20] Among the few houses located outside the city center was the Marconi, which opened in 1908 and was backed by Italian migrants. Opera also extended to the southern working-class suburban areas. In 1904, the Roma Theater opened its doors in Avellaneda and mixed opera with spoken theater. The Argentino Opera House in La Plata, the Buenos Aires State capital, was inaugurated just ten years after the city itself, in 1891.[21]

Workers, Monster and Mobs

In 1910, while El centenario celebrated the elite, two concurrent events tried to tarnish its image and show the rest of the world that the victories of the local oligarchy were based on the exploitation of its workers. The opening of the country to flows of imports and exports also meant an increase in human traffic and conflicting ideologies. With the mass immigration of Italians, Eastern Europeans, Jews, and Spaniards came socialism and anarchism. The latter provided the spark for two organized attacks on the Colón.

One occurred on June 26, 1910, soon after the murder of Police Chief Ramón L. Falcón[22] by the Russian activist Simon Radowitsky,[23] when a bomb exploded in the Colón. Investigators were sure that the bomb had been, not placed in the lower levels, but thrown from the *paraíso*,[24] the cheaply priced, men-only floor of the opera house, "where the enemies of society are located." No one died, but the attack left ten people injured, and media outlets fueled the legend by reporting that the bomb was planted by a couple of "poorly dressed people in the *paraíso*" (Salas 1996, 241). The next day, the audience showed up in impressive numbers, but this was not the high bourgeoisie's sole response. That morning, Congress met in an extraordinary session to pass a law prohibiting anarchist individuals, groups, or ideas from entering the country. Although anarchists had succeeded in killing the police chief and had tried to blow up the traditional Del Carmen Church and kill Presidents Quintana and Figueroa Alcorta, it was not until the attack on the Colón that a consensus for draconian measures against anarchist immigrants was achieved. The second attack occurred fifteen years later as part of a protest of the gala to honor the twenty-four-year reign of the Italian king Vittorio Emanuelle II.[25] While the explosives used were less powerful than those used in 1910, anarchist propaganda was attached to them. This seemed to confirm the connection between opera and the elite.

However, the relationship between the diverse migrant populations and the culture of the elites was more complex; attacks on the physical space and its audiences were just one tactic. Socialist workers appropriated opera, not only by frequenting the different houses, but also by making arias and other opera fragments (e.g., Boito's *Mefistofele*, the instrumental parts of Rossini's *Guillermo Tell*, and fragments from Mascagni's *Iris*, including the "Sun Anthem") a central part of their public rituals and celebrations. Silvia Sigal (2006, 199) and Blas Matamoro (1972, 89) show a thirty-year span over which such socialist activities took place at the Colón, from May Day lectures and celebrations to the 1928 commemoration of the death of Juan B. Justo, the Socialist Party's founder and leader.

Even though the image of an exclusively homogeneous, high-class population persists, plebeian publics have long been a part of the Colón's audience. Take, for example, this classic text describing the introduction of a young man to the ways of society during a 1942 performance of *Parsifal*:

> "*We* say 'to Colón,'" María Zuñiga added, with the definitive emphasis of someone who closes a debate . . . and this time she highlighted *we*.
>
> The teenager went mute. *We* he thought. *We* would mean the Gonzalvez and the Zuñigas? And there will be some others. Those who don't say *to the Colón* (as it should be) but *to Colón* (like *we* say it). Do we say it like this in order to distinguish ourselves? Is it a code? Do we talk in code? And Salvador promised from that moment on to keep an eye on who said "to Colón": this would help him classify them. Meanwhile, he was ashamed of not having been initiated in this particularity of his own clan, of his own people, of *us*. He gazed around and wondered if the surrounding people would be included within *we*. (Mujica Láinez 1979, 65)

This excerpt from a novel by the paradigmatic writer of the Colón is the last among a long series of texts by elite writers who refer to the "invisible" parts of the audience. In 1866, Estanislao del Campo, an habitué of the first Colón, wrote a gaucho poem based on the fictional impressions of a gaucho who mistakenly attended the opera for the first time. While witnessing a performance of Gounod's *Faust*, the gaucho believes that what he sees onstage is happening in reality.[26] The difficult-to-translate text begins Anastasio el Pollo's visit to the Colón with a description of the moments before the performance starts. He describes "how the audience crowded like cattle, pushed desperately to get to the box office," and complains about the size of the entrance: "If the place was so small . . . why do they enclose so many sheep in the corral?" He goes on, lamenting that, in the shoving, his boots and pants were torn, and he is surprised to notice that "someone had stolen the knife from [his] belt." After a while, "tired and sad," he climbs "101 steps" all the way to the top floor, "where the country folk [*la paisanada*] go, which was the lowest layer in the stoving of people."

The cattle-like experience surprises del Campo's alter ego; he gets pushed, shoved, and contained. Moreover, as Aguilar (2003, 87) analyzes, del Campo's word games play with the fact that, at that time, Argentina was one of the main exporters of wool; at one point, he compares the filling of the last floor to the stowing of wool. The gaucho is also surprised by the poor moral quality of the house inhabitants as his most precious and honorable possession as a male rural laborer, his knife, is stolen.

The suspect character of the people on the uppermost floors can also be gleaned from at least four other texts from the modernizing period. In 1879, a social reporter for the satiric magazine *El mosquito* described the top floor of the recently inaugurated Politeama as "a heterogeneous group of men dressed in diverse ways, but with a generally somber character" (cited in Pasolini 1999, 248). A year later, the cultural critic Carlos Olivera wrote that the uppermost floor was the place "of the coarse common people, composed evenly of well-known thieves and small-time crooks who take for themselves the right of more-enlightened people to clap and whistle for the artists" (quoted in Pasolini 1999, 239–40). In 1885, Eduardo Cambaceres, the owner of an *avant-scène* box at the old Colón, published a novel, *Sin rumbo*, centered on the romance between a young visiting Italian diva and a young bourgeois heir whose life revolves around both the aristocratic world of private clubs and the international world of opera. In this book, the male protagonist partakes in exotic adventures with dubious characters, including the diva, her husband, an opera impresario, and other adventurers. However, he saves his greatest repugnance for the audience on the top floor, which he calls "the dirty crease of Paradise" (Cambaceres 1885/1980, 112). Later, in 1907, another journalist called this part of the audience at the Coliseo (the social equivalent of the Colón until the latter reopened) the "crowded mass" and the "mob-monster" owing to its increasingly coarse behavior (see *La vida moderna* 1, no. 2 [1907]: 23–25).

Elites, Italians, and City Authorities

In his seminal work on how the Boston Brahmins managed to create a new organizational basis for high culture and, in the process, reclassified opera as art and became a social class, Paul DiMaggio (1982a, 1982b) describes three processes through which the higher class of Boston bounded certain cultural practices and made them sacred, exclusive, and artistic. He labels these *entrepreneurship*, *classification*, and *framing*. DiMaggio describes the first as organizational structures that gave members of the elite a certain level of power and control; the second as the erection of clearly defined boundaries between art and entertainment, with high culture being appropriated by the elite and the upper middle classes; and the third as the development of a new etiquette of appreciation.[27]

Let us take these dimensions into consideration and observe how they unfolded in Buenos Aires and how much social currency the elites managed to produce via opera attendance at the Colón. In terms of cultural entrepreneurship, the Colón was born as a mixed project that involved an Italian impresario, Angelo Ferrari, city authorities who were part of the elite that attended the opera, and a few families that bought long-term subscriptions for the most expensive and prestigious boxes. However, Ferrari's many failed attempts to raise money, the costs of the extended period of construction, and the small size of the contributions given by the elite families (which amounted to less than 15 percent of the total cost of construction) made the municipality the key player in this three-pronged structure. The participation of the city state grew with time, up to the point where, in 1925, the Colón started housing an orchestra, conductors, and singers backed by the city budget, and, in 1931, the house was municipalized, meaning that the city would take over its budget and fund it. Consequently, the impresario's influence waned as a committee named by the city made artistic decisions regarding budget allocations, hiring, and repertory and eventually reorganized the seasonal structure.

Even more important was a 1906 municipal decree that took the power to distribute and allocate seats away from the impresario and the elite. Because of this rule, the tickets had to go to the municipal office, where they would be marked and numbered before they could be sold. The second article of this decree established that tickets could not be sold without the municipal stamp or outside the theater box office. What was actually a fiscal measure to increase tax collection had two consequences (Pasolini 1999, 246). First, it transformed the once-personalized, prestige-based relationship that opera-goers, especially women, had with the impresario into a market-mediated relationship that took away the impresario's ability to distribute "extra" tickets among socialites on the basis of their influence. Second, the creation of the "general entrance" ticket enabled anyone with enough money to attend the opera. This resulted in a more mobile audience and modified who could access the Colón.

The Colón was highly successful at presenting only operas, concerts, and ballets while excluding popular genres. This did not mean that the ruling elite defined what opera meant or even determined the preferred repertoire. The many debates among members of the elite during the late nineteenth century and the early twentieth about the place Wagner should occupy in the opera pantheon (Pasolini 1999; Sanguinetti 2002) did, however, mean that operas by the German composer would be finally heard in Buenos Aires. But it was not until 1922 that they were actually performed in German; previously, they had been performed in Italian.[28] This anecdote calls attention to a very specific phenomenon: the influence that poor Italian immigrants, who brought with them idea of opera as popular culture, had over the genre in Buenos Aires.[29] While this audience shared the sacred character of opera, which also stood for their nationality, they lived quite separately from the elite who attended the Colón and challenged their accepted concepts of theater etiquette.

Two Colóns?

The modern history of opera in Buenos Aires can be traced to a mixed practice that was pursued as much by the local oligarchy as by poor people from immigrant communities (Pujol 1989). The British historian John Rosselli (1990, 168) calls attention to how the opera audience of Buenos Aires was divided into an elite, fashionable portion and a popular portion composed almost entirely of the local Italian population. The expansion of the audience meant a diversification of tastes and genres. However, even then, opera had a central place. For instance, in 1905, almost half a million spectators attended opera in a city of 1.2 million. The genre surpassed *zarzuela* (sung theater of Spanish origins) as the most attended by the *porteño* audience, constituting 17 percent of overall theatrical consumption (over 2 million spectators) and 29 percent of the four most-attended genres. Other theatrical genres were important enough to have grown from 222 performances in 1897 to 1,222 in 1910 (Diego 1983, 146). The expansion of the audience meant, obviously, the transformation of house etiquette as new people appeared even in unexpected parts of the house. Posters announcing performances began appearing in languages other than Spanish, and some houses became known by other names, such as the "Teatro della Vittoria" and even the "Theatre Colón."

From 1908 to 1968, the Marconi was the "poor" opera house of Buenos Aires. Backed by Italian immigrants, it presented Italian operas, operettas, and "Neapolitan dramas." In almost sixty years of existence (1903–60), only fifty-four titles were performed there, although some seasons included up to sixteen titles. The repertoire looks even more limited if we take into account that nineteen titles were performed only once and a few others only two or three times. Among the comic operas, only *Barbiere* was performed, and titles such as *Andrea Chenier* and *Manon Lescaut* were discarded because of their complexity or large casts. After 1934, there were sixteen major scores: seven by Verdi, three by Puccini, and one each by Donizetti, Rossini, Mascagni, Leoncavallo, and Ponchiello; the remaining title was the Italian version of Bizet's *Carmen*.[30]

While poor Italians had their own opera house, some of them ventured to the Colón for the cheapest tickets available, which did not require any kind of subscription commitment. They were not the only ones; a list of subscribers from the inaugural seasons shows that, among the sixty-three Hispano-Argentine names, there are five Italian names (Rosselli 1990, 169). Furthermore, in her study of the Colón playbill, Sforza (1990) shows that Italian names gradually multiplied; in 1910, there were eight families among the box subscribers and a few more if the *tertulia* seats are included (Pelleschi, Gazzolo, Zambelli, Bernasconi, Zamboni, Demarchi, and Pini).[31] A playbill from 1909 reveals a few other Italian names among the orchestra seats (Tedeschi, Galloti, Estefanelli, and Marzoni).[32]

Unlike immigrant patterns seen, for instance, in New York City (Baily 1985), Italians incorporated themselves into the life of Buenos Aires by spreading into many different areas and interacting in a new public space, known as the *barrio* or "neighborhood," created by local cultural and political associations (Romero 1983; Gorelik 1998).[33] Local historians (Sarlo 1988, 1991; Gutierrez and Romero 1995) have shown how the networks that produced a plebeian, integrating culture continued all the way into the 1940s. These networks—press houses that published cheap mass translations of classic books, innovative newspapers, and clubs that popularized science, radio, and technology[34]—were behind the expansion of cultural goods during the 1920s and 1930s. Such institutions were run by poor immigrants who thought that high culture was as much a means for upward mobility as a tool for spiritual growth. In producing these cultural and artistic products, they undermined as much as they confirmed the values of the dominant culture and bridged and integrated the culture of the middle and popular classes. Since opera became increasingly much more expensive than these other high-culture realms, organized migrants usually pressured the Socialist and the Radical parties to maintain the government subsidy.

A Set Stage

Historical and organizational sociologists remind us that the defining years of an institution are important for the understanding of how specific elements imprint themselves and remain for decades or even centuries (see Stinchcombe 1965; and Johnson 2007). If we were to stop here and think of the characteristics that make Buenos Aires a particular setting in which to understand the love of opera, there are two key elements to call on. First, the fact that the elite promoted opera as a way for the nation to enter the modern world made the Colón a key player in the globalization of opera as a genre. Second, despite that civilizing character, opera was consumed in the same setting by a very heterogeneous population. The ambivalence among elite, civilizing, and plebeian forces has survived throughout the years and framed the potential for attachment. A more populist approach—like the one undertaken by the Peronist regime in the late 1940s and the early 1950s, which affected most high-culture institutions in the country—should have resulted in breaking down that stratification. Instead, even Perón and Evita kept the public subsidy, maintained the pricing scale, and respected the gala traditions down to the last detail (see figure 3).[35] They also had special performances for the unions, opening a free summer house in a public park.[36] On the other hand, a more exclusive project would have closed the five hundred to one thousand spaces that currently provide the cheapest paid spectacle in Buenos Aires (even cheaper than standing room for a second-division soccer game). Nevertheless, after the failed original project by the twenty-five elite families, never has such a thing been proposed, not even under the military regime that governed the country from 1976 to 1983.

In 1908, the most expensive seats cost thirteen to seventeen times more than the cheapest, a trend that continues today.[37] This was expected during the nineteenth century, when theaters depended on market returns for their survival and usually mixed opera with other less-prestigious cultural practices (Weber 1976; DiMaggio 1982a; Levine 1988). In most European countries, opera followed a clear trajectory, from the genre being owned by

FIGURE 3. Evita in an *avant-scène* balcony box. July 9, 1950. *Source*: Archivo General de la Nación.

a few patrons but consumed in the same way by everybody, to a distinction game that involved the cultivation of specific tastes (the development of high culture) that corresponded precisely to positions in the social structure. Unlike these cases, opera in Buenos Aires has kept alive the tension between its exclusive and its democratic character since its inception.

In the following pages, I will develop more thoroughly the third characteristic that makes Buenos Aires a special setting for understanding the love for opera: the lack of status payoff for fans as the Colón budget diminishes drastically and opera is extended to other minor opera houses and is consumed by people from many backgrounds. This happens despite growing economic constraints.

Numbers

The history of the political economy of the Colón is marked by its transition from a seasonal opera house (with a standard set of titles offered yearly by touring companies brought in by an impresario) to one focused on production. That meant a reduction in titles, since works are not repeated season after season; the creation of workshops for costumes, wigs, and scenery; and the establishment of a house orchestra and chorus and a collection of singers, conductors, and voice coaches. It also meant that artistic decisions were taken away from impresarios and put into the hands of an artistic director or commissioner. The full municipalization of the Colón was decreed in 1935 (Caamaño 1970; Rosselli 1990).

Its current budget, after the economic and political crisis of 2001,[38] which eroded the value of the peso against the U.S. dollar, is estimated at less than 60 million pesos (some US$20 million). Despite the fact that it is a public institution, the Colón's finances are hard to figure out. According to the *New York Times*, the budget for the 2005 season was US $22.5 million (Rother 2005); an internal report from 2002, while inconclusive, appears to show a budget for that season closer to US$15 million. Meanwhile, a report from the University of Tres de Febrero estimates the 2004 budget at around US$13 million. Before the crisis (1996–2001), the budget used to fluctuate between US$42 and US$52 million,[39] and many independent critics and producers still estimate the annual budget to be around U$40 million. Currently, the city covers 82 percent.[40] The crisis of 2002 slowed down both production and consumption; the total expenditure for soloist contracts decreased from a peak of over 7 million pesos in 2001 to 2.7 million pesos in 2002 (or less than US$1 million after the crisis eroded the convertibility laws that pegged the value of the peso to the dollar), and only sixty-nine thousand spectators showed up for operas that year. To put this number in context, in both 2000 and 2001, over ninety-five thousand spectators attended opera performances.[41]

The hall seats 2,500 people and has enough space for 620 more[42] in standing-room areas behind the orchestra seats or on the upper three floors.[43] Performances are offered through five subscription series. Operas are usually premiered either on what is called a *gran abono* night, when those in the boxes and orchestra seating still must wear black tie, or on an *abono nocturno tradicional*. These two series have been around since the beginning of the opera house and attract longtime subscribers. More recent subscribers often attend the *abono extraordinario* and the *abono nocturno nuevo* series. Every title (nine to twelve, depending on the season) is performed four to six times. Subscription seats are held for a long time and are nontransferable. The only way to get into the house without a subscription is to get a partial-view seat or a standing-room ticket. In 2005, eleven titles were offered, including the summer season, for a total of fifty-two performances.

The Many Houses of Opera in Buenos Aires

Nowadays, the Colón's programming is complemented by three other opera houses—the Argentino, which accommodates 2,200 people, is located forty miles away from the city and is subsidized by Buenos Aires State; the Roma, with space for 560 people, is located in the southern industrial suburb of Avellaneda; and the Avenida, located ten blocks from the Colón, seats 1,100 and has standing room for 150 more—and five opera companies. Ticket prices for these houses are less expensive, ranging from US$5 for a seat on the upper floors to US$25 for an orchestra or box seat. Offerings have multiplied since 1999, when Juventus Lyrica presented *Don Giovanni* at the Avenida and was the only opera company other than the Colón or the Argentino. During 2004, this circuit offered fifty-four titles and 134 performances, and producers estimate that over 110,000 spectators attended.[44] The opera houses and companies work mostly with local singers and conductors, who usually play supporting roles at the Colón and perform on it as replacement soloists or principals of the second cast. Off-Colón circuit companies and performances have grown significantly over the last five years, from twenty-nine productions in 2001, to forty in 2002, to forty-three in 2003.

Newspapers (e.g., Liut 2002, 2003, 2004) have covered this explosion of the opera in the city. The most common explanation for this expansion is supply, not demand. The limited activity of the Colón (fifty-four performances a year on average during the 1990s), its preference for international soloists, and the lack of opportunities for artists (conductors and singers but especially stage directors) who are not part of the official roster has led national performers to venture outside the main opera house. Critics compare the growth of opera after the crisis of 2001–2—which "nationalized" the Colón's season as the house was forced to cancel all foreign hires and to debut soloists who had honed their skills off-circuit—to its pinnacle in the city in the 1920s.

In the 270 days of the opera season, which runs from April to December, there were almost two hundred nights when opera could be heard in the city. Opera people take advantage of the extended circuit and go to most houses, although the apex of the system, despite its decreasing status, is still the Colón. The current opera environment operates as a particular ecology, one where a combination of the availability of opera and the decreasing quality of what is offered on the main stage lowers the entry cost (especially symbolically since the other opera houses are not as intimidating to neophytes as the Colón) and results in the decline of the status payoff associated with attending.

The Architecture of Fandom

The heterogeneity of the opera audience can be best understood when observing the Colón's architecture and the way the audience is spatially stratified. Maintaining an internal boundary between the two groups at the opera house allowed for its association with high culture while, paradoxically, making it available to everybody. Only the audience members in the boxes and orchestra seats have access to the foyers, the receiving hall filled with busts, and the White and Golden Halls. The spaces between the orchestra seats (called *sillones de patio de platea*) are wide, and the small foyer for each box can seat as many people as the box itself. The *cazuela* still has a small hall since the space was historically reserved for women, who could not sit in the orchestra seats alone, but the other spaces have only narrow hallways. Even the chairs are upholstered in different fabrics and colors according to floor: dark scarlet for the boxes, ruby for the orchestra seats, and dull brown for the upper floors.

In his dissertation on the history of U.S. opera houses, Clancy (2005) establishes a distinction between houses that spatially reinforced social privilege and those that rejected it. In order to do so, he outlines a series of explicit criteria, including whether there were different entrances and stairs for different floors and ticket levels and whether it was possible to access certain parts of the theater, such as the balconies, from the lower-priced rooms (figures 4 and 5 show how different the seating arrangements are in different sections of the Colón). To these features, the Colón Opera House adds two more divisions. The first is the enforcing character of the bars and rails on the top floors of the house. The second is a gender division between the standing-room-only floors: in the *paraíso*, people stand together, regardless of gender, while only women occupy the *cazuela* and only men the *tertulia*. This division has been part of the Colón tradition since the construction of the old opera house in 1857, when the whole floor, including 240 seats (Sanguinetti 2002), was for women only; it was seen as a way of protecting women who were attending alone.

Unlike the Milan Scala, for instance, the spatial division at the Colón has been maintained and is, even today, reinforced by the audience, the ushers, and the box office. The only people who wander together to these standing areas are tourists, who have a hard time understanding the persistence of this division and who usually get upset when removed. Because of the separate entrances, upper-floor patrons usually must be content with seeing each other during intermissions.

Getting to Paradise

It is especially telling that the name given to the upper floor of the house (with most of the standing-room spaces and the cheapest seating) is *paraíso* (paradise). José Luis, one of my older informants and an amateur writer, makes the link between heaven and the opera experience explicit in a beautifully written piece: "Sometimes, when I look at the house's ceiling, I remember the words of Erich Kleiber, who used to tell the orchestra that, when he died, he would still be there, hanging from the ceiling, to make sure they played well. I would also love to stay there, not controlling (I wouldn't know how), but standing as an audience member, on the ceiling, even higher than the *paraíso*. If Borges thought of paradise as within 'the library class of things,' I would like to imagine it within the 'opera house class of things,' as our beloved Colón."

FIGURE 4.
A *tertulia* chair.
Photograph by
Marina Nougués.

FIGURE 5.
The balcony box
section. Photo-
graph by Marina
Nougués.

While *paraíso* might seem an ironic name, it makes perfect sense both when used in staging and in terms of its location, near the ceiling of the opera house. It is common for *regisseurs* (stage directors) to use the upper floors of the house, or parts of it, to stage their performances. A presentation of *Lucia* in 2005, for instance, had the tenor singing from inside the chandelier; a 2001 version of *The Rake's Progress* had the two main male characters (Ramey and Groves) singing from the upper floor. However, what several interviewees remember vividly is the 1999 staging of *Mefistofele* when "the chorus voices were coming from heaven!" Marcela, a woman in her late forties who is studying to be a lawyer, offered details of that experience: "There were three choruses singing: the Colón's, the Children's Choir, and the one from La Plata. The one that was singing from above seemed like it was singing from heaven. I don't remember who the director was, but it really registered in me. I loved it. I was impacted by the staging, but mostly by the sound of the three choruses singing in unison. How it did sound because they put the chorus from La Plata upstairs!"

The location of the *paraíso* makes its name appropriate both as the floor next to the beautiful ceiling of the house (see figure 6) and as the site of the best acoustics in the house. People emphasize the fact that the ceiling is so close that it gives them their "own little roof," which works as an acoustic chamber, making the *paraíso* the best place, not to observe, but to listen to opera. Some critics (Enzo Valenti Ferro)[45] and artists (e.g., the renowned international stage director Margarita Wallmann) have also romanticized this space as the one from which "balconies of heaven" hang. In 1976, Wallmann published *Balcones del cielo*, a memoir and reflection of her many years as a *regisseur* and choreographer around the world. A large chapter of the book is dedicated to the Colón, where she worked at different times from 1936 until the early 1980s. The preface to the Argentinean edition, written by Valenti Ferro, makes explicit the connection between a verse from the poem "Recueillement" by Charles Baudelaire that she used for the title and the never-ending nostalgia attached to the upper floors of the house. The part of the poem in question, which also serves as the epigraph of the book, reads:

> My Grief, give me your hand; come this way
> Far from them.
> See the dead years in old-fashioned gowns
> Lean over the balconies of heaven.

The name *paraíso* can be traced to a very specific origin. It has been inherited from Spanish theaters, where it combined both the location on the highest floor in the house and the gaiety of the experience. This last quality

FIGURE 6. The chandelier and the ceiling painted by Antonio Berni.
Photograph by the author.

can be best observed by looking at figure 6, in which the light comes down from the most beautiful part of the house, the mural on the ceiling by the local painter Antonio Berni and the chandelier, to democratically bathe, first and foremost, the people and spaces in the upper floors. Despite this happy coincidence between name and lighting, which makes for an obvious analogy about the civilizing character of the beauty that comes from above and touches the less fortunate first, the space is also known by a second, less poetic name that underscores its plebeian character—the "Chicken House." That name is derived from the old Italian houses in the city, like the Marconi, which early in the twentieth century wired their upper floors to keep the audience from throwing things (especially eggs or other food) onto the stage (Pollini 2002).

The dual character of these names elevates us to our object of study: those fans attracted by the beauty of European high culture and its civilizing power who nevertheless behave in an intense and passionate way usually reserved by scholars for consumers of mass or popular culture. The centrality of these passionate fans in the many practices and processes that go on at the Colón can be best seen in one of the closing paragraphs of *El Teatro Colón* (1972) by Blas Matamoro. Published during the revolutionary 1970s by a nationalist and populist press, the book is a harsh critique of the opera house as the site of a European-oriented oligarchy. It ends with a proposal to close the theater so that the poor people from the far provinces will no longer have to pay taxes to support the luxurious tastes of the millionaires. However, when the author wonders who would truly be damaged by this, he does not point to the anachronistic elite or even to the artists from abroad who come to work at "a museum of foreign art." He points to the "sick fans" who wait for hours before and after the shows to get an autograph, chat—just for a moment—with the artists about their last performances, ask them what they think of the city, follow their cars to learn where they are staying in hopes of continuing their conversations. Matamoro despises the Colón and what goes on in it, attributing all its diseases to its oligarchic character, frozen in an era long past, tied to a society of rich landowners that has ceased to exist. Yet he chooses to end the book by referring to a species that he cannot reduce to the generality of character he attributes to the rest of the theater: passionate people who read opera newsletters, listen to radio shows, ask their favorite artists for pictures by mail, buy records, scream for their favorite diva, and despise her rivals. The nuance in Matamoro's argument leads to an interesting question: If the existence of these fans cannot be explained by status concerns alone, what can explain it? Who are these opera fans? Where do they come from? How did they arrive at the Colón? The next chapter will address these issues.

CHAPTER TWO

"It was love at first sight"

Biography and Social Trajectory of
Standing-Room Dwellers

The Ghosts

The Argentinean writer Manuel Mujica Láinez has contributed to the Colón Opera House in many ways, including the idea of painting a ring in the dome, the libretto for an opera (Ginastera's *Bomarzo*), and a novel about the theater (*El gran teatro*). However, his most important contribution is, perhaps, the proposition outlined in this paragraph from his "Mis memoria del Teatro Colón" (My memories of the Colón Theater): "If all of those who have been closely connected with it at some moment in our lives (and who have something of our own to relate) decided to write down the testimony of our experience, I feel that the joint fruit of our heterogeneous contribution would produce unthought-of riches. Perhaps we might then understand who the ghosts are, where they are, where dreams of intangible signs of hope and disappointment come from, what secret dwellers inhabit the theater" (1983, 56).

This chapter takes up the challenge he proposes, recording in ink the biographies and testimonies of the fans who occupy the upper floors of the opera house. However, this was no easy feat. This kind of material was difficult to collect as their stories were revealed only during in-depth interviews. Opera people tend to hide their backgrounds from others, and what they usually shared with me during my fieldwork was only a part of their personae as operagoers. While I spent countless hours with them in ticket lines, at intermissions, and in conversations over coffee, it was not until I explicitly asked what they did for a living, whether they were married, or where their parents were from that I got to learn something about them that did not pertain to opera.

Passion for the opera attracts a wide range of people to the *cazuela, tertulia,* and *paraíso* floors, confirming the role those spaces have played historically. On the basis of most of the sociological literature available, however, I had imagined that I was going to find a population of local fans from the upper middle classes who have always lived in the core or better-accommodated neighborhoods of the city and have been educated about opera by parents who brought them to the Colón.[1] However, the life stories of the group point in a different direction, to a random act of initiation sometimes during the adult years—made possible by a family member (usually not a parent), a friend, or a public educational institution. They also reveal that we are dealing with people from diverse backgrounds, from many parts of the city and country.

Fans' life trajectories range from the story of uneducated, semiemployed Tito, the forty-eight-year-old son of Italian immigrants who never fostered his interest in opera, to that of Andrea, a physician in her mid-sixties who lives in one of the most posh areas of Buenos Aires and was sent to the city by her rural, Jewish parents. There is José Luis, a sixty-six-year-old record collector and amateur critic from a wealthy Spanish artisan family who never finished college but went "crazy" for classical music after hearing a random waltz on the radio, and Natalia, a thirty-one-year-old political scientist who "fell in love" with opera after falling in love with an amateur musician. Natalia's father never finished high school, worked in a factory, and to this day does not own a record player.

Unlike with professional vocations that require a formal process of initiation, be it that of a musician (Becker 1953), physician (Becker 1961; Friedson 2005), boxer (Wacquant 2003), or tattoo artist (Sanders 1990), it is difficult to follow the trajectory of a novice opera fan. Opera fans are hard to identify; they are not isolated spatially within the opera house; they do not go through a series of formal steps to change their status and acquire proficiency; and, even when I did find people who were attending for the first time, there was no guarantee that they would return. To summarize, novice fans display no outward signs (be it in dress, makeup, or the space they occupy) that identify either their separate or their marginal (or liminal) status.[2] This posed a conundrum: How could I understand initiation stories if I could not also witness them? I opted to capture the peculiar character of the initial attraction to opera through life stories and interviews. People told me how they started attending opera, what they remembered from the first performance they attended, and how long it was until they decided to attend again.

This chapter presents the life stories of six of the many fans I spoke with and interviewed during my fieldwork. The retrospective character of these narratives does not invalidate them. However, I do not want to present these vignettes as self-explanatory. The profiles related here are what Charles Tilly (1998) would call *standard stories*, that is, "the sequential, explanatory accounts of self-motivated human action." As such, these narrative self-portraits present a fusion of "unified time and place, a limited set of self-motivated actors, and cause-effect relations centered on those actors' deliberate actions" (6), and, thus, cannot provide a complete sociological explanation for the development of an opera fan. Paraphrasing Auyero (2006), if we want to understand why these fans do what they do, we are in trouble because cause-effect relations are not only the intended consequences of individual actions. I refer to these stories as a collection that may illuminate some of the traits that appear repeatedly and that may transcend the personal teleological narrative, helping us better comprehend how these individuals are constructed as fans, why they are attracted to opera in the first place, and why they intensify their investment with the art form over time.

My story choices are based primarily on how well they make explicit and illuminate three background patterns that most passionate fans share: (1) While there are no explicit class and education patterns, almost all the fans come from a plebeian and immigrant family, regardless of their current social position. (2) They have migrated to mostly middle-class and upper-middle-class areas of the city from other parts of the country and the metropolitan area. (3) Most of them live alone.

"COMING DOWNTOWN . . . WAS A BIG THING"

Julio is sixty-two years old. He lives with three cats in a small, one-bedroom apartment on the third floor of a building close to the Pacífico train terminus, an area to which workers from the inner country seeking work in the city have historically flocked but that has in recent years been the site of intense gentrification efforts. As soon as I arrived, he asked if I minded animals. Because of the low light and the brown couch cover, I had some difficulty locating the cats seated on it. At first, I thought he was referring to the stuffed animals—a Garfield and a basset hound—on another loveseat. "Those are gifts from my students," he explained.

Julio is a voice coach, and his house is full of LPs and CDs. (He used to spend almost $300 a month on CDs.) His living room is mostly occupied by a piano, with a small bookcase for scores behind it. The rest of the living room consists of the two loveseats with some vintage French posters and a portrait of Verdi on the walls. A second room is filled with old playbills, photographs, scores, LPs, and other papers.

Julio is six foot one, weighs some 250 pounds, and has thinning hair. His striking light blue eyes contrasted sharply with orange short-sleeved shirt and brown pants that he wore for the interview. He was also wearing sneakers because he has had issues with his legs for years and cannot stand other shoes. He seemed eager to talk and became even more lively and animated when I turned on the recorder for our interview, which lasted just shy of two hours. When the interview was over, he put on a jacket and a driving cap.

All Julio's grandparents were Italian immigrants who resided in Buenos Aires State. His father's parents lived in Carlos Casares, where his grandfather had a horse sulky shop, and his mother's lived in Dolores, where they worked the land. At ninety-six, Julio's mother, a housewife who used to sing in church, still remembered the time a touring opera company came to her town to present *Tosca* and she almost died from the shock caused by the onstage death of Cavaradossi.

Julio's parents lived in Lanús, an industrial suburb in the southern part of the city. His mother took him to the opera for the first time when he was only eight. "Coming downtown from Lanús," he said, "was a big thing." While he saw several operas for children, like *Hansel and Gretel*, it was not until he was seventeen that he decided to attend the opera on a regular basis. It was a 1962 production of *Barbiere* with Victoria de los Ángeles that sparked his interest, so much so that both the opera and the singer became his personal favorites; he followed her all to the way to Montevideo in 1977. Julio still remembers the timbre of her voice and the pastel-pink and sepia-red dress she wore. By then, he was already studying piano with a neighborhood teacher and had dropped out of high school to help his mother and brother with their small family business, a work-clothes shop that they had inherited from his father. Julio made a career out of the piano, passing the exams at the municipal conservatory and teaching music. When he was thirty, he decided to give singing a try, and, though he managed to sing well enough to win a prize from a Wagner society, he confined himself to being a voice coach, teaching a holistic method that involves techniques for the entire body.

Although Julio has met many people at the Colón, he has made only one or two friends there. One is also from Lanús and used to buy work clothes from him. Julio lives alone and, like many of the other interviewees, did not talk much about his personal life, although the intimacy he has with music suggests that, in many ways, *is* his personal life. When we talked about friends, he spoke mostly of his students, with whom he shares his passion for music in general. He appreciates bossa nova, jazz, and string quartets in addition to opera.

I approached Julio about an interview after four or five conversations in the standing room of the *tertulia* floor at the Colón, where he goes because his legs are so long and he has gained so much weight that he cannot sit comfortably on the orchestra floor. However, even this is difficult for him because his feet are often sore. He says that, at this point, he goes to see only something he does not know well, like Massenet's *Don Quichotte*; something he loves, like Wagner's *Die Walküre*; or something too big to miss, like the recitals by Maria Guleghina and Juan Diego Flórez. "It's not like when I was in my twenties and went to everything opera, but I believe there are a few works that deserve to be listened to more than once."

"IT'S ALL MINE. I DIDN'T INHERIT ANYTHING FROM MY PARENTS"

Franco is forty-one years old. He lives alone in a big apartment next to a very traditional church in the northern part of the city. He's tall and fit, as he likes to exercise, and very approachable. If he is coming to the opera from work, he wears a suit, although for the interview he donned a blue polo shirt and designer jeans. I met him as I did most of the other interviewees, in the standing-room area of the *tertulia* floor. Franco attends every opera performance in the city and was a constant presence throughout my field-work. In fact, he graciously introduced me to many other fans and occasionally accompanied me to and from operas outside the city. The first time we made phone contact, he asked whether I was going to Avellaneda to attend a seldom-performed opera by Vivaldi; he had just returned from another performance at the Roma House and had gotten lost when he was detoured by protesters commemorating the third anniversary of the deaths of two activists who had been killed by police. He concluded, "It's the risk you run if you want to attend everything!"

Franco's apartment is a new two bedroom in the upper-middle-class neighborhood of Barrio Norte. He had just moved in when I conducted the interview, so the apartment was not fully furnished. He said he wanted to keep the house free of things as he likes to be surrounded by beauty. There was, however, a big table in the living room, a designer couch, and a music system. All throughout the interview, he was very cheerful and excited.

He offered me a spiced tea and started talking on his own without much prompting. Franco told me that his family was never interested in classical music and that well into his teens he liked the local genre *rock nacional*. During his fourth year of high school, however, a music teacher at his small rural school suggested to students that, if they wanted to listen to something that would never fall out of fashion, they should consider something like Vivaldi's *Four Seasons*. Franco told his mother, and the next time she went to Punta Alta, the closest city, she brought him back a tape of that work, followed soon after by a few other classical works. When Franco went to La Plata to study medicine, he saw that *The Magic Flute* was playing and decided to attend. He did not understand much but felt compelled to go back. His first memory of it was the "Queen of the Night Aria," and the day after he passed by a record shop and bought a version of it by Maria Callas. At that time, he was, in his words, "an absolute virgin" and "completely ignorant." His second opera, one month later, was *Lucia*, and, soon after, he bought another record by Callas. He was so curious that he started attending multiple performances of each title, sometimes attending all the dates a particular opera was offered.

The first time he came to the Colón, for Wagner's *Tannhäuser*, Franco had already been living in Buenos Aires for four years. When I asked him what took him so long, he said that he was scared; he had believed that opera was for the elite and that, if he did not have enough money or social status, he was going to feel out of place. Those days are long gone. Now that the Colón is like home, the real challenge is getting to the secondary houses, like the Avenida. Franco has met many people through opera, but he does not socialize with them; he says that they are like those "imaginary friends [*amigos invisibles*]" he had when he was a child.

Franco's family never shared his passion. "It's all mine. I didn't inherit anything from my parents." They didn't have a stereo system, classical radio broadcasts did not reach all the way to the southern part of Buenos Aires State, and they never had much spare time for leisure activities anyway. His father was from a German family that worked the land; his mother was a housewife in Villalonga. Although his sister occasionally joined him at the opera once she moved to the city, for a long time his family disapproved of his interest in opera because they did not consider it an appropriate activity for a rugged rural man.

Franco is one of only two fans who came out to me in conversation. However, he made a big point of separating his operagoing from his sexuality. To him, opera is a sacred space that he would never taint by doing "something stupid, like making a pass at another guy in the *tertulia*." His personal transition became complete when he resigned from his job at a public hospital and started studying art history. Soon after, he found a job with a public relations firm that enabled him to work more closely with design and the arts in general. Although he never disclosed the actual amount, Franco said that he spends about a quarter of his income on opera-related activities. He usually goes three times a week and buys CDs, books, and DVDs. He also listens to the radio constantly. He has enough money to purchase subscription tickets at the Avenida and at the Buenos Aires Philharmonic, but, for him, opera at the Colón is a standing-up activity, although he does occasionally manage to find an empty *tertulia* seat. In his life, and in everything he does, he asserts, "Music takes precedence."

"GOING TO THE OPERA IS EASIER"

Luis is forty-seven years old. Despite his sad eyes and a few gray hairs in his thick beard, he looks young for his age. However, the death of his mother and a couple of economic setbacks gave him heart complications, and now he needs to exercise frequently. For the interview, he wore gym clothes since he had just returned from physical therapy.

I first met Luis in the *tertulia* on a Sunday afternoon while attending the first part of *Don Quichotte* for the second time before leaving to catch the beginning of *La forza del destino* at the Avenida. I had seen him frequently at the off-Colón circuit, usually with a group of opera radio producers whom he has befriended.

Luis lives by himself in a cozy, one-bedroom apartment in Flores, a traditional middle-class neighborhood. The apartment is a bit disorganized, and the furniture is made out of cheap wood and looks precarious. When I visited, there were scores of playbills and pictures on the floor in addition to several hanging on the walls and set about in small frames. Mixed among the mementos were photographs of international stars like Frederica von Stade, regional divas like the Brazilian soprano Kalinka Damiani, a couple of local sopranos and friends, and a scene from Boito's *Mefistofele*, one of his favorite operas. Luis's face brightens when he talks about opera, although, by the end of the interview, he seemed a little sad and the wrinkles in his face were more obvious after he had recounted all that he has pushed aside in his life for opera.

Before going to the opera for the first time, Luis simply thought it was something that started at 5:00 P.M. and lasted until midnight. His grandparents were Eastern European Jews who never cared much for classical music. One of his grandfathers was Russian and delivered oil; his wife was a housewife. His other grandfather was Polish and worked as a rag picker who sold fabric pieces to tailors. Although his parents had a few records, including the suite from Bizet's *Carmen*, they listened mostly to AM radio talk shows. His father was a tailor, and his mother assisted him but mostly stayed at home. Luis's mother sent him to study piano when he was a child, but he quickly got bored and quit. He tried again when he was thirty but did not have the talent or the patience necessary to excel. Luis's family lived in Villa Devoto, a residential neighborhood on the western outskirts of the city that did not have good public transportation to the city center. Because of this, he seldom went downtown, and there were few incentives for him to leave the neighborhood. Luis sang in the elementary school choir and went to the Jewish-oriented high school. In his youth, he liked mostly Argentinean rock and folk music with nice harmonies and big voices.

When Luis was twenty-seven, his ex-brother-in-law told him that he sometimes went to the Colón and asked him whether he wanted to go. The first opera Luis saw was *Carmen*, and, as he put it, "It was love at first sight." He did not know much about the singers but fell immediately for the sound of the opera house and the size of the stage. He started going constantly soon after and never stopped. Eventually, he actually preferred standing up to being seated. After a while, going to the Colón was like going to his mother's house. It took him ten years to start frequenting the off-Colón circuit, traveling to La Plata and, later, Cordoba and Rosario.

At a gala in Avellaneda in 1998, Luis met Bela, a radio producer and stage director who became his best friend and the person he admires most and from whom he takes his cues when it comes to opera. Luis used to bring friends, especially women, to the opera, but he now mostly goes with other amateurs involved in radio shows and off-Colón productions. Like other passionate fans, he crossed to the production side of opera. However, he suffered a mild stroke while trying to help stage *Dido and Aeneas* at a theater on the fringes of the off-circuit, La Manufactura Papelera, due to the stress caused trying to raise enough funds to repay loans, investors, and the orchestra musicians. He currently works as a salesman and debt collector and also collaborates on the radio show that Bela produces.

Because of his radio work, Luis gets a free seat at the off-circuit operas, so he attends the Roma and the Avenida more frequently than the Colón. He has stopped going to each opera more than once, although he makes an exception for a seldom-performed title like Zemlinsky's *King Kandaules* since there was a big chance that he "would never get to see it again." Luis has also stopped booing, although he still passionately discusses staging, costumes, and voices with his friends. Music has been his loyal companion over the years, and it has helped him through bad times. However, he reflected, his engagement with opera has at times been borderline pathological; he has abandoned other activities, and it has been a while since he has dated. At the thought of meeting an unknown woman in another social scenario, Luis confessed, "Going to the opera is easier."

When two other habitués of the *cazuela* floor introduced me to Alicia during an intermission, I had already heard about her monthly trips from Azul, two hundred miles south of the city. After several phone conversations, we arranged to have coffee the day after she attended Juan José Castro's *La zapatera prodigiosa*.

In her late sixties, Alicia has transparent green eyes and dyed blonde hair that lightly touches her shoulders. She cried two times during the interview, shocked by the emotions her memories awoke. The first time, I had asked about her favorite opera, and she was explaining that *Butterfly* affects her the most emotionally. The second time, she was explaining what opera does to her physically and how it actually gives her goose bumps.

Alicia started going to the opera when she was young. Her parents took her to a spring-season performance at La Rural, where the Colón presented some operas in the 1950s as a way to expand its audience. Her first memory of going to the Colón was for *Traviata* when she was six years old. That performance included, not only the renowned but aging Beniamino Gigli, but also his daughter Rina.[3] Although Alicia tried to instill a passion for opera in her own children, bringing them all the way from Azul on the bus—three hours each way—none of them became interested. Now that she is older, she stays overnight at her son's apartment in the city.

Alicia's father had a small business in Liniers, a lower-middle-class commercial neighborhood in the western part of the city. Her mother worked with him, and they listened to classical music around the clock in the shop and their home. Although both of Alicia's parents were Italian, they did not learn about opera in Italy. Her father had started going to the Marconi with his boss and eventually moved on to the Opera and the Coliseo. When there were two shows on Sunday, he attended both. Alicia's mother also liked going, but she attended more *zarzuela* than opera. They would always go to the *paraíso* standing room.

Alicia had begun studying ballet and piano at age four, but, once she finished elementary school, her father advised her to choose a more practical career path. Although she is grateful for her father's advice, she still deeply admires performers. To her, a conductor has one of the best jobs in the world.

Working with other musicians, she said, has to be a doubly rewarding experience; you get to work with instruments and enjoy them and also enjoy the audience's applause once the job is done.

While attending a public normal school[4] for girls, Alicia went to the opera with friends. When she began dental school, her husband, who was also a dentist, began accompanying her. They eventually moved from Buenos Aires to Azul for his work, but she still came to the city regularly to see the opera. During the 1970s, they lived in Philadelphia for four years, but, to her, no foreign opera can compare with the Colón. When she and her husband first returned to Argentina, Alicia no longer had a subscription, so she would wait in all-night lines to get tickets. In 1990, a flood in Azul prevented her from renewing her subscription series on time. Although the theater's foundation intervened and gave her two orchestra seats, for her and her mother, Alicia did not feel comfortable there, preferring the view from the *cazuela*. Now, she is back in the *cazuela* and organizes her professional life around the Colón calendar. She stopped coming with her family a while ago, when her mother became too old to travel on the bus, but now has a few friends that she always talks to during intermissions and on the way out. Alicia fell in love with opera when "she was really, really little," and it remains a central part of her life. At the end of the interview, she thanked me, saying, "I was so happy to be able to tell someone all this."[5]

"I DISCOVERED A WHOLE NEW WORLD"

Irma is seventy years old. She has permed hair that is dyed red, and she was wearing a red sweater and dress pants for our meeting. She also invited her friend Rina to the interview, explaining, "If the Colón was ever sold, they would have to take Rina too because she is part of the inventory." Irma put out pastries and tea, and, for the next three hours, I barely said a word, except to answer questions about myself, my project, and my interest in opera. The interview had a unique intensity due to the constant counterpoint between the two women, with Irma always protesting that Rina did not let her speak.

Irma's apartment is a small two-bedroom in the neighborhood of Once, the traditional Jewish garment district of the city. The apartment is decorated with numerous paintings that Irma did herself, and the table where we had tea was covered with music and theater magazines, among them one that the Colón published until 2003. Before I left, Irma graciously offered her collection for my research, and the two women promised to introduce me to some other female fans as well as their regular usher, who had recently been promoted to the orchestra seats section. He knew their names, their tastes, and a bit of their family histories, and, if they were late, he would sometimes open a box for them.

Irma has come a long way since first hearing and falling in love with Chopin's polonaises on the Radio Municipal when she was twelve. From that point on, she wanted to listen to that music or at least to a radio station that played that music. However, her father disapproved. He was a manual worker who would paint and do decorating jobs on the side, and he managed to build a small house for the family in Lanús. He thought that Irma would be single forever if she went to the opera or sang *zarzuela* or the occasional *canzonetta* in the house. Whenever she sang a nocturne by Chopin that she had learned in the school choir, he would say, "There she is, the old maid candidate." His disdain for high-culture pursuits was confined to music, however; he was a fervent reader of Russian authors and taught Irma to read at a very young age. Such confrontations only confirmed for Irma something she said several times during the interview: "Life is an opera."

Despite her father's concerns, Irma started going to the opera at the Marconi in 1957. Her mother was the daughter of Spanish immigrants and loved *zarzuela* so much that she took Irma to the Avenida to see a famous tenor, Ramón Contreras. Irma also heard Contreras sing in the 1958 Colón summer season and joined his fan club soon after. Every Monday, she went to the small auditorium of the national radio to see him perform.

Thanks to the women she met at the fan club, Irma learned about the standing-room area of the Colón. She had been surprised to see that those other women, who did not seem to be that well off, were going regularly to the opera, and she decided to ask how they managed to do so. For the next few years, her life revolved around the world of all-night lines. She took her then boyfriend (who later became her husband) along to her first-ever Colón opera: the double bill of *Cavalleria rusticana* and *Pagliacci*. She remembers running up the stairs to get the best possible place in the *paraíso* and being mesmerized by the monumental dimensions of the stage and the lights. She had never seen anything like it, and the impact it had on her was powerful. Reminiscing, Irma explained, "I discovered a whole new world."

Unlike Rina, who was single and used to go to the opera five times a week, including dress rehearsals, Irma had to care for her husband and daughter. They would alternate Sundays out, with Irma going to the opera one week and her husband going to watch soccer the next. Recognizing her passion for opera, her husband bought Irma a modern LP player so that she could invite guests over to listen. Sadly, he died when their daughter was only three. Although Irma took her daughter to the opera many times, she did not develop the same love for it. Irma, however, has only extended her activities over the years to include off-Colón arenas, conferences, and participation in an amateur choir. For her, not only is life an opera; opera is a way of life.

Néstor lives by himself in a small one-bedroom apartment in an elegant area on the border between Barrio Norte and Recoleta. In his forties, he is tall and quite fit, although he has some obvious plastic surgery scars next to his ears and eyes. While he studied both veterinary medicine and architecture, he now makes a living as a personal trainer, and, during the interview, he was wearing gym clothing. I actually met him through another fan who goes to the same gym. They had become acquainted at the opera house and consider each other friends, but only so far as to share an occasional coffee or visit when they run into each other at the local market. The centerpiece of his apartment—which is otherwise rather old-fashioned, with a big flowery couch and curtains—is a home theater system with a DVD player, speakers, and a large screen. There were at least a hundred DVDs and VHS cassettes out when I visited and an even more extensive collection in a wooden cabinet beside the theater system.

Néstor comes from a wealthy family from Carlos Casares, a town located 150 miles to the west of the city whose economy was dependent on the cultivation of sunflowers. His family played the radio and LPs constantly when he was growing up. His father, a Ukrainian Jewish civil engineer who built the Liberty Temple in Buenos Aires—one of the main synagogues of the Ashkenazi community—inherited "lots of Beethoven, Schubert, Mozart, and a bit of opera" from his family and was, as Néstor said, "very cultivated." His grandfather, also a fixture of the Jewish social world, helped organize one of Buenos Aires's two main cemeteries, in Liniers. Despite this, Néstor grew up as a Catholic, much like his mother, a housewife whose father was English and mother Spanish. His family regularly visited the city during winter break, and, in addition to the Holiday on Ice skate shows, they would take him to the Colón. The first opera he saw was the double bill *Cavalleria* and *Pagliacci*.

At the age of twenty-one, when he was in the city to study architecture, Néstor decided to repeat that experience. He attended the 1980 performance of *Pagliacci*. Since then, he has been going to as many performances as possible, including dress rehearsals. In 1992, he decided to buy a subscription series, first for the gallery next to the *paraíso*, and eventually upgrading in 1998 to the *cazuela*. Whenever he decides to attend a repeat performance, he still goes to the *tertulia* standing room. Unfortunately, he said, over the last few years, he has felt less compelled to see multiple performances of the same opera because he feels that the quality has diminished. However, he has ventured to Avellaneda and La Plata and has also acquired a subscription to the Buenos Aires Lírica season at the Avenida.

The first time he went to the Colón on his own, Nestor was hooked by the acoustics, the voices onstage (if he were to be reincarnated, he says he would love to be an opera singer), and the passion of audience members—people like him whose enthusiasm never wavered, even after years of going to the opera house. He misses what he called *the follies of the opera*, those people who suffered from it and whom he would see whenever he would attend a performance, be it at the Colón or another house. He seldom brings people from the outside, be it partners or friends. He would rather run into the people he barely knows who greet him and chat whenever possible. As he says, "I've always liked to go alone. I never get bored." Néstor seldom shares how much he loves opera with people he knows from work, sensing that he "might detect a hint of disrespect." He has not befriended many people from the Colón, but he stays in touch with one or two by phone, and they usually meet when he goes to an off-Cólon performance. In his opinion, opera mediates those relationships.

Is There a Social Location for Passion?

Is being a passionate opera fan reducible to a particular position in the social structure? Can any background pattern provide us with a full explanation of the intense attachment these fans feel for opera? Is there any right combination of economic, cultural, and social capital that predisposes an individual to fall in love with opera? If the question here is whether there appears to be any class-specific form of fandom, I am afraid that the final answer is no. However, if we look for patterns beyond social class and education, a few indicators do repeat themselves. Let me first discard the answers we look for initially as sociologists and then proceed to examine other factors that might help us understand who these fans are and what it is they look for in opera.

Most of my interviewees come from diverse segments of the middle class, ranging from the petty bourgeoisie to a few who are considered upper-middle-class.[6] Some are petty accountants (e.g., Alfredo).[7] A few of them are minor lawyers (Gustavo, Daniela, Juan Manuel). There are also a dentist (Alicia); two physicians, one who has her own private assisted-fertilization clinic (Andrea) and another who works in a public hospital (Fabiana); a psychoanalyst (Eugenio); a few high school teachers (Antonio, Esteban, María);

two journalists (Bianca and Ernesto); a physical trainer (Néstor); a public relations specialist (Franco); a semiretired small shop owner (Rina); a theater director from the independent scene (Guillermo); and a debt collector (Luis). Five of them are public employees (Natalia, Diego, Andrés, Ludmila, Eduardito). A few of them have already retired and live off small pensions (Irma, Ethel) or are still working part-time with their elderly parents (Tito), as freelance translators (Roberto), in public offices (Alejandro, Maria Luisa), or as schoolteachers (Diana). One of them is a voice coach (Julio). Another is an aspiring singer (Luciana). Others have also translated their passion for music into work as music journalists or radio producers (Bela, Germán, José Luis, Gustavo).

Unfortunately, the number of people for whom I have complete background information (thirty-nine) is too small to play the number games with gusto. However, if we look at, not only the professions of the fans, but also the highest level of education that they have achieved, we find that 40 percent (fifteen) finished their university studies.[8] Another 13 percent (five) dropped out of college, and the remainder only went to high school (nineteen), including two people who dropped out before finishing.

Looking at these numbers, one might be tempted to think that opera fans represent an educational elite, but this would be incorrect. The high literacy rate of the Argentinean population (near 96 percent) has distinguished it from other Latin American countries for many years. As of 2004, for instance, over 1.5 million people were enrolled in college (*Alfabetismo y educación* 2004). However, widespread access to education does not make Argentina a developed nation. Economically, it is an impoverished country that had high unemployment rates throughout the 1990s and the early years of the twenty-first century (more than 16 percent), a shrinking gross national product until 2003, and an increasingly recessive distribution of income. The economic and political crisis of 2001, when the national currency plummeted to a third of its value and the country had five presidents over a ten-day period, has affected most of society. As most recent studies about the diminishing economic power of the Argentinean middle class have shown, many Argentineans are in an awkward position that combines high educational capital with low economic capacity.[9] More than a few of the opera fans with whom I spoke are included in this category, and their habit of occupying the cheap seats is a matter, not just of pride and preference, but a necessity if they want to attend regularly.

How different are these passionate standing-room fans from the general Buenos Aires population? How do they fare in comparison to other members of the Colón audience? According to the National Marketing Association and the city government,[10] 51 percent of the city population can be considered upper-class (21 percent), upper-middle-class (13 percent), or traditional middle-class (17 percent). The remaining 49 percent is divided among upper-working-class, lower-class, and those outside the labor market. Nevertheless, the city is an oasis. A quick comparison of Buenos Aires proper with the surrounding metropolis gives us a snapshot of the brutal process of dualization the country underwent during the 1990s.[11] In the Buenos Aires Metropolitan Region or Gran Buenos Aires, the middle and upper classes (21 percent) are surpassed by the marginal class (23 percent), which, along with the upper working class and the lower class, constitute three-quarters of the area's total population.

Most of the interviewees in my study represent three specific groups: the upper middle class,[12] the traditional middle class,[13] and the lower middle class.[14] Only three interviewees belong to the upper working class.[15] It is hard to say how this sample compares to the overall Colón population. The authorities do not keep a register and have prevented researchers from doing so.[16] However, as the prices presented in the first chapter suggest, a large portion of the orchestra seats and the lower boxes and balconies belong either to the upper class or to the upper middle class. In fact, two of the standing-room fans in the group own orchestra-level subscriptions but go upstairs for repeat performances of a single title, and four others have subscriptions for *tertulia* or *cazuela* seats. A survey from the Avenida, conducted by Juventus Lyrica, gives us a better understanding of the composition of the population at the city's second house: 45 percent are upper- and upper-middle-class, 31 percent are traditional middle-class, 14 percent are lower-middle-class, and almost 10 percent are from the upper part of the working class.[17] Many of my interviewees maintain that the Avenida audience includes some people from the lower floors of the Colón but otherwise closely resembles the composition of both the seating and the standing areas of the upper three floors. Among the most common occupations represented at the Avenida are teacher or professor (11 percent), employee (9 percent), lawyer (7 percent), physician (7 percent), housewife (6 percent), and student (6 percent). Retired people make up almost 10 percent.[18]

The Deviating Background of Love

As we can see, the class composition of the population of passionate fans who populate the higher floors of the Colón (and better seats at houses where the price ranges are not so extreme) suggests a heterogeneous population. What all of them share, despite their differences in income, education, and age—from the doctor with a country house to the fortysomething high school dropout still living with his parents—is their affiliation with the urban-middle-class imaginary of a country based on social homogeneity, as produced by a series of institutions including public education, access to universal health care, and the promise of upward mobility. This middle-class vision aligns high culture with civilized ideals and practices and meshes well with the embellished picture of Argentina's liberal and mesocratic rule that is central to the middle-class imaginary (Semán 2006). Is there any reason why this diverse collection of people shares a particular and idealized vision of the world of cultural goods, including opera?

"My grandmother took me to the Colón a few times when I was nine or ten. She was a Spaniard, and, though she wasn't exactly poor, there was little extra money, but she had it in her head that this was the culture her granddaughter should be a part of. She thought it was proper and appropriate for me, so I went to the Colón." The story María describes is a very familiar one, tracing the origin of high culture—and opera and the Colón in particular—to the fans' plebeian or immigrant backgrounds. Many fans come from families that either brought their definition of culture with them from Europe or accepted the dominant idea of culture as a set of prescribed appropriate practices, like learning an instrument (piano, for both boys and girls; violin, for boys) or attending classical music and dance performances or lessons (ballet, for girls) at an early age.[19]

All the interviewees come from immigrant families; some are Italian, some Spanish, and some Eastern European Jewish.[20] Only one comes from a family that has been in Argentina for more than two generations. This is the same person whose geographic origin (Tucumán) is beyond the influence of the city suburbs and the area commonly referred to as the Pampa Gringa. As we have already seen in the testimonies, most of the interviewees' mothers were housewives, while their fathers worked in factories, owned small family businesses or craft shops, or worked the land. In the few cases where the family was already well-off economically, they either were not interested in high culture—like Rina's or José Luis's families, whose money came from a successful craft-related business (jewelry and furniture)—or came to Buenos Aires only once a year and had sporadic contact with high culture and its etiquette, as in the cases of Néstor and Andrés.

This plebeian or immigrant family origin was symbolized during the interviews mostly through turns of phrase that referred to geographic distance. Julio and Luis associated going to the Colón with "coming downtown." Others, like Franco, linked it to "finally having arrived in the city." They were hardly alone in expressing this spatial dimension as few of them lived close to the opera house as children. As I already hinted, there are two groups to which these expressions of geographic mobility can be attributed: those coming from noncentral areas of the city or from the metropolitan region and those coming from the areas where most immigrants settled to work the land—the south of Cordoba, Entre Ríos, Santa Fe, and most of Buenos Aires State.

Throughout the history of Buenos Aires, most of the its upper- and higher-middle-class families have remained in the city or, at most, retired to the northern suburbs along the river.[21] Land use has taken the form of concentric rings spreading outward from the historical center, where most of the financial services and the headquarters of manufacturing companies as well as most government institutions are located. A complex yet antiquated transportation system connects the rest of the city with the core through six subway lines and three main railway terminal stations. The working-class periphery developed thanks to public transportation subsidies[22] and state loans for lower-class property ownership.[23]

It is precisely in this working-class periphery, be it on the southern or western outskirts of the city or in the first of the three rings of suburbs, that we can place the fans' family origins. Places like Villa Devoto, Floresta, San Martín, Barracas, La Boca, Liniers, Lanús, and Avellaneda repeatedly came up during the interviews, forming the picture of a shared social trajectory that brought fans to the Colón. These neighborhoods were the result of three processes: the expansion of transportation systems,[24] especially the trains and tramways; the consequential placement of industrial plants along those railways; and state efforts to create good and affordable housing for the working class and the lower middle class. This three-pronged process manifested itself differently in each area. In the suburbs, the early expansion of the railway toward the south encouraged the opening of many industrial plants during the 1910s, which consolidated during the process of import substitution from the early 1930s through the 1960s (Auyero 2001, 48). Meanwhile, the extension of the western railway had a different effect on the neighborhoods on the western outskirts of the city. Flores, a summer vacation area for the rich, was quickly surrounded by lower-middle-class homes and commercial areas, including Liniers, the home of the city's main slaughterhouse; Bajo Flores, which housed one of the biggest garbage dumps in the city; and Floresta. The subway system has historically ignored the southern part of the city, but, in 1904, the tramway began serving the factories and poor households of areas like Barracas, Pompeya, and La Boca (Scobie and Luzzi 1983).

Farther away from the Colón—and from the other big regional cities that housed opera houses, like Rosario, Santa Fe, La Plata, and Cordoba—were those fans and their families from the Pampa Gringa (Gallo 1984). Although the name has sometimes been used strictly for the rural areas of the center, south, and west of Santa Fe State that were colonized by migrants from Piamonte, Friuli, Saboya Switzerland, and Germany, it is commonly used to describe a larger area that includes Buenos Aires State, the south of Cordoba, and Entre Rios as well as Santa Fe. These areas are also heavily populated by immigrants, including Eastern European Jews, Basque, Dutch, and Irish peasants, who dedicated themselves to working the land or participating in local agricultural commerce. Cities and towns like Ramallo, Carlos Casares, El Paraíso, Arrecifes, and Chabas were constituted as "small hygienic cities" (Hourcade 1999) organized, not as mini–agrarian societies, but around markets and social institutions like ethnic mutual-aid associations, sports clubs, bars, and a few high-culture establishments like a local opera or theater group.[25] Operas were usually performed in fragments or in concert, without scenery or costumes (Sanguinetti 2002), which partly explains the surprise fans from these areas felt the first time they went to the Colón.

For those whose families were not that interested in opera, and for those whose families (e.g., those of Natalia, Fabiana, Franco, and Irma) were actually against it, their initiation into the world of classical music took place through the democratizing efforts of public institutions, including the radio and the schools. The classical music programs of Radio Excelsior, Radio Municipal, and Radio El Mundo, which had its own orchestra and auditorium by the 1930s, were followed a few years later (1947) by the classical music service supplied to the whole country by the state radio. Meanwhile, public schools provided students a music education centered on the history of classical music and, sometimes, provided cheap subscription tickets.

Thanks to the radio, those who had never attended live opera were able to familiarize themselves with it, regardless of how far they were from the city center. Many of the fans' narratives emphasize the active role of radio in their music educations. The most extreme example might be José Luis, whose Spanish parents were absolutely oblivious to opera. For him, the road to the Colón was through radio and records. When he was eight years old, he discovered a Viennese waltz show broadcast by the state radio. He fell in love with the waltzes and had his parents buy him as many records as they could, and, whenever his family's prosperous jewelry business kept them away from their Flores home, he would spend the whole day listening to the radio with the cleaning lady. In 1950, one his favorite conductors, Arthur Roshinski, came to Buenos Aires to conduct Rimsky-Korsakov's *The Golden Cockerel*. He thought that Roshinski would be conducting the symphonic suite drawn from the opera, which lasts twenty minutes. To his surprise, it was the whole opera. After attending with his mother, he was entranced by what he calls "the spectacle of opera," and, by 1952, he started going on his own to every performance.

Music teachers and school programs appear to be other stepping-stones by which these fans get to opera. To Franco's teacher extolling the eternal powers of classical music, we can add José Luis's public high school, the Colegio Nacional de Buenos Aires, and its music program, which put him in touch with fellow student opera fans and provided discounted subscription tickets. Andrea was able to learn about opera at her normal school and Daniela at the Nicolás Avellaneda. At the Mariano Acosta, Gustavo followed the advice of his music teacher and bought a student subscription, which included the 1977 performance of *Eugene Onegin*. One year later, he traded his subscription and started going to the upper floors, the *segunda tertulia lateral* (the second row of lateral *tertulia* seats), with a school friend who clued him in to the low quality of the student subscription, which was called *extraordinary* but paradoxically included mostly performances with second principals and national performers. Gustavo stayed there—because "those tickets were as cheap as the *paraíso*"—until 1990, when he bought the extraordinary subscription again, this time for orchestra seats.

"Because I love it"

More than a few of the fans I interviewed described the intense feeling they experienced their first time at the opera house as something explosive, something that was meant to be, or something they had been waiting for their whole lives.[26] A smaller but still significant number mentioned the second way in which they affiliated with the *dramma per musica*. This experience seems to have less to do with their inherited dispositions than with the personal relationships involved in their introductions to opera. These stories are less related to family and schooling and more to those who were their friends and lovers at the time and the role they played in charging opera with affection.

Although there are many stories of childhood and high school friends bringing fans to the opera house for the first time (Diego, Bela, Gustavo, Rina, and Daniela) or meeting one's partner at or coming with him/her to the opera house (Mario and Ethel, Roberto and his wife, Irma's first date with her husband) and of operas that seemed directly related to a fan's personal life (Luis's friendship with Bela and Rina's with Irma), perhaps the most striking story is Natalia's. I ran into her first at a performance of a chamber opera (*Der Kaiser von Atlantis*) that the Colón staged at the Coliseo and then a second time at the *paraíso* exit for a Sunday performance of *Barbiere*. She did not think she would be of much help to my research since she had "never hooked up with music until [that] year." When I asked her why she had suddenly decided to start going by herself, she confessed, "There is a whole story behind it. There was this guy who lived in Strasbourg, and he came to Buenos Aires to work for a bit, and we went out, and then we decided to keep in touch. . . . He once sent me an MP3 file with *Poppea*, and I became fascinated. I mean, I had never heard it before, and, all of a sudden, a whole new universe opened up, and I had to go and buy *Poppea*. And then, after that, I decided to give something that involved the stage a chance, too." In other words, her initial experience was more than a matter of just listening to music or missing a loved one. Her appreciation of the music grew even stronger when she attended a live performance. In that transformation, listening to music on her own, disembodied from the stage, became more of an exercise in preparation and anticipation. "I loved how the movements, the rhythm, and the voices were sewn together on the stage. It was what impacted me the most." The last time I saw her, she asked me which operas I would recommend and whether it would be smart to take one of the appreciation classes or attend one of the conferences. From the titles playing that season, she already knew she wanted to see Strauss's *Capriccio* and Puccini's *Turandot*.

Despite the importance of personal bonds in their introductions in opera, most of the passionate fans interviewed currently live alone. A little less than a third live with a permanent partner.[27] Those who are married often expressed how difficult it is to keep up with the intensely demanding rhythm of opera fandom. Some have compromised with their families and attend only once a month (Alicia), while others have set their limits at once a week (like Gustavo, after his wife had their second daughter) or once every other week (as Irma did when her husband was alive and she had to take care of him and their child). A few others, like Roberto, alternate going alone with coming with their spouse. Guillermo bought *tertulia* subscription series for his whole family and, meanwhile, goes on his own whenever he feels like it, although that is never more than once a week. Victor and Alberto go to the *tertulia* floor together as a couple, but they are more an exception than the norm.

The release from family responsibilities has a direct relationship with the increase in the investment in opera. Irma came back to the Colón with a vengeance after she split from her partner of twenty-one years, while Andrea added an opera subscription to her frequent but scattered forays into the music world after her husband passed away. On one occasion, I heard divorcé Germán speaking candidly with another audience member before a performance of *La forza del destino*. He humorously admitted that there are many ways a newly single man can fill up his life. He has chosen music, going to three concerts a week, for example, rather than engaging in more profane activities. He said, "Yesterday I went to see Joshua Bell, on the weekend I went to the Colón. Last week, I came to the Avenida for Juventus [Lyrica, the opera company]. I mean, what are you supposed to do if you are a lonely guy [*un tipo solo*]? There's soccer, you can go to the tracks, have a drink here and there, masturbate [*la japa*]. There's not much else to do. I'd rather go to all the concerts." Despite this confession, Germán has ceased his many opera activities since his daughter had a child.[28] Being a grandfather decreased the amount of time and energy he could spend on opera and reinserted him into the world of family obligations.

Armando is a friend of Germán's and was actually his boss at one of the radio shows he used to produce. Armando is a renowned radio sports journalist in his early sixties who goes to everything he can fit into his schedule and takes advantage of his travels around the world to attend opera. Here, he reflects on what it is that makes people intensify their investment in opera and other classical music activities as they age and withdraw themselves from other activities and circles of affiliation:

> When you are older than forty or fifty, it is an extraordinary relief. If only people would learn to listen, or better yet, train. . . . You don't learn the pleasure of opera just sitting there for three or four hours at a time. . . . When your kids are gone, when your body stops responding and you do less physical activities, you can find great comfort in music. To be out of yourself is the great possibility that music allows. Being with yourself all the time is a little bit boring, especially when you're old and you've been with yourself for a while. Seeing a performance and stepping out of myself for those few hours fills me with pleasure.

"Se non é vero, é ben trovato"

"Coming downtown . . . was a big thing." "It's all mine. I didn't inherit anything from my parents." "I discovered a whole new world." "I've always liked to go alone. I never get bored." These statements are neither capricious nor naive; instead, they point to a specific direction in social origin, providing some hints at the answer to the question of whether fans' backgrounds can help predict the shape of their connections to opera. Are opera fans "made out of clay" solely by some of the key informal institutions of the opera machine—the all-night lines, intermission conversations, fan clubs, shared trips, and debates in newspapers, newsletters, and forums? Or are they somehow predisposed to such heavily personalized investment in their passion, as I will describe in depth later? Fans bring from their place of origin a sense of distanced respect for high culture as something they initially contemplated from afar; they cherish the initial moment of surprise they felt when first confronted by the voices and stage of the Colón. They also bring the hardworking, individualized perspective for which those of petty bourgeois origin are known and that is, as I will show, smoothly transformed into an idea of the activities that surround opera becoming a kind of career and of a performance as something to be enjoyed, elucidated, and confronted individually, one-on-one with the music. The sense of opera as a personal adventure (Simmel 1958)—something outside the realm of profane, quotidian life—and its threading as a narrative bildungsroman, which makes them loving beings as much as it makes of opera a constitutive experience for them, can be seen as a predictable way of relating with an activity, given opera fans' social backgrounds. But is that all there is?

While lower-middle-class and middle-class audiences behave similarly to the way in which Bourdieu expected in *Distinction*,[29] his description falls short when it comes to making sense of the classificatory battles that take place within the opera house and the intense initial attraction (characterized, as we have seen, by a "love at first sight" reaction) that fans feel or remember having felt when they were first confronted by an opera. Their allodoxic attraction to opera is, to a certain extent, the attraction to a strange, new world. However, pointing this out does not explain why certain things that should, in consequence, be patterned homogeneously are actually heterogeneous; for instance, why opera fans' families lack the same attraction to opera, why people of the same social position enjoy opera in different ways, or why others who come from the same background as the opera fans are more attracted to wine tasting, movies, soccer, or going to the tracks. We must ask, in the words of the French sociologist Bernard Lahire (2003), how these dispositions are activated in a specific context to the point that appetence becomes a passion.

Thus, to complete the explanation of why fans engage with opera and not movies or jazz, it is necessary to move from the background to the foreground factors, along with the mediating institutions, the socialization instances that make of opera something delectable and enjoyable, helping amateurs[30] shape their initial attraction. The second part of this book follows this path. The next chapter begins to do so by moving from the level of self-report presented in the life stories to themes and issues that might be known by the opera fans only in a prereflexive way, drawing on theory to engage in a different kind of storytelling about being and becoming an opera fan.

PART II

FOREGROUND

CHAPTER THREE

Becoming an Opera Fan

Cultural Membership,
Mediation, and Differentiation

Homeless at the Doorsteps

One of the two side entrances of the Colón Opera House faces a walking section of Viamonte Street renamed Arturo Toscanini Street. The entrance is a tall, white door beneath a large facade supported by a solid pair of Ionic columns. The once bright-yellow walls surrounding it have faded and reveal humidity stains. Passersby leave leaflets there offering all kinds of services, from weight-loss programs to cheap toner replacements for office printers, and, once performances are over, homeless men find shelter from the cold on the three gray steps (see figure 7). This is where those seated in the *cazuela* and *tertulia*—the upper floors with the cheapest tickets—gather in order to enter the opera house. Depending on the opera being performed, people congregate anywhere from an hour and a half to twenty minutes before the door opens for the opportunity to claim a good spot on the standing-room floors—one with an unobstructed view of the stage. There is an elevator, but, because it does not leave the ground floor until a good number of people are on board, most ticketholders forgo the long wait time and choose the stairs. Fans of all ages march up the four or five flights in a silent but fierce competition to get to the best spots.

It is winter in Buenos Aires, and there is a constant drizzle. Today, there are far more people than the usual fifty or so that gather before the opera

FIGURE 7. A homeless woman sits next to the side entrance of the Colón. Photograph by the author.

house door opens. The pull of Wagner's *Die Walküre* seems too much to resist. There are over a hundred people, and there is still a good forty-five minutes until we get to enter the hall. Spectators either shield themselves with umbrellas or try to stay as close as possible to the wall, taking advantage of the many balconies, ledges, and sculpted figures above. About fifteen minutes before eight o'clock, a woman passes by and distributes flyers to the people in line. They are advertising *Un ballo in maschera*, Verdi's opera, which is playing at the Avenida, the city's second opera house, at the same time.

The flyers immediately become a catalyst for conversation among strangers. I am standing next to a woman in her early sixties who looks briefly at the flyer before exclaiming, "I heard the first night was a disaster." She adjusts her large glasses and goes on, "I haven't gone yet, but my girlfriend went and said it was a mess. I'm going on Sunday. Have you gone already?" Before I can reply, the woman is rhapsodizing about how good "she" was the first time she saw the same opera at the Colón. Soon, our conversation is joined by the older gentleman in front of the woman and the young man behind me. It seems that everyone knows who "she" is but me. Before I can embarrass myself by asking, the older gentleman says, "But La Piscitelli [Maria Pia Piscitelli, the star of the Avenida *Ballo*] was extraordinary. It's hardly a surprise, if you consider how good she has been before." Before I can say something about how I remembered her in *Norma*, the three of them start exchanging notes. "I think that what she did in *Simon*[1] was amazing," says the young man, to which the older man responds, "Yes, but I thought she fared even better the time she went toe to toe with June Anderson as Norma!"[2] The woman—I would later learn her name was Noemí—says she thinks that Piscitelli was most memorable in *Don Carlo*.[3] The older gentleman goes on to voice his dissatisfaction with the rationale behind staging *Ballo* yet again. "Why do they need to stage an opera like that one? So many great singers have come to do it. How do you compare her with La Mitchell,[4] for instance?" To this, Noemí answers that, although Piscitelli has a great voice and a nice presence, she saw an incredible *Simon* at the Colón, with a different soprano.

She cannot remember whether she was Ukrainian or Polish, "but it was at least some eleven years ago. And it was definitely better."[5] The line has finally started to move, and the small group becomes quiet as everyone prepares to bound up the hundreds of steps that separate them from a complete and unobstructed view of the stage.

A scene like this is typical at the door of the opera house and often repeats itself inside. Fans engage in informal conversations about what they are about to see or other recent events in the local opera scene. In doing so, they point to certain topics and themes and extend an open and almost automatic invitation to talk. These conversations usually happen in small groups, mostly one-on-one, as it is the fans who are by themselves who tend to speak to one another. If it is opening night of a particular opera, the questions are about the dress rehearsals, and past-season productions are used for comparison. If it is any performance other than the first, the obvious question is whether you have already seen the opera. Regardless of whether they are discussing what they have come to see or another recent production, fans engage in comparisons to recent performances, other operas in which the featured singers appeared during past seasons, and—especially if the opera has never been performed in the country—standout recordings.

The Blind Spot: High Culture and Initiation Processes

A significant body of sociological and anthropological literature has reflected on what it means to be initiated and how we traverse diverse stages in a transformative way until the moment in which we become one with the practice and transcend our previous status within a given community. Sociologists and anthropologist have looked at the processes by which people pass through certain rites of passage that move them from one status and role to another. Generally, the focus has been on political communities, rituals of masculinity among members of segmentary societies, or the membership rituals one must pass through to be integrated into a profession (see Becker 1961, 1963; Van Gennep 1961; Turner 1967, 1974, 1977; Myerhoff and Moore 1975; and Wacquant 2003). This perspective has not been deployed, however, in order to understand how someone becomes a devoted and engaged consumer of a cultural product.

The purpose of this chapter is to explicate the processes of initiation into a practice usually considered high culture by North American sociology. It differs from other accounts of cultural consumption in that it is concerned, not with the correspondence between social background and taste, but with the processes whereby taste is assembled, the diverse spaces where this happens, and the diverse stages through which it happens. It asks, not only what people bring with them (their backgrounds and dispositions), but also what they see in a cultural product and how they learn to intensify their attachment to that product both internally (as they learn how to feel and be moved) and externally (as they learn where and how to display their appreciation publicly). While sociologists concerned with the capacity for converting culture into capital have signaled the importance of the family in reproducing the taste for high culture, they have fallen short in explaining how it is that certain characteristics of a cultural practice are rendered so meaningful as to mobilize someone to partake in it.

How They Learned What an Opera Was

The first question I posed to fans like those who conversed outside the opera house was: How much do you need to know to actually enjoy opera? At the beginning of my research, some of my informants were very concerned about downplaying how much they have attended. They always pointed to someone else "who actually has been going forever and really knows about it." However, some of these people were at the opera house every time I attended, and, when they finally told me how long they have been going, they would say, "Just twenty-five years."

This highly experiential character of learning makes for a complex system, one that proposes opera as an activity that (*a*) looks to the past for reference and comparison, (*b*) demands extensive and intensive attendance, (*c*) encourages people to attend conferences and lectures, listen to the radio, read related books, and buy records (although these activities are always complementary and never a substitute for attendance), and (*d*) makes for an almost automatic and informal apprenticeship process in which the older members school the younger ones and are recognized and revered for their knowledge.[6]

I do not want to make of opera—at least for these fans—an activity that is learned following the classic model of affiliation and initiation into cultural practices that Howard Becker (1953) established with his case study of marijuana use. This model makes sociability, or contact with other participants who already enjoy the activity, the turning point and suggests that the activity is ambiguous at first and does not produce the desired effects until one learns how to consume and enjoy it properly. By contrast, I extend this model by including various settings in which fans learn the effects opera has on them and complement it by including an instant of revelation not contemplated in Becker's model, in which they are attracted to opera, not *solely* by and through the company of others, but by an intense attraction (visual, corporal) that they *subsequently* must socially learn how to control and maximize.[7]

As established in chapter 2, fans do not initially reject opera or get confused by it. Instead, they feel an intense attraction that they are compelled to explore and organize in order to maximize the pleasure it produces. The compulsion to talk about, to listen to, and to learn about opera—always embodied in the phrase "I don't know enough"—signals, not a cultural deficiency, as could be thought at first glance, but the active intention to find a more complete effect, one that goes beyond any personal, physical sensations experienced into the realm of the work and explanations of it yet results, paradoxically, in an intense one-on-one relationship with that work. While this involves many occasions that imply forms of sociability, grouping, and exchange, passionate opera fans are not led hand in hand into the social aspects of the activity; on the contrary, they give in to it in a highly individualized way.

Various studies of audiences and spectatorship have shown the role of surprise and the suspension of disbelief in enjoying a performance. The trope is as much a part of opera scholarship and criticism, which preoccupies itself with the notion that something we love can become disfigured by our excessive knowledge of it, as it is of cultural sociology, whose authors suggest that audiences are props, that they can be conned by staged scenes of authenticity, and that they need to have a fresh take on what is being performed, devoid of background information, in order to enjoy it.[8]

Drawing on my ethnographic work, I set two aims for this chapter. First, I show that passionate fans enjoy opera, not because they want to be swayed by it in their ignorance, but rather because of their belief that it is something that must be learned in order to be properly enjoyed. Herein, I emphasize that, while learning about opera is an eminently social activity, what is learned is a romantic understanding of opera consumption, one that teaches how to be one with the music in a highly personalized and individualized way, sheltered from all possible obstacles, including other people, the current political problems at the house, and even staging considered controversial.

Second, I describe three diverse settings in which people learn about opera. One type is informal. It involves the surrounding, nonmusical moments of the performance: ticket and door lines, intermissions, bus trips to other opera houses. A second kind is more formal, including as it does classes, lectures, and conferences. A third kind takes place at the opera house as novices follow the lead of older fans who either clap, sit silently, or boo, indicating the etiquette and the appropriate moments for each action. Passionate fans learn to enjoy opera *in foro interno*, responding internally to parts of the music that are supposed to demand an emotional reaction, and *in foro externo*, reacting publicly in an appropriate way.

The resulting "listening contract" gives us a thorough idea of how music is listened to by the fans, when and how they react to it, and what dimensions they emphasize, isolate, and engage with (the emphasis on vocal effort and volume, the recognizable character of a music fragment over its quality, and the musicality of the work, focused on the warmth and expressivity of the voice) and the diverse situations in which they resolve the contradiction between some of the dimensions.

Let me now present the diverse settings through which fans learn to organize their initial attraction, internally (settings 1 and 2) and externally (setting 3).

Setting 1: Opera Talk

Fans, in their initial confrontation, feel an intense attraction that they are compelled to explore and organize in order to maximize the pleasure it produces. Much as in Turner's (1967, 102) analysis of the liminal period in Ndembu ritual, in which 'initiation is about, not just acquisition of knowledge, but transformation of being, in learning how to absorb the powers that the cultural practice engenders and how to control what they already feel *fans transform themselves*. The movement from novice to fan is complete when the powers of music are activated again after their social status is redefined and the tools to decipher the experience and control it are in place.

"So, did you come on Friday?" was a question that I often overheard during my fieldwork. Passionate opera fans love compulsive conversation, and what better opening gambit than asking another person in the standing-room line (or already in the standing room) for their opinion of opening night (always a Friday)? Doing this helps fans establish complicity. They will continue: Was the soprano good enough? How did you like her? Were the tempi by the conductor appropriate? And what about that flying ship in the third act? While initial questions refer to the current performance, the conversation will soon venture into other terrain: Do you know this opera? Have you seen it before? Have you seen it before at the Colón? Have you heard the singers in other parts? Fans are curious about how these performances fare in comparison to what we have witnessed before and, if we have not been able to see the opera in this country,[9] how they fare in comparison to the recording. When attending a more contemporary and esoteric opera, like Berg's *Wozzeck*, the conversations can veer into even more complex terrains, like the influence of Strauss on the score and the tension between expression, atonalism, and theatricality. The questions are far from aggressive and are always inclusive, inviting. Questioners assume fellow audience members have the same level of knowledge and believe that, even if this is not the case, their enthusiasm is the best way to proselytize and teach others how opera should be appreciated, evaluated, and enjoyed.

These conversations range in character according to the interlocutor. With some of the older and more pedagogically oriented fans, for instance, they always felt like a highly illustrated lecture with as many cross-references as possible, mentions of the names of famous conductors from the past and their facility with the work at hand, the best recordings, and some obscure details from the composer's life meant to illuminate the choice of words at the end of the third act or a repeated motif, all adorned by literary quotes. On the other hand, younger fans made more sarcastic comments, poking fun at the most obviously run-down details of the staging, the poor casting choices, and the tenuous relationship between the stage director and the conductor during rehearsals. Tito exhibited such sarcasm as well as knowledge at a performance of *Die Walküre*—playing with the well-known fact that Wagner's operas are supposed to be performed without interruption and are usually long by comparison to other operas—saying, "We are lucky there are no applauses in Wagner; otherwise we would never get out of here."

I wasn't the only one receiving the attention of these other fans, who saw me as an especially curious addressee for their exchanges since I always had a notebook in my hands during the performances; a few of the younger fans explained to me how they were slowly initiated through conversations into a more in-depth understanding of what to look for in an opera. While many of them seemed appreciative of the conversations for deepening their understanding, some find the experience overwhelming at first. For instance, during her second visit to the opera, Natalia's neighbor in the *paraíso* tried to strike up a conversation with her and a group of women that began with eager questions about what parts of the opera they had and had not enjoyed and solicited their opinions as well. Natalia felt so new and had so little to say that she decided to go out for a smoke during the second intermission. Franco, on the other hand, described a happier relationship to this conversational integration into the community of fans. He was initially educated by radio, but, once he moved to the city and started attending operas, he wrote down and took the advice of older fans. He interacted with audience members, especially the older men, who had witnessed singers like Nilsson or Colo. "At first I always kept my mouth shut," he reminisced. "I aligned myself with other people up until the moment I decided I knew enough to take the muzzle off of my mouth to share my thoughts with other spectators." Tito has personalized this kind of relationship to the point that he recognizes Archimedes, a man in his neearly seventies, as his opera and music mentor. "He's like an open book. I always try to talk to him before we get in, and I look for him during the intermissions." Tito legitimizes Archimedes' authority by citing his background: "He came as a kid from La Paz, a small town in Entre Rios, and saw Toscanini conducting!" Since then, Archimedes has been a fixture at the Colón and on the off-Colón scene. Tito had a late start; he did not come to the opera until he was in his late twenties but has now been attending for some fifteen years and is eager to follow in Archimedes' footsteps. As I mentioned before, he also offers his tidbits of opera knowledge to those interested in listening to him and engaging in conversation.

There are short yet constant bits of instruction and commentary exchanged throughout a given performance. Fans talk for the half hour they might share at the door, standing in line, leaning against the dusty side wall; they talk at the box office, waiting for tickets to an almost sold-out show and complaining about the slow, lone clerk and about the casual fan who does not know the layout of the Colón by heart and takes forever to choose a ticket. They talk while waiting for the performance to start, situating themselves in ideal positions on the top floor, and go at it during the intermissions, when they either sit on the stairs outside the rooms or roam through the hallways in search of a familiar face. Few say more than a few words at the end of the performance. Instead, they run down four or five flights, filling the stairwells to the brim, singing praises or shouting disapproval, and, thus, synthesizing what they expressed during their more elaborate previous conversations, before flooding the few forms of public transportation—usually buses—still available so late at night. Only a minuscule group will stay at the artists' entrance waiting for the performers to leave in order to exchange a few words or ask for a picture or an autograph. The intense sociability established at the opera house disperses once the show is over and all go their separate ways.

The buses from Buenos Aires to La Plata—a forty-five-mile trip that takes over an hour and a half each way—constitute a more intense and concentrated version of what happens in the opera house. First, there is a self-selection process since only a handful of people travel from the Colón to the Argentino.[10] As Violeta, one of the women I met on my first trip, reflected, "This is a small circuit. We all come to the Colón, to the Avenida, to La Plata. After a couple of rounds, you recognize most of the faces. It's always the same ones." Though producers like Bela spoke of a time when eight buses (some five hundred people) made the trip, there are usually between eighty and two hundred fans who traverse the forty-five miles looking for more opera. Second, because people are forced to be together in a secluded space for a longer period of time on the buses, the conversations that occur on board are also longer. The trip back resembles a dinner conversation among strangers, in which the performance is dissected and more reasons and information need to be conveyed in order to fully do so and convince others of a point of view.

Since most of the productions are local, bus conversations do not revolve around big names, international singers, or canonical versions. Rather, they explore the intense, particularized knowledge of those who frequent the scene. For instance, coming back from *La bohème* in La Plata in 2003, fans offered the names of singers they felt were better suited to play Rodolfo than the last-minute replacement who "butchered" the part and was, nevertheless, applauded at the end. Some fans were able to go so far as to suggest singers who not only performed regularly at the Argentino but lived in La Plata. They did not stop there, either. Because the company from La Plata was staging *Carmen* later that month at Luna Park, a stadium usually utilized for boxing matches and rock concerts, debates soon ensued about whether Luis Lima, a famous yet aging Argentinean tenor, was still good enough to play Don José, as was announced, whether there were better Escamillos available, and whether the amplification and venue would make the show something other than opera. Such conversations usually end just a few moments before the buses arrive at their final destinations, when people break away from the enchantment of opera and begin focusing on where they are going and the taxis or buses they are going to take.

For someone with a limited knowledge of the local world, these conversations can be hard to follow. While people reflect on what they like personally, they also take cues from others. As I mentioned before, the bus trip is an intensified version of the initiation environment. Because of the self-selection process and the extended period of time to talk, those with a more complete knowledge can borrow from many shelves and decide when to talk about the past, when to refer to a comparable production, and when to focus on the details of the current production. While other initiation settings also involve an imbalance between those already belonging to the small local scene and those in the process of becoming a member, the trip to the opera makes the novice a passive receptacle for the details of how opera affects others and how intimacy with the object can help us attain both a more complete understanding and a thorough enjoyment of it.

For those for whom these informal situations are not enough, there is a more formal way to learn opera internally: the many conferences and opera-appreciation classes that have multiplied alongside the increase in opera and opera-related activity in the city. Unlike intermission conversations, classes make explicit what fans should be looking for in opera, what features of the experience they should privilege, and how they should act during a performance. In the next section, I examine this second setting for becoming and learning.

Setting 2: The Maestro in Action

Several institutions in Buenos Aires schedule conferences that follow the opera season. The Colón Opera itself has a free lecture series by its in-residence critics, as does the Italian Circle. Both opera companies residing at the Avenida (Juventus Lyrica and Buenos Aires Lírica) have started their own lecture series, one at the national library, the other at a private cultural foundation that also sponsors an "Opera for Kids" series at the Colón. Some eight hundred people pay up to 25 pesos (the equivalent of a seat on the top floor of the opera house) to see Marcelo Arce, a music critic, discuss the current Colón season on a giant screen at the Avenida Theater. Arce actually has three different lecture series and "music-didactic" shows, as he calls them, although they do not always focus on opera. A few other music critics also have their own classes and lectures. Some, like Esteban Saavedra's, feature live singers who are part of the official roster of the Colón, while others, often for wealthier patrons, culminate in a trip to the Met in New York, a European house, or, even better, the Bayreuth Festival in Germany. Meanwhile, numerous amateurs offer appreciation classes in their apartments, during which they show DVDs of the current season's titles or focus on special cycles like Wagner's *Ring*.

I closely scrutinized the cycle of conferences at a small, local university located close to the Avenida. Most of the lectures there have between thirty and seventy students, depending on the opera and the speaker. Many of those who attend are preparing themselves to go to the opera house that week, trying to remember a forgotten story line or anecdote, or just hoping to enjoy a free screening of an opera.

Sketches at an Opera Class

On a Wednesday night in July 2004, I entered a small room in the basement of a private Buenos Aires university. The room was usually used as a lecture hall, and the seats repeat the disposition of a pedagogical institution. Most of the people were already seated and gazing toward the front, where a blackboard, a television with VCR, and a desk were set up. There were some fifty people in the room, most of them in their fifties; only eight or nine were younger than thirty. They were all eagerly waiting for the "professor" to come. The class, one of the many given during that week in Buenos Aires, is not an adult education seminar but a public talk on how to properly appreciate La fanciulla del West (The girl of the golden West), an opera by Puccini.

The professor enters. He is the feared critic of one of Buenos Aires's historic yet declining newspapers. He is about six foot three and wears his hair slicked back; he is dressed in a light gray suit and carrying an attaché case.

He smiles gently when he enters. A woman sighs a little; some others recognize him now that they see him. He also recognizes some people from a previous lecture.

He comes with a colleague, another critic, an ex-singer who has recently developed a free newsletter that covers with praise most of the music season in Buenos Aires, focusing on opera. Before the tape starts rolling, he starts talking, giving some background ("The opera was performed at the Colón in 1911, 1915, 1920, 1930, 1951, 1979, and 1986").

The professor keeps talking:

> If you have to define Puccini, the basic words to understand him would be lyricism, symphonism, harmonic beauty. . . . OK, fast-forward to the leitmotif. . . . See, that's the leitmotif of the opera; it's in this aria at the beginning but also at the end and in one of the middle scenes. Isn't it a splendid phrase? . . .
>
> I hope you understand this is a unique scene. . . . Now it travels through the Puccinian language, so dynamic. It has passion, emotion.

The professor points to a couple of other scenes. He repeats one of the key passages and for an hour and a half gives a talk in which adjectives abound and in which the description of the plot is interspersed with some references to the context of creation, the careers of the singers in the video, and the luck of the various versions of the opera performed at other times at the Colón.

(Field notes taken July 14, 2004)

This scene gives us a good idea of what goes on in these classes. A figure who performs an authoritative role explains bits of a work using a vocabulary that conforms to the romantic music experience: harmony, melody, and accompaniment; intense emotion; the essence of music beyond words. Such classes offer a definition of *beauty* as "a harmony of composition and the production of a sense of inwardness that enables audience members to enjoy the piece individually and in silence." At the same time, such talks laud the singers as gifted people to be admired for their embodiment of beauty, perhaps as much as the music that produces such emotion. Not much can really be said of the music since language and music are two distinct systems and music is comprehensible only through metaphor and the concentrated effort of the listener.[11] Because the speaker cannot say much about the music beyond the information he can provide that may give listeners the tools to decipher the composer's intentions—another key element of romantic listening— he talks about all that surrounds its production: dates, casts, and personal anecdotes from the life of the composer and well-known singers. Then, he also gossips a bit about the new production of the opera on the basis of his viewing of the dress rehearsal.

Most serious classes focus on what is being presented that season in Buenos Aires and utilize past performances in the city's "First Coliseum" as references. During a class from the same series of lectures as the example given above, another "maestro," a critic from the same newspaper, covered the most important arias from Donizetti's *Lucia*, playing versions from other Colón performances or by then-headlining singers. He mentioned that Titta Ruffo and Maria Barrientos premiered it in 1911 but chose to play a 1930s version by Lily Pons, who was the first singer whom people identified with the part. He then summarized the singers of the 1950s and played a version from 1972 by Beverly Sills and Alfredo Kraus, remarking, "This was the last one we were able to see live, like things used to be, with the live, canonical versions that the Colón used to have all the time. Those two artists made a mark in their time, so this is undoubtedly one of the best versions of *Lucia* you could listen to." At the end of the aria, the sixty or so people in the audience applauded along with the roaring audience on the recording. "Do you remember this?" he asked. "We were a part of that audience," to which a few people in the audience nodded. "Do you remember Tulio Boni?" People in the audience answered, "Yes!" loudly and promptly. "The chorus was prepared by Tulio Boni," he reminisced. The class continued with a version from the Metropolitan sung by Caruso and Alicia Galli Curci from 1911, which the professor considered part of the house tradition, "since they also sang it at the Colón in 1915."

Opera's relationship to its past as a genre and as a practice is taught through references to the Colón, even when recordings do not refer to the opera house directly. The narrative includes the names of the great ones who made the Colón and opera something worth engaging in. It shows the continuity between past and present, linking voices like those of Caruso, Pons, and Kraus, who sang *Lucia* at the Colón, to the international Argentine star

Marcelo Alvarez, who recorded it abroad. In doing this, the lesson makes sure the audience understands that the height of the Colón was the early 1970s and that the present is a period of downfall but proposes that the traditional Colón way of doing opera is still alive in the great Argentine singers who cannot come because of economic reasons (Alvarez, Cura, Lima) but who triumph abroad. As such, this reenactment of the past, with its inclusive tones and its rhetorical questions, is another way of delineating the boundaries of cultural membership for the opera community. As in other instances of initiation, neophytes are taught content in small units that are easily recognizable (singers, voices, casts, titles, authors), thus providing them with a grasp of categories (melody, harmony, emotion) that allows them to think in the abstract and with the ultimate standards of reference (the Colón, great international and national voices).[12]

As we can see, the enthusiasm and knowledge of the professor, despite the special reverence granted to him by the members of the community, are not so esoteric. It is only a more intensive and extensive gradation of the knowledge that any fan could have. In fact, in some of the classes, some people already know what they are supposed to be learning. They attend just to refresh their memories before going to the opera or, even, *instead* of going to the opera as it has become either too expensive (most of the people in the audience are retirees) or too taxing (standing up for four hours at a time is something their bodies can no longer take).

Another scene from a class taught by a radio commentator and critic for Buenos Aires's English-language newspaper underscores the equivalent knowledge of some critics and fans. When discussing the Buenos Aires offering of Massenet's *Don Quichotte*, he was corrected three times. First, he referred to Strauss's *Rosenkavalier* as Stravinsky's *Rosenkavalier*. Next, while summarizing Massenet's most important works, he included the seldom-performed *Cléopâtre* but forgot about *Werther* and was reminded of it by a woman in the audience. Finally—and this is actually one time where we can witness the availability of this kind of knowledge—when he referred to the last time the same composer's *Thaïs* was performed in Buenos Aires and said it was sung by the famous local soprano Delia Rigal in 1950, an old man in the audience corrected vehemently, "1952!" which was accepted as the right date by the critic.[13]

Teaching a class like this does not involve special skills, like reading scores or playing an instrument, or serious studies that certify professorial status, like musicology or a thorough understanding of music theory. It means putting together, in the most diverse manner, lists of dates, casts, soloists, and works. However, it does involve a specific kind of knowledge derived from experience: the comparative understanding of what a good performance is; the classification of the voices not only in terms of register (soprano, e.g.) but also in terms of style (light, lyric, dramatic, coloratura, etc.) and peculiarities (whether it is better in the lower areas, whether it cracks at the highest part of its range, whether the voice has range, etc.). As I said before, this kind of knowledge can be acquired by anyone who is interested in investing in the opera world. However, as I observed when talking with critics and while attending many performances as part of my fieldwork, it is a work of habituation that occupies most of an opera fan's nonworking time.

Actually, most of the "professors" or "maestros" are not trained musicians or musicologists or even historians. They are lawyers, accountants, and physicians who fell in love with the bel canto and achieved a higher rank within the opera community, to the point where they started exercising their power through paid activities for newspapers, radio shows, public lectures, and, sometimes, free newsletters. Such newsletters guarantee them, not only the recognition of the community, signified by the term *maestro* or *professor*, but also free circulation among the institutions that constitute the opera social world. As a former press secretary of the Colón told me, one of the worst problems with keeping track of attendance is the number of free passes people get because of these connections. Many think that "the theater belongs to them" since they have been involved in it for so long and, according to this logic, are already "a part of it." In order to establish their credentials they usually invoke some obscure music newsletter or radio show they once wrote for. Moreover, my informant told me, even when he tried to banish some of them from the house, their knowledge of the institution virtually guaranteed that they would know someone (the hall chief, an usher, a guardian) who would let them in for free.

To summarize, the maestros play a dual role. On the one hand, they are the supreme beings of the community of appreciators. On the other, they are in charge of didactically guaranteeing that new audiences learn both the proper interpretation of the intentions of the music and the proper behavior attached to it. Nevertheless, lively conversations and music lessons are not the only ways in which fans learn how and what to appreciate. These other ways can be abrupt and sometimes even violent.

Setting 3: Collective Connoisseurship

Older fans utilize silence and booing as strategies for indicating whether a performance is worthy as well as when appreciation can appropriately be shown. As any habitué of the opera house knows, there are specific parts where, regardless of how good the performance, it is not appropriate to demonstrate one's appreciation. This particular point is critical in understanding how fans learn to appreciate opera *in foro externo*, that is, learn the kinds of behaviors that are and are not appropriate.

There are many moments in which older fans silence newer ones as an out-of-place noise can distract them from the experience of being one with the music. There are three main types of disturbances: (*a*) an intruding noise like a cough or candy being unwrapped; (*b*) applause at an inappropriate moment; and (*c*) undeserved applause. In the first case, the older fans tend to scold the candy opener with a stern look and will more explicitly indicate that that is inappropriate behavior if the offense is repeated. Some fans, like Ernesto, suspect that such interruptions occur only when the viewer is not interested in the music and fails to make an effort to concentrate on what is going on onstage. He offered the example of a winter performance by international Peruvian star Juan Diego Flórez during which no one coughed. This indicated, for him, that people were really focused. In the second case, confrontation escalates, and older fans try to shame novices into understanding that a choral part, an aria that has not ended, or an aria during which fans do not traditionally express emotion is not a time to celebrate. The immediate response is generally an exasperated "Shhh!" that is often even louder than the clapping.

Interesting negotiations happen at seldom-heard operas like *Don Quichotte*, *I Lombardi*, or *Der Freischütz*. During the first intermission of the latter, which ended up being a success, one of the stage assistants worried about the audience's apparent lack of enthusiasm but rationalized that the minimal applause was due to its lack of exposure to the title and consequent doubts. In this case, the power of self-censorship was so strong that no one clapped anywhere but at the end of each act and after the grand finale. Producers often worry about the behavior of less-regular fans. For instance, when producing *La traviata* at Luna Park—a stadium seating, as we have seen, over eight thousand people—Bela was excited that "people clapped when they had to clap, liked what they had to like, and were moved by what had to move them." His remark demonstrates how etiquette, appreciation, and emotion go hand in hand as part of the same complex system whereby rules of civility both constrain and enable emotion and allow for its proper public display.

Finally, we have the final and most contentious type of behavior censorship. In it, we see the attempts of passionate fans to socialize the rest of the house into their understanding of opera. This education involves delineating what is worthy about opera and the appropriate moments and spaces in which to show the kind of appreciation elicited by a good fragment, that is, establishing boundaries for the community of connoisseurs. Silencing and booing work as tools for individual and communal boundary setting and as mechanisms for reproducing the romantic understanding of music. The sensation of being cut off from the music has both collective and individual dimensions.[14] In the collective sense, it is a matter of affirming oneself as part of the deserving community of those who truly understand what opera is about; a moral lesson is taught to the noisemaker and opera polluter on behalf of the community. Individually, it is about being separated from the object of one's intense affection.

What I call *collective connoisseurship* is composed, then, of more and less implicit doses of persuasion and coercion. In the first account, younger and solitary fans tend to accept the legitimacy of both the formal and the informal maestros who teach them about opera and partake in numerous personal exchanges through which the boundaries of the appropriate features to look for are drawn. This does not happen overnight; it requires a long-term commitment to listening to commentaries and to learning dates, casts, names, and registers, comparing what happens to oneself with what happens to others, and noting whether the effects we are looking for result from the highlighted elements. As I have explained, seasoned fans make no effort to hide what they think is the appropriate etiquette for enjoyment and how it links to their understanding of opera and to the moments in which we should be moved by it. The furious gestures and fleeting yet intense glances that aim to silence all noise beyond the stage clearly demonstrate the coercive nature of how opera knowledge (and cultural membership) is achieved.

The success of a performance appears to be based on certain routinized expectations that help opera fans decide whether they have enjoyed it. But how does this mechanism work? What features do novice opera fans learn first?

Listening Contract

If we look at audience reactions in even more detail, we find some interesting rules of thumb about opera enthusiasm. One is that, contrary to the adage *primo la musica, poi le parole* (music before words), opera fans (and I am talking here about most of the fans) always prefer singing over the instrumental sections. They treat the instrumental interludes at operas, and especially at recitals, as moments when they can relax their attention, when they are allowed to comment on what they have just witnessed or even just take a breath. Chatter from the top floors usually covers the first few bars after an explosive aria and the instrumental beginning of most acts.[15]

The end of an aria is received in one of two ways. Sometimes, fans clap loudly, as is the case after a Verdian cabaletta (the fast final part of any vocal ensemble, usually a duet) or Alfredo's first aria of the second act in *La traviata*; they start freely doing so a few bars into the instrumental ending. On the other hand, they may exhale and wait a second or two before finally expressing their appreciation after a *finale piano*, usually executed by a soprano.[16] While it might seem as though appreciation follows form, certain fans police these moments. For instance, Juan Manuel, a lawyer and amateur musician in his early thirties, hates people who start clapping and screaming over a delicate ending and always tries to silence them. Others, like Franco, who becomes pensive after a delicate aria that ends, not in exclamation, but in a *pianissimo* lament, try to make sure everyone else respects the moment in which the singer exhales before the end. This distinction between *forte*- and *pianissimo*-ending arias is erased, however, if the singer performs a high note near the end of his or her solo. If that is the case, as in the death scene of *Lucia*, fans do not hold their breath, despite the aria's sad and pensive character, and start clapping and cheering immediately.[17]

Fans learn harmony and melody as the keys to unlocking the vault of enjoyment. It was significant that during a 2003 performance of *Bomarzo*—an opera from the late 1960s by the Argentinean composer Alberto Ginastera that is considered the pinnacle of Latin American high modernism—not only did the new subscribers stay much longer than the more partisan and traditional audience, but they also clapped loudly at two moments: when the venerable singer Ricardo Yost sang the Sorcerer scene and when a child sang a fifteenth-century madrigal at the beginning and at the end. In fact, one of the older audience members told me: "You know why they clapped? They liked the boy 'cause they like melody, harmony, something that while they don't know they can understand, and maybe, maybe—look what I'm saying!—enjoy." The lack of melody disfigures *Bomarzo* as an opera up to the point where, according to Alfredo: "It's just one note after the other. He doesn't write for singing. They should have played in concert form. I mean, the dance in it is OK, and so is the staging, but there is so little activity and so little music that it doesn't make any sense as an opera. Opera is Alfredo in *La traviata*!"

While lunching in front of the second most important opera house in La

Plata, a couple of elderly middle-class operagoers gave me a similar definition while discussing why it was not smart to send schoolboys and -girls to
see the latest contemporary opera:

> Can you believe taking people to see that instead of an opera! Why not
> take them to see *Traviata*? So they can see something beautiful. Which
> memories will the kid bring home? Do you know *Traviata*? Do you know
> the beginning of the first act when they start with the toast? . . . That's
> beautiful, isn't it? A boy, a girl, sees that and takes a memory with him.
> The problem is that many people don't know the Colón. They don't know
> what is underneath it, what it is good for. High school kids think it's a
> monument, like the Obelisk. It's not the same to listen as to see and listen.
> But people don't know about this and refuse to come. Out of ignorance,
> because I'm sure that if we took somebody with us tonight to watch this
> [*La Bohème*] they won't ever want to leave. This is like that. It either gets
> you or it doesn't.

Julio also emphasized the link between melody, harmony, and initial attraction and his intense contempt for *Bomarzo*. He was shocked that students
were taken to see it; he said that, after that, a child never comes to the Colón
again. "They are crazy! Absolutely out of the loop, I can't believe there isn't
anybody that indicates to them that the week after *Lucia* and *Elisir d'amore*
were playing. Do you understand me? *Bomarzo*. . . . What a drag!"

Novice fans are taught to respond to a recognizable fragment. For instance, if the aria performed is Verdi's "Celeste Aida" and it is awful, it does
not matter—by the end they already know they have to clap for it. Appren-
tices should also clap after the scene with a toast (*brindisi*) and Violetta's
solo "Sempre libera" in *La traviata*, Tosca's "Recondita armonia," the "Si,
mi chiamano Mimi" aria in *La bohème*, Nabucco's "Va pensiero," and "Una
furtiva lagrima" in Donizetti's *Elisir d'amore*. These are the basics. Afterward,
they can add some German arias to their clapping repertory, especially the
love duet from *Tristan und Isolde*. Since they are not knowledgeable enough
to recognize mediocre performances or even really bad ones, they tend to
respond with great enthusiasm to that which they can already recognize. A
great example is the more than warm reception given to the last-minute-
replacement Rodolfo in a 2003 performance of *La bohème* at La Plata's opera
house. He cracked every high note and was stiff onstage owing to the lack
of rehearsal, but when he sang "Che gelida manina," people hummed along
and started clapping before he was done.

Yet the last situation also serves to exemplify the second category: sheer
effort, especially if translated into voice volume, no matter how out of tune,

is treated by novices as beautiful and deserving of recognition. This seems to happen, not only with opera, but also with symphonic music. For instance, consider the free concerts at the Law School Main Hall, which houses the main youth orchestras of Buenos Aires—a venue and a music institution occupying roughly the same place in the orchestral field as those discussed above do in the opera world. The end of Tchaikovsky's *1812 Overture* or any other spectacularly loud work guarantees a clapping return for the programming investment as much as a shouting *Pagliacci* novice singing "Vesti la giubba" in front of a novice audience.

Despite the common description of new lovers as favoring high-pitched notes and inordinately big volume, there is also a reason behind the search for volume in other venues than the Colón. Compared to Europe venues, the Colón is a really large opera house,[18] dominated by a repertory in need of big voices. The famous Spanish soprano Teresa Berganza once complained about its size, comparing it to a bullfighting arena. Because of this, Julio maintains that people are impressed because "singers knock walls down with their voices." The appreciation of big voices at other smaller houses is based on what happens at the Colón. So, when the tenor Antonio Grieco sang Manrico in *Trovatore* in May 2005 at Avellaneda, a hall that seats only six hundred people, the off-Colón fans applauded and were intensely excited because, in such small space, as Bela said on that occasion, "the voice makes your ears bleed."

A Few Words on Taste, Attachment, and Initiation

I am arguing, not that all fans at Buenos Aires's opera houses, or even those populating the upper floors, behave in the same way, but rather that there is a certain commonality in how opera is understood to be transmitted, learned, evaluated, and reproduced. My account of the instances fans pass through and the categories through which they learn is a modeled stylization of the whole process. Not all fans learn through the same fragments. Moreover, once fans accumulate a stock of knowledge, they are free to improvise and deviate from the learned norm without being punished for it. They are able to abandon themselves to their own whims, explore more contemporary work, exhume the less-frequented operas by renowned composers, and look for the subtleties of smaller voices.

This chapter extends and refines the model for cultural affiliation that Howard Becker (1953) established when discussing the initiation of marijuana users. However, unlike in Becker's original formulation, in this version fans not only get interested in the practice once they are socialized into it;

they partake in a cycle of enchantment that starts with a visceral connection to the music or an interest in opera as spectacle. Fans get hooked[19] when they are still outsiders, before having an active apparatus developed to interpret the experience, or before being thoroughly socialized in what constitutes the enjoyment and how they should decode it. While there are intense instances of sociability and socialization, the temporality structure is different here than in the original model. Learning through interaction happens, not at the beginning, as expected, but as the logical continuation that helps shape the initial attraction. The production of opera fans continues mostly outside family ties and through many informal channels: bus trips, intermissions, and the lines at the door of the opera houses.

The *tertulia* and *cazuela* spaces trigger and cement the socialization process as the individuation one is supposed to achieve in one's relationship to the music is presupposed by the space (the structure of the house and standing room make someone in those spaces an individual divided from others) and by the fact that the *tertulia* and the *cazuela* make it hard for people to go in groups, thus stimulating the possibility of one-on-one conversations among strangers. The classes, which are the most formal[20] means of bridging the gap between initial surprise and an intense, studious commitment to opera, make opera a meaningful experience anchored in a specific place (the Colón Opera House) and time (an elusive golden past) while showing a model for affiliation—the maestro, who enjoys opera thoroughly because of his extensive but not esoteric knowledge.

The process that I have just described results in learning a specific kind of opera and also how to be a specific kind of fan. But which kind of fan? Since it is obvious that not everyone relates to opera in the way passionate fans do, what kind of relationship do these fans have with other ways of enjoying opera? How do they differentiate themselves from other parts of the audience? Which groups do they choose to distinguish themselves from, and what does that say about them? Which strategies do they pursue in order to do this, and what are the personal consequences of this search for recognition and distinction? I focus in depth in these issues in the next chapter.

CHAPTER FOUR

Moral Listening

Symbolic Boundaries, Work on the Self,
and Passionate Engagement

Opera Thugs

Franco calls himself an opera thug. He says that sometimes, because of his love of opera, he finds himself acting in ways he would not even consider on the street or in any other public venue—shoving, pushing, screaming, or violating norms of intimacy. He expends so much energy at the opera house that, during our interview, he complained to me: "At some point I'll have to stop, or I'll get sick." The week of the interview he was attending Wagner's *Die Walküre*, Brahms's *German Requiem*, Lully's *Armide*, and Verdi's *Ballo in maschera*. He was also thinking of returning on Friday to listen to the *Ballo* second cast, which featured a different soprano and a different mezzo. "But my body has its limits. I'm too tired and would like to have dinner at home from time to time. Though on Sunday I wanna go again to *Walküre*."

Franco claims that he is a professional opera fan. "After the show is over, I continue at home; I read, I study." He dedicates at least two hours of his day to opera outside the performances themselves, one in the morning and one in the afternoon. He also listens to music while cooking or ironing his shirts before going to work. He leaves the preshow preparation for the weekends, when he has more time, is a bit more relaxed, and can focus intently. Despite this intense labor of love, he tries to avoid reading reviews before attending an opera for the first time so as not to cloud his critical judgment.

He can attend up to five shows a week if his schedules permits. There was a time when he used to do other things, like go to the movies. But that has come to an end: he now thinks movies are nothing compared to the power of opera.

The love Franco professes for opera is not satisfied by his many hours of listening or his abandonment of other artistic forms and media; that comes through his intensive and extensive attendance. The week before our interview, for example, he had driven for hours in order to see a seldom-performed opera at Avellaneda's Roma Theater. Even that story pales in comparison to his account of sleeping three nights on the street just to be able to buy tickets for Plácido Domingo's last appearance in 1998.

What makes people like Franco invest so deeply and passionately in opera? It is not, in fact, his profession; he is not a singer, a coach, a producer, or even an amateur critic. If he were any of these, that would certainly help explain the vocational, calling-like structure of his disciplined investment. He is not a performer, which would explain his sensuous immersion in certain bodily aspects of the experience. No, he actually works at a public relations firm. And he is investing in an "old" or "residual" (Williams 1977) art form, one without immediate and explicit rewards in a country where signs of distinction have shifted away from the opera house.[1] Yet others like him invest themselves in it in a similarly intense way.

For the purposes of this chapter, I will focus on showing how and why people like Franco present a case of intense and passionate engagement with a practice. In order to do this, I will show how passionate fans shape an image as worthy selves through a laborious, sustained, long-term engagement with opera that is founded on claiming opera as their own and is based on an ethic of sacrifice, refined knowledge, and bodily attachment; that works through strategies to distinguish themselves, partly from what they perceive as the outside, but mostly (in terms of symbolic boundaries) from other parts of the house audience; and that is presented and performed through intense sociability with an audience of equals.

What distinguishes audience members in this case is, not that they are listening to a different cultural product than other people, but their belief that, while they are listening to the same thing as other people, they are listening better. Passionate opera fans present themselves as superior selves, using a range of discourses and practices that involve other people *within* the opera world to do so. The distinction tournament is played out, not against outside actors, but against other audience members in the quest to define how the experience is best practiced, understood, and enjoyed. Passionate fans recognize the existence of diverse audiences within the opera house (such as those who attend only for entertainment or out of social or professional obligation), but they simultaneously criticize the presence of those others by pointing out how they do not practice opera in the right way. This right way can be best seen in the categories that passionate fans use to understand the performances and in their conceptions of what constitutes appropriate etiquette for consumption. These involve (*a*) an emphasis on the live voice as the producer of emotion, mediated, nevertheless, by a discursive understanding of voices and the experience, (*b*) a bodily component of opera appreciation that goes beyond the connection with a singer's voice, (*c*) the use of spaces within the opera house, and (*d*) an alternative etiquette, one that combines both passion and restraint to distinguish them from other audience members.

Lyric Spinto, Please!

Passionate fans enjoy what they call "the melodic part of the opera," but it is through their emotional response to the singer's voice that identification with the opera truly takes place. At first glance, one might think that they would more fully identify with the characters or the dramatic quality of the plot (especially now that surtitles dominate the opera stage and audience members can more easily follow the libretto), but fans—and academics, too, as I will show—discredit this line of inquiry. Fans dismiss opera plots as stupid, minor, unbelievable, or soap opera–like. Bianca, a journalist in her early thirties, says: "I couldn't get unhooked from everyday life if it was just because of the stories. *La traviata* is a stupidity [*una boludez*], *Le nozze di Figaro* is a stupidity, and *Barbiere* is another stupidity. It is something else that does it to me." Alicia maintains that she enjoys every scene of every opera, but not because of any identification with the characters: "I basically follow music fragments, usually from the best-known operas—*La traviata*, *Bohème*, *Tosca*, *Madame Butterfly*. I hum the whole day. It's crazy! It's like I have them recorded in my mind; they are the ones my parents hummed when I was a child. I hum the whole day, even when I'm working [she has a dental office]." Andrea continues the idea: "I liked some arias a lot before I knew what they said. I like the voice as an instrument, as *the* instrument. I don't care about what is going on. 'La donna è mobile' used to produce a lot in me, like a feeling of gaiety, nothing cynical or ironic like when I found out what it was about. The libretto is just an excuse. They are really dumb; they are always about gossip and prohibitions. Just like the 2:00 P.M. Colombian soap opera."

The historian Paul Robinson (2002) contests the notion (which became popular during the late 1980s, when the idea of text was the favorite metaphor of cultural analysis [see Groos and Parker 1988])[2] that the meaning of an opera can be found in its libretto. On the contrary, the unintelligibility of singing (be it because it is in a foreign language, because the operatic voice distorts text, or because the voice competes with even as it complements other voices and a symphony orchestra) means that the opera, or a fragment of it, is beautiful and moving because of the music alone. To paraphrase the, rock critic Grail Marcus: "Words are sounds we can feel before they are statements to understand" (quoted in Frith 1981, 14).[3]

As a consequence, it is central for the core argument of this study to understand why dramatic voices are audience favorites. Among sopranos, spinto and dramatic are *Fächer*[4] favored over lyric voices, and the same happens among tenors. When given the option between beauty, pitch, perfection, and lightness and tone, expression, messiness, and warmth, people opted for the latter. For most of the passionate fans, *deeper* meant a better interpretation and also a voice that would put them closer to a transcendent state. We can observe this in the language used to describe the passage from a regular, everyday state to the intensely frantic one in which the subject loses control and becomes the passive object provoked by an outside force with transformative power: "It transmits something," "It gets to me," "It drives me crazy," "It freezes me," "It moves me," "It kills me," "It fills me up," "It makes me stupid," etc.

Guillermo, a theater director in his early fifties, is the first of my respondents to focus on the voice as the dramatic instrument most able to communicate transcendence and produce the emotion that helps explain why opera has overtaken theater as a passion in his life: "Everything seemed larger than life. The voices made it enormous; they filled me up. It was three times, five times more powerful than dramatic theater. The musicality, the voices, the music; it was all like . . . it filled me up. And I was really emotionally moved. To me, it was an emotion I felt every time I attended an opera."

Bianca elaborates on this issue: "I'm a very rational person and can't stop thinking about the laundry list or things to do at work. But, when the music wins me over, it makes me cry. When I lift up the barrier that impedes the music from getting me or winning me over, then the combination of music and the scene does it for me." In discussing their favorite *Fächer*, Irma and her friend Rina arrive at the same conclusion: "We like dramatic sopranos and dramatic tenors. Don't get me wrong, it's fun to hear some high notes and lots of fioritura. I recognize they are wonderful, but eventually they end up boring me. We like the dramatic part of opera. Interpretation." They conclude almost in unison: "And dramatic interpretation belongs to the deeper voices!"

Fabiana, a forty-three-year-old doctor at a public hospital, agrees:

> I go to the opera because of the combination of the voice with the music. It generates something in my chest. I call it good company; it generates lots of good emotions in me after the performance is over. The stepping-stone is always the same. The dramatic soprano does it well and the lyric spinto, also the dramatic mezzo and the baritones; all the deeper chords and the deep parts of the higher chords. I like high-pitched voices too, but they don't move me at all. I admire the technique, but they don't move me. I value how a person can be a wonderful instrument, but they don't excite me or overwhelm me emotionally at all.

Drawing on his professional expertise, a voice coach I met on the *tertulia* floor explained to me how the fascination with a singer such as Maria Callas derives from the link between deep voices, interpretation, drama, and transcendence:

> People love lyric spintos because they have a lyric voice but the voice has a push; they are deeper and stronger, have more volume in certain parts, so after they look like they are fragile and without defense they surprise you. With Callas it is like with [Carlos] Gardel—the legendary Argentinean tango singer. She sings better every day! When you are twenty-two, you say, "She's an awful singer," but, when you are thirty-five, you start loving her. You understand how visceral singing is, to sing and leave your truth onstage. . . . I really admire her. And the other woman, [Renata] Tebaldi, she has the most beautiful voice I have ever listened to, and the most boring, too. Very limited, as boring as it is beautiful.[5]

Bodily Opera

As we can see from the preceding testimonies, there is a movement in focus that makes of the voice the locus of the transition from the body of the performer to the body of the audience member. In this transition, the body of the fan is framed as a surface for the inscription of effects, which is, nevertheless, productive as their own bodies engage in many activities during the performances. Because of this, I paid particular attention during my research to physical behaviors: Do people always stay in the same part of the theater? Do they speak during the music? Are they a "respectable audience" that can restrain their feelings and remain silence? Do they keep an uptight posture, or do they keep challenging the spaces around them? Do they shout loudly after a well-known aria? Do the audiences at minor opera houses behave in the same way? Is there a spatial division of behavior at the minor opera houses between the galleries and the balcony? These questions have, indeed, informed the work of many historians who have focused on the relation between the development of a silent audience and the disciplinarian character of the theater in the construction of respectable behaviors among middle-class men and women (see, e.g., Sennett 1977; Levine 1988; Johnson 1995; and Ahlquist 1997). As we can see in the following testimonies, opera fans recognize their physical and emotional responses to music:

> I feel there is some music that vibrates to the same frequency I do. It happens close to what we call the heart, but it actually does something funny to your breathing too. (Andrea, sixty-four)

> I get transformed. I get emotional when I feel something is excellent. . . . There are some finales that always make me emotional. When *La bohème* ends, there isn't one time I haven't cried! (Santiago, forty-one)

> I feel it in the chest. It's like I become vulnerable to lots of conflicting emotions. It travels with me everywhere afterward—if I feel sad, if I'm happy, or even if I'm just all right. (Fabiana, forty-three)

> Music generates emotion in me. It's like a chill runs through my body, and I get goose bumps. It's like I feel it on my skin. [After saying this, she starts crying, and we have to suspend the interview for a few minutes.] (Alicia, sixty-nine)

> Opera is the best thing there is. I love standing there for four hours. You always get something in return. Sometimes I feel like I'm having a heart attack, especially in the really high notes of the bel canto arias. They drive me crazy! (Diego, thirty-four)

> At the end of [Modest Mussorgsky's] *Khovanshchina*, I listen to every pounding on the timpani, and I feel as if every pound hits my body. It's something visceral that takes you to the greatest fullness of yourself. (Maria Luisa, seventy-one)

Passionate fans spoke as if music had taken their body over, occupying the space where the core of the self used to be with such force as to make them forget who they are or at least forget their daily problems. They see themselves as becoming passive vessels for a superior force, even if they can actively observe themselves from the outside and reflect about it later. Sometimes, they are overtaken by sensory sensations. Fabiana told me that the first time she went to the Colón, for a performance of *Tannhäuser*, she was so overwhelmed that she smelled jasmines the whole night, although the flowers were nowhere to be seen. Diego was so moved by the experience of seeing Mirella Freni singing *Fedora*, in a performance with Plácido Domingo, that he was like a madman when he left the Colón. "I couldn't sleep because of the euphoria. I really admire the singers who sing very well, mostly because of what they give me; they transmit something. I really couldn't fall sleep. It was so special."

But the body is not just a passive canvas to be transformed by the voice; passionate fans also engage actively with their own bodies. They establish a relationship with others through delicate negotiations over the limits of proper intimacy and norms of respectability. While people try not to mix among floors and are very respectful of other people's space, especially when interacting with or among seat holders, the standing-room crowds participate in an implicit battle to stake out better spots that guarantee a good view. They elbow themselves in, establish territory by grabbing the handrail and flexing the arms, take little steps to move other people's legs and gain a better position—as if they were going for a basketball rebound. This happens both on the men-only floor and in the mixed area, where women participate in this social game, too. One of the regulars from the men's standing area captures the flavor of these interactions: "The real problem is short people. They manage to invade your space through the side, from behind; they push you, destabilize you, and once they have done that—*Bam*! They have occupied your spot."

This does not mean that people push and shove or that they force their bodies against one another. On the contrary, fans do this as an almost automatic "breaching experiment"[6] that shows the accepted boundary for intimacy. I have witnessed people protesting the extreme closeness of others, such as an angry woman demanding that a man leave as he had violated the unspoken agreement granting unobstructed views to people who occupied the space first. In sum, any outside interference that interrupts their one-on-one relationship with music is considered a breach.

In this proximity to music, operagoers inhabit a contained space within themselves in which the engagement with music is demonstrated through a very specific repertory of gestures: the eyes closed to show concentration, a kneeling pose with the hands on the railing and the knees on the floor, covering the eyes with a hand while looking down to the floor. The body tends to close into itself, the back curving, the navel pushing to get close to the spine, the free hand usually making a fist. In doing this, people have told me that they try to contain themselves within the space they feel music builds for them. On some occasions, these gestures get more extroverted, the body opening up at arias or sections where the rhythm tends to over-flow the melody. People do so while mimicking the energetic gestures of the conductor, following the beat with their foot, or, in the most extreme cases, mimicking the singers. These extroverted states can be best understood if we take a look at the larger spatial patterns that opera fans produce.

Spatial Tricks

As explained in chapter 1, the Colón is an opera house that has spatially reinforced social privilege, with different entrances and stairs for different floors and ticket prices. It is impossible to access the balconies and orchestra seats from the upper floors (in fact, even the *tertulia* and the *cazuela* are divided from the galleries and the *paraíso*), and there is a gender distinction in two of the standing-room spaces. The upper floors are also divided between seating and standing areas, and the bars and rails reinforce the division of space, making its disciplinarian character even more evident.

The audience on the top floors recognizes these patterns of spatial segregation and differentiation, and, though they can do little about the former, they do their best to alter the latter through many tricks. As Becker (1998, 6–7) suggests, these tricks are ways of interfering with what would otherwise be the routines imposed by the opera house. However, after some time, these tricks themselves become routines that are learned and passed on through intensive and extensive habituation. There are two kinds of tricks. One has to do with using accumulated knowledge about the house and its personnel to better your viewing arrangement, up to the point where you can even sit in the standing-room-only areas. The second trick has to do with avoiding or violating implicit and explicit rules for occupying and circulating through the space.

Ushers act as guides who help audience members, especially the new ones, achieve the complicated balance involved when buying cheap tickets and trying to decide between standing or seated (the latter would actually cost between five and seven times more, depending on the opera house). At the Avenida, ushers tend to advise you where to sit (e.g., in partial-view seats they know have not been offered for sale), and, if you are late, they usually seat you in a better spot so that you will not have to walk through rows and disturb the rest of the audience. The same thing happens when the performances are not too full.

Unlike the Colón, with its different entrances, stairs, and foyers for the stratified audience, the Avenida has a single entrance. Taking advantage of this, some of the younger house regulars buy the cheapest tickets (10 pesos, or a bit less than US$4) and spend the first act looking for vacant seating at the orchestra level. When they have a proper idea of which seats are empty (especially since only 10–20 percent of those seats typically are not occupied), they do what they call a *bajada*: they all descend together, usually after the first intermission, to occupy the empty spots. This move counts on the complicity of the ushers who let them go and do not ask for a ticket. But it happens so often at the Avenida that sometimes people venture in off the street just to see a specific aria during the later part of an opera.

Over time, fans also develop an acute sense of which tickets are not usually offered for sale; they transmit this kind of informal knowledge to newer members.[7] The first time I found out about it was at the Avenida, when an older man told me, "You should sit over there. Those partial-view seats are not sold by the house." People wait outside the standing box to see if they can capture a free space among the seldom-sold seats. They also make use of this knowledge if they are in the mood just for listening (without being concerned about seeing the stage) while being seated or to alternate between really uncomfortable locations by coming once to the right side and the next time to the left in order—as one regular said almost as a joke—"to avoid developing a stiff neck."

The second kind of trick involves men buying tickets to the women-only area and women to the men-only area. The ushers and ticket agents help make this work since they sell women's tickets to men and let women go into the women's area with men's tickets.[8] This usually occurs if tickets for one of the same-sex standing areas are sold out (which happens a lot). For instance, women were on line early in the morning for Maria Guleghina's recital, buying out the tickets, not only for the *cazuela*, but also for the *tertulia*. One of the ushers explained to me that the *tertulia* was not as full as expected that night because there was an overflow of women on the lower floor who had entered the women's floor with men's tickets.

This trick is innocuous compared to the explicit violation of occupancy and fire-code standards, especially in the men's standing-room-only area. People block the exit areas, sit on stairs, balance their backsides on handrails, and sometimes hang from the side rails. They also stand close together, violating norms of intimacy and personal space in a way that would be scandalous in other settings. On the opening night of *Lucia*, there were so many people standing on the stairs and in the vestibule that four people decided to hang sideways, grabbing the handrails at the end of the standing box and the three seating levels. They balanced the full weight of their bodies while holding themselves up by wrapping their left hands and legs around the thick metallic tube. One of them hung like that for the entire first act (see figure 8).

FIGURE 8.
An opera thug
standing up
next to the outer
border of the
tertulia floor of
the opera house.
Photograph by
the author.

These occupancy and fire-code violations are reproduced at the Avenida, where people also block all exits, sit on the steps that take other audience members to their seats, and fabricate seats using bags or jackets in the space between the rows of seats. Franco summarizes it better than anybody: "We are the crazy ones, the irrational ones. We don't respect anything. Before, the entrance and the steps used to be empty; now, when people are trying to enter or exit, it is a mess."

The fabrication of seating spaces next to the steps is a well-known trick at the Colón, especially among women. They bring folding chairs and have done so for a long time. A director of the house tried to stop this during the late 1990s but gave up after two months following a strong protest by the *cazuela* women. Most of them argued that it was their given right since it was such a long-standing tradition and since, as they aged, most of them could not stand for hours anymore. Though some men bring folding chairs—they put them to the front of the lateral *tertulia*—the standing box makes it impossible to fit them. The women-only *cazuela* space is not boxed in the same way and makes it easier to bring folding seats. There is there a straight view to the stage, without rails to impede the view.

It is not hard to understand why men avoid the standing box (see figure 9). They dismiss it by calling it the *jonca* (a slang word meaning "coffin" that is *cajón* [box] spelled backward), and many of them hang around the fringes of it for a long while until somebody else occupies the middle. The space is so small and really just for one person at a time. The ceiling is really close to the head, especially if you are over six feet tall, and it forces people to bend their bodies over the rail on top of the box.

FIGURE 9. Seating (mixed) and standing (men only) arrangements at the *tertulia* level. Photograph by the author.

People also circulate in other ways. They run—regardless of age—up the stairs to guarantee the best standing arrangement possible and walk around the open *paraíso* area while performances are in progress. People who do so stop their constant movement to sit on the side areas (no view at all) or on the floor at the back of the *paraíso*. They approach the viewing area when something big (an aria, or the finale, or a whole music fragment they deem worthy) is coming. As a result of all this, the official diagram of the seating chart (see figure 10) and the actual use of the space (see figure 11) are somewhat different.

This is not the only way in which passionate fans depart from the sober and detached etiquette that we have learned to expect from an opera audience. They also manifest their passion by exploring the boundaries between the self-restraint necessary for consumption and the feelings aroused by what happens onstage. We can see this in the booing and hissing from the upper floors of the Colón, which go hand in hand with forms of appreciation and expression usually considered more legitimate, like clapping or shouts of *Bravo*!

Passionate Etiquette

Booing is not considered ill-mannered when compared to clapping and shouting bravos as all are deemed to be an expression of emotions awakened by the performance. In one of the many messages Roberto posted to an online opera forum, he wondered: "Why is it that to approve of something by shouting 'bravo' is considered good taste while to disapprove of it by booing is considered rude?" He went even further and turned the perceived aggressor—the fan who boos—into a victim: "Why do I have to listen to somebody else's approval of something I think is really bad or unpleasant?"

Booing matches and confrontations between audience members have led to fistfights. During my fieldwork, fans almost started a fight on two occa-

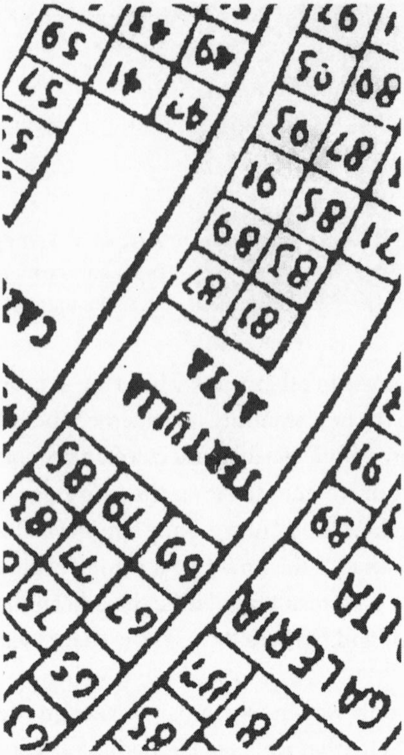

FIGURE 10. The
official Colón Opera
House seating chart.
The white areas
behind the numbers
are the standing
areas. The labeled
area of the floor is
supposed to be kept
open.

FIGURE 11.
Detail of the "free"
area of the *tertulia*
floor. In this case,
there are 27 people
occupying the area,
sitting on the stairs
or on the handrails
or standing or sitting
on folding chairs.
On the occasions I
went, the number of
people varied from
12 to 43. * = seating
on a folding chair.
■ = seating on
handrails.
● = standing up.
▲ = seating on
stairsteps.

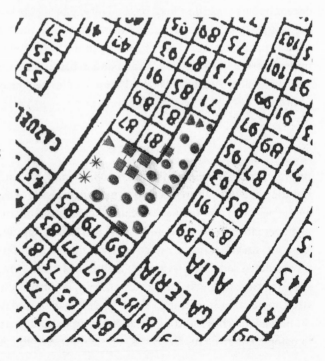

sions: the modern staging by the Argentinean painter Guillermo Kuitca of *The Flying Dutchman*,[9] which included an airport baggage line to represent a contemporary version of an endless journey, and a staging of *Il barbiere di Siviglia*[10] that featured a hippie singing the aria "Pace e gioia" (Peace and joy), a disco ball, a first act inspired by *West Side Story*, and fragments of the popular Italian song "Volare." At the beginning of the second act of the latter performance, when people already knew what was bound to happen, someone shouted from the top floor: "Bring the real Rossini back. This is an outrage!" Hernan, a student in his early twenties, was so upset by this as to tell me on the way out of the performance, "It was too aggressive. The more one group clapped, the more the other booed. By the end, there were two gangs, one trying to drown out the other. It's a miracle we haven't all finished with a massive, collective fistfight! How long can you discuss and shout before you end up fighting? It was like a soccer stadium."

A more violent episode took place at a provincial opera house in Bahia Blanca, where opera had not been performed for a long time. Patrons decided to throw stones at the theater's box office after a performance of *Madame Butterfly* was sold out and a large number of people could not get in.[11]

An interesting paradox about opera fans who demonstrate a physicality more akin to soccer fans or pop culture lovers is that they declare moral superiority on the basis of their music-listening habits.[12] For instance, during one of the first times I was discussing my project with people at the opera house, someone who identified himself as a Wagner fan directed my attention to questions that pertained to the embodied qualities of opera listening (or so I thought). He asked me whether I was going to take into account the effect that music has on people. I started to respond, saying that, yes, there are cognitive and physical effects.[13] He stopped me and explained: "No, actual effects, that music elevates you, that it makes you a better, more spiritual person."

Audience members reconcile these kinds of physical practices with the culture-as-cultivation-of-the-soul discourse through what I call *moral listening*, a rhetoric that emphasizes the never-ending, detail-oriented, experiential process of learning in order to be emotionally moved and affected by opera, which, they believe, consequently makes one a better person. Despite its exclusionary undertones, most of the fans are convinced that one achieves this spiritual character in a very democratic way: by attending the standing-room-only spaces (for less than two dollars) as frequently as possible. There, according to Victoria, a fan in her mid-fifties who now sits in the box seats: "You will always be well received and schooled." This perceived democratic quality allows the passionate fans to contrast the spiritual elitism of the standing-room-only space with the economic elitism of the orchestra seating and the boxes.

Upstairs, Downstairs

In claiming opera as their own, passionate fans not only distinguish themselves from the outside world; they also deploy microstrategies that distinguish them from other parts of the audience. These emphasize the instrumental character of the consumption of opera of the more well-off members of the audience and their consequential lack of passion and engagement. This does not mean that there are not upper-class audience members in the boxes or the orchestra seats who have a fan-like commitment to opera. What I am presenting here is mostly the ways in which upper-floor fans conceptualize and classify other audience members. Fans use stereotypes to typify the world around them, and, because of this, I use these classifications to interpret the ways in which my informants reconstruct their world, rather than taking them as a faithful representation of what the patrons in boxes and orchestra seats do.[14]

Interaction between the two audiences is shaped by the architecture of the Colón. With three different entrances and stairs for different floors and ticket prices, audiences are not only stratified but spatially secluded; it is impossible to access certain parts of the opera house, such as the balconies, from the lower-priced rooms. While standing-room fans and orchestra-seat ticketholders are in the same building, their interaction is only visual and happens strictly during the performance, with fans from the upper floors looking down (see figure 12).

Passionate fans summarize the attitude of the audience from the lower floors with the adjective *formal*. Franco offers a thorough description:

> I like how people live opera on the upper floors [*arriba*]. They discuss it; they have passion. I don't see that downstairs [*abajo*]. I think it is because those who dedicate three or four standing hours to this do it because they really want to; if they take on such a sacrifice, it is because they love it like crazy. . . . The people who are seated look at you as if you were invading a physical place and generating disturbances for them. Same thing if you are standing up on the orchestra floor. They look at you in a selfish way, as elitists who think you have infiltrated their environment or something like that. . . . This is for a sensitivity elite, not for the people who go because of social obligations, who need to be seen leaving the Colón.

FIGURE 12. The boxes and orchestra seats as seen from the *paraíso*.
Photograph by Fabián Mosenson.

Diego, a public employee in his early thirties, could not agree more with this evaluation of the people from "downstairs": "They go because they feel obliged to, not because they are interested in it. They need to for social reasons. As soon as the performance is over they run out. You can notice it at the singers' recitals; whenever there are encores, they miss them; they are already out the door." Even some members of the orchestra-seating area agree. For instance, an older lawyer who subscribes to orchestra seats at the Colón told me: "You do well to go upstairs. That's where people really like and learn opera. They read scores." He made a gesture as if he was reading in the dark with a flashlight while flipping the pages of an orchestra score. "I used to go there, too. Now I have some more money and can afford a good seat, but I still feel as if I were upstairs."

Passionate fans contrast the spiritual elitism of the standing-room-only space with the economic elitism of the orchestra seating and the boxes and convert their fanaticism into the source of their superiority and real attachment to high culture. Things that should rightly be discredited from a sober and detached high point of view (hooliganism, bodily responses to music, sacrifice, and dedication) make them feel more worthy of being opera lovers. In this case, opposition to the outside is less important (since people from the outside either do not care about opera at all or care little about their claims to be superior beings because of it) than opposition to other insiders, whom they disqualify because of their lack of genuine interest.

As much as passionate fans exclude the rich for their lack of love, as expressed in their sober manners, they also exclude the newer audience members because of their lack of proper judgment, using a discourse of aesthetic sophistication to distinguish themselves from the newcomers.

The New Audience

Opera fans discredit the new audience members by categorizing them according to three distinguishing features: First and foremost, they participate in other cultural practices besides opera. Second, they engage in automatic applause, which shows an absolute lack of sophistication. Third, they have no self-restraint, something the opera fans associate explicitly with the cultural degradation of the outside world.

Esteban, an art high school teacher in his mid-sixties, gives us his two cents on the new audience: "Audiences used to have a deeper knowledge. Now I see a light take, kind of like the apprentice that is always coming to it for the first time. That makes them like or approve of everything. I feel like the media controls the new audiences, like they would accept anything that looks like a show, be it movies, TV or theater. Opera is just one more thing."

His testimony pales next to the anger manifested by some of the passionate fans about the 2006 version of the magazine the opera house produces and sends to its season subscribers. They were deeply suspicious that the ideal reader the publishers had in mind was not them but rather a new and omnivorous cultural practitioner for whom opera is only part of the menu.[15] Susana, who claims to have been attending opera for thirty-five years, complains that the magazine is like a mixture of weekly magazines for the nouveau riche, like *Hello* or *People*, with gourmet and style guides. She summarizes her claims in a highly ironic mode: "So after reading the pages of the new magazine, just because I go pretty frequently to the opera house as a subscriber, I will become part of this exquisite group of bons vivants to which the magazine is addressed. I suggest, then, that to accentuate even more its mundane character they should include actual articles about music and art such as 'The Importance of Golf in Leonard Bernstein's Life,' 'Why Did Luciano Pavarotti Abandon Playing Polo?' or 'The Day José Carreras Met the Stewardess Who Years Later Became His Wife.'"

Another subscriber, Monica, seconds the assessment: "I feel ashamed of receiving it. I feel offended they think of the opera fans as a bunch of snobs or superficial people." Her lament transitioned into an indictment of the rich audience. "They really don't make any effort to hide that for them classical music just belongs to people with money. How big is the ignorance and the spiritual poverty of these cheap marketing people."

A third fan, Ana, goes back to comparisons with the past and to the class of magazine an audience composed of people like her actually deserves: "We could live without this magazine; it's so superficial. It's funny; lately I went back to look at issue 46 of the Colón magazine from 1997. I wanted to stoke my memory a bit. . . . To think we used to complain about the size of it; it's true it is a bit of hard work to move it, but you get everything you need: a discography, the libretto, notes written by Miguel Ángel Veltri.[16] I feel ashamed to get the new one."

Néstor points to the convergence of two other characteristics in the new audience, a lack of depth and misplaced passion:

> I notice an automatic applause. It drives me crazy; any stupidity, and they start clapping. When I first came to the opera, bravos weren't like they are now. It was a well-deserved applause. You used to jump from the upper floors! Now I listen to people shouting "Bravo!" and I have to dig deep into my memory to remember the last time I thought a bravo was justified. Either people have amnesia, or they haven't heard enough. I don't want to put myself in a superior place, but if you haven't listened to versions of the opera, if you don't know the parts, the curtain rises, and you think everything is great. With an ignorant audience you end up reproducing the shitty performances!

José Luis draws an explicit connection between the automatic applause and the degradation of the outside world. In doing so, he refers, not to soccer, street pickets, or the corruption of politicians, as others have done, but to trash television. He sees the representation of this in the popularity among new audiences of the staging of *Barbiere*. He writes: "We had a *Barbiere* full of stupidity, with collectible cars and gangsters onstage and so many other things it is impossible to number them. Do opera as it's supposed to be done! If you don't like it, don't do it. Go to TV to do trash and bad skits."

Daniel, a critic and lawyer in his mid-thirties, links the new audience behavior more generally to all the maladies of the outside world. He says that, in the same way a man drinks coffee with water full of chlorine, rewards his worst employee because he is the most flattering, eats a mass-produced burger for lunch and convinces himself that he tastes something different every time, drives two hours just to get home every night, and watches the same television show once he gets there, the opera audience of the Colón has forgotten its proud past, which combined ruthless criticism with a warmth and welcoming reception, and has since given way to the most absolute lack of discrimination.

While most of these testimonies refer to the transformation of the Colón audience, the extension of the Buenos Aires opera world since 1999 (when another major opera house, the Argentino, reopened and a new opera company, Juventus Lyrica, had its first performance at the Avenida Theater) has meant that passionate opera fans must now confront other audiences that previously had access neither to the Colón in particular nor to opera in general. The expansion of the circuit is best observed in venues like Avellaneda's Roma, a small, six-hundred-person house that features singers and musicians from the fringes of the Colón circuit. Opera at the second tier of the off-Colón circuit is imprinted with the limitations of amateurism. New audiences go to it at the same time as old fans, who find in these venues new possibilities to engage with their passion. Nevertheless, this circuit produces both opera that is criticized by most passionate fans and the kind of audience these same fans have been fighting to distinguish themselves from. So how do opera fanatics respond to the off-Colón experience and, more importantly, to the audience it produces?

The Chicken House within the Chicken House

A stage director from the Colón Opera, Mariano Perez Rabal, referred to the Roma's working conditions for the Verdi opera he was staging with equal amounts of appreciation and disdain. He said:

> It's a crazy place; I have to do the lights! There is nobody there to do them [for the show], so I have to go backstage and take care of it. I also have to bring my own tools; otherwise, there are no hammers to put the nails in the floor. On the other hand, people have a crazy enthusiasm. For instance, one of the nuns from the chorus, when I said to them I didn't have enough costumes for everybody or that some of them were torn apart, asked for the pieces that were destroyed and sewed them back together. Can you believe that? Now I have more people onstage—the dimensions of the stage are really small; there is no sense of depth—than I care for or than I can manage.

On another occasion, Mariano told me that he actually liked the second tier of the off-Colón circuit better than the upper tier: "The second circuit is more fun; they are really fresh. You already accept that things are not like they used to be but have some fun with it." Then he went on and repeated the anecdote about the hammer, but this time he made it part of the marriage between some passionate fans and the amateur production of opera.

Nicolás Carballo is always there if an opera is being performed, especially on the secondary circuit. On the occasion of a Verdi opera that Mariano Perez Rabal was staging at the Roma, he was hanging out in the foyer, chatting with a few opera people ("Everybody is here," he said), and explaining to me what he saw as the advantages and limitations of this way of producing opera: "It's crazy in here. There is a warmth you don't see anywhere else. Granted, you have to change the light bulbs yourself, do the lights, take care of everything, but it doesn't matter. You'll see it; it's crazy how they applaud the performances. It's like the Marconi."[17] In linking what he does and the kind of opera he likes with the Marconi Theater, the Italian working-class opera house that competed against the Colón early in the twentieth century, Nicolás transforms the understanding of the experience. Instead of viewing opera houses like the Roma as resource-deprived imitations of a lavish and metropolitan golden past, he sees them as the continuation of a competing way of doing opera—working-class opera with a truly popular audience, or at least with the behaviors attached to it. Mariano alluded to this when he was surprised to see me attending a third performance of the opera he was staging: "What are you doing here? This is the chicken house [*gallinero*] within the chicken house."[18]

By telling me, "This is the chicken house within the chicken house," Mariano portrayed the Avellaneda's audience as an even more intense version of the passionate characters from the Colón's upper floors. This description, however, includes a series of behaviors that put the local audience at odds with the opera people: taking flash pictures in the middle of performances, making cell-phone calls while the music is playing, and—worst of all—talking and applauding excessively. Unlike opera people, who usually reserve conversation for the end of an aria, or members of the new audience, who will occasionally applaud at inappropriate places, the people from houses like Avellaneda get shushed constantly, both for their intense (and misplaced) enthusiasm and for their constant chatter. These "popular fans," from a working-class part of the city, are considered by the passionate fans to be a run-down version of the new audience and, as such, are almost as abhorred. Nevertheless, whereas they rage against the new audience in general, their rage being based on the economic advantages of a well-off audience with a more omnivorous pattern of cultural consumption and less of an investment in opera, the fans from Avellaneda are forgiven. It is not their fault that they do not know how to appreciate opera—it is just that they cannot.

Fans like Violeta use *provincial* as the key adjective to explain what goes on in Avellaneda. She said that it reminded her of what opera was probably like in the small provincial houses of Italy or in the early twentieth century; it also reminded her of a *kermesse*, a popular festival for families where games, music, and dance were mixed with abundant food and heavy drinking. Franco, again, offered the best definition: "At the Roma, things are completely different. From time to time, you feel a family-like climate, like if you were at a fair in a small provincial town. You see lots of love for doing things, but the people from the audience behave too informally. The solemnity you see at the Avenida and at the Colón is missing." The level of amateurism apparent in off-Colón opera houses contributes, he says. "I see it as something almost homemade, and you change as a spectator because of it; you forgive all the imperfections, all the weird noises behind the curtain, backstage. You cross the Riachuelo,[19] and you install a filter in yourself, a cushion, a buffer, and you can stand anything."

Franco's testimony illustrates not only the paternalistic tone with which fans like him refer to what happens outside the city boundaries ("You cross the Riachuelo . . .") but also a more important feature: that, in extending their passion to other locations, they have to adapt to the run-down versions without giving up their status among the diverse audiences of the local opera scene. Passionate fans adopt three attitudes when confronting the world outside the Colón Opera[20] (they exclude the Buenos Aires Lírica, the first company at the Avenida, which, because of its professionalism, artistic goals, style, and budget, is considered to be a mini-Colón). In speaking about the secondary circuit, they (1) swear never to enter the world outside the Colón, (2) compare it immediately to the Colón and despise the spectacles they witness, and (3) think that it is a low-quality show but go anyway because they appreciate the passionate efforts of the organizers and performers.

José Luis, like most of the older fans, tries to avoid the secondary circuit as much as he can, even though he gets invited frequently and could go for free: "They don't have my level as audience. I'm not a musician, but they are not up to my level. The new companies need to leave the big works alone, stop with the cheap, pseudoinnovative staging. They pretend to innovate, but that is because they don't have any money. They try to sell it as if it was an act of genius, but they would be better off recognizing that they don't have one dime. . . . The day they did *Fledermaus* at the Avenida I thought it was the end of it; since they didn't have money for costumes, singers were all dressed in cardboard. They showed their asses and underpants. I don't get scared by it. . . . Opera needs money; there's no way around it. You can't do it on the cheap."

Julio, the voice coach who is a great admirer of Maria Callas, laughs at the way these shows are reviewed by the critics: "They need to stop! They say things like, 'This was a praiseworthy representation, a commendable work.' Don't do operas like those! Do Mozart, Donizetti, Bellini; do Weber; do something less complicated. Don't do Strauss or something like that if you don't have the appropriate voices!" Even critics share this concern. Esteban, one of the professors with the most opera students, confessed that he writes reviews of such productions with an understanding of the context. He cannot just say that "the tenor was really bad" or that "his voice felt short" without explaining how laudable it is for these houses to be producing pretty satisfactory operas without the Colón's resources. In cases where the performances are too bad to report or impossible to hide under euphemisms, he chooses not to publish a review.

Other fans participate as much as they can in the secondary circuit but always make a point to criticize what they have just witnessed with a combination of irony and detailed elaboration. Tito made fun of the diverse companies of the secondary circuit on three different occasions when I ran into him. Watching *Il trovatore* in Avellaneda, he made fun first of the limited resources and the small orchestra pit by saying, "What will happen if they try to do Wagner? There won't be any audience, from the space they will take from the seats to fit the orchestra!" Later, when he saw that the stage had a black background and floor with a centerpiece that changed from act to act (the first one was a big yellow medallion), he said, "There is no change of scenery! Unbelievable! Well, if you think about it, what are they going to trade for the cheese (referring to the medallion)—a giant mozzarella pizza?" At the beginning of the third act, he said, "Now they have taken out the cheese and put a birdcage." On another occasion, after Juventus Lyrica's production of *Tales of Hoffman*, his comments were not so ironic, but they still stung: "She [the local rising soprano Soledad de la Rosa] wasn't great. She's too hyped. You can see she needs to train some more; her voice got tired and worn out by the end. She wanted to sing all the parts, but you have to take lots of soup before doing that.[21] Also, the conductor wasn't that great. You could see he lacks a hand for French music—too much Italian opera in his life." On the third occasion, after he criticized a performance on the secondary circuit (*Ballo in maschera*), one of the ushers admonished him: "It's funny. You never like anything. You always complain, but you are always here! You should stop coming."

Fans like Tito are ubiquitous at secondary houses because being there allows them to participate in the world of opera as much as they can without renouncing the Colón as the paradigm for comparison. The third kind of passionate fan, however, quickly articulates the vast distance between the

Colón and the secondary circuit. These fans enjoy the particular character-istics of the other stages without worrying about what they lack and focus on the pluses. They emphasize the need for a contextualized understanding of the experience. Ernesto is one of those fans:

> When I go to the Avenida, I leave 100 percent full and happy. They don't sell it like "the great opera." You go to see Juventus Lyrica or Buenos Aires Lírica, and you might like it, or you might not, but you see the hours and hours of rehearsals behind it. It's like in Avellaneda; they don't pretend to be something else. I hate pretentious things. If the Colón says it is going to stage a gala, I go. But I expect a good pianist and a singer of superlative character, and then you enjoy it 100 percent, but, if you don't, then the word *gala* doesn't make any sense. At Avellaneda, they don't lie to you. I go and come back happy from it.

As we can infer from this testimony, the impossibility of the Colón fulfilling a fan's expectations can drive someone like Ernesto to displace his interest to a minor opera setting, which cannot exactly replace the Colón but can, nevertheless, provide him with enjoyment. But other fans like Néstor do not stop there, finding in the off-circuit a continuation of the kind of opera the Colón cannot or will not stage anymore. As he said before, Néstor loves to attend performances by Adelaida Negri: "I have lots of respect for the lady. That is a whole different story. When I go, I make deaf ears [*oídos sordos*] to many things and enjoy how she gives herself away onstage. I'm very nostalgic and like to pay homage to the great figures of the past. To me to attend is a way of paying homage."

While the repertory of evaluation is local, the extension from the original locus—the Colón—to an extended stage, with multiples sites and scales, provides new challenges that were solved by means of homology (the love of the amateur producers for opera is like our love) and through new means of differentiation that are, nevertheless, more sympathetic to this impoverished new audience than to the wealthy new audience from the Colón.

"I doubt whatever a reviewer says immediately"

The accusation of indiscriminate judgment does not stop at the new and off-Colón audiences. Passionate fans distinguish themselves by engaging in a highly adversarial relationship with the critics. They have two ways of confronting them: First, they link the critics indirectly to the maladies of the outside world, by associating them with the new audience through a shared lack of proper judgment. Second, they link the critics directly to one of the key features of "Argentinean downfall" — corruption.

Some sociologists (see Becker 1982; Bourdieu 1984, 1992; and Zolberg 1990) have argued that the difference between high and low culture lies, not only in enacting the proper etiquette for appreciation, but also in the discursive mediation of the former, in which critics act as gatekeepers to the arts world, assuming a negotiation in which what is exchanged for status is the right to a personal opinion. Other sociologists (e.g., Shrum 1996) have brought nuance to this idea by showing that the importance of reviews lies, not in their evaluative function, but in the visibility they provide. However, Shrum emphasizes that even this kind of mediation is limited to the world of highbrow genres, like theater or opera. But, if this is the case, why does the Buenos Aires opera world have such an adversarial relationship to professional music criticism? Furthermore, why do passionate fans focus their efforts on improving their evaluative skills, sometimes, paradoxically, taking classes with the same critics they despise?

One the one hand, fans distrust critics as they might be friends with the artists, be paid to celebrate mediocre performances, review the minor opera houses according to effort and not quality, or make factual errors. On the other, they look for the review to confirm that they have been right in their own critical judgment (though sometimes they scoff anyway).

As Franco reflects in relation to his review-reading habits: "I read *Clarín* and *La Nación*; I wait two days after the premiere. It is like a ritual; it is the first thing I read from that morning's newspaper. There might have been an explosion in London, but the review of *Die Walküre* goes first! It's like I need to know if what I thought or how the work impacted on me coincides with the critic's view. Sometimes I think I should write a synthesis of the show so I can compare it afterward, to see if I have a good critical eye."

This need for outside validation transitions to a more common theme: "I feel like there are some spurious interests going on, that you saw something that stunk badly and all of a sudden they find a phrase to transform it into a sweet and delectable elixir. Like [the Argentinean baritone Luis] Gaeta in *Ballo*. His voice was too strained, though he is a good artist. But, when you read the review, they say he showed his professionalism, his good phrasing. They don't really talk about it so they don't have to criticize him. They really go the distance not to criticize him, to protect him."

Andrea, too, lumps the critics into a single group. She has a subscription for an orchestra seat but goes upstairs when she "needs" to see an opera more than one time. "All of them are a disaster, an absolute mess. They write without any basis!" Ernesto continues this line of thinking: "Critics in Argentina are too friendly. There isn't any independent reviewing; there is no objective criticism. I'd rather pay more attention to what another guy from the audience tells me. I doubt whatever a reviewer says immediately." Juan Manuel, a lawyer and amateur musician in his late twenties who arrived in the city from the north of the country not so long ago, rants, "The newspaper's reviews lack a certain level. You read them, and you realize the people writing don't know music. You don't have to be a musician to judge, but they should at least be serious about it." He further fuels the discussion by pointing to a specific example of a reviewer's gaffe: "There was a concert where they were playing Bartok's *Contrasts* and another piece that included a flutist, and the guy starts writing about how good the flutist was in the *Contrasts*. You start doubting whether they actually come to the concerts at all! He was raving like crazy about how great the flutist was in a work that includes only piano, violin, and clarinet! You feel like sending a letter to the editor. These are objectives things, not subject to interpretation! It feels really unprepared." But that is not all he has to say; he also complains about how he thinks there are critics who get paid on the side.

Regardless of the perception of music criticism as a corrupt enterprise, it is still utilized as the yardstick against which to measure one's judgment. Even Andrea, who talked about the critics' lack of foundations, told me how she usually gets together with the people from the opera house to comment on the recent reviews and how they are pleased if the review coincides with their opinions. Arnaldo, the vice principal of a high school, does the same thing: he tries to go to a performance without reading anything and then reads the reviews to see whether he "nailed it" with his own critical judgment.

There Are No More Critics!

Irma and Rina have experienced so much through the Colón. We talked for over three and a half hours, and, late in the conversation, they gave me their opinions on music criticism:

    R: *I have to say there are no more critics. They are a thing of the past.*
    I: *Not only among music critics. The same thing happens with the theatrical ones. There are lots of interests at play.*
    R: *There is Pablo Kohan, and Coda, who I think is the section editor, he might be a bit better. . . . I don't like how Montero writes. And I also know*

him a lot, so I don't have any faith in him; he goes to wherever the sun
is warmer.
I: *A friend of mine told me that you have to listen to the critic first and*
then form your opinion; I told her she's absolutely wrong!
R: *You have to go by yourself. But I think people follow the reviews.*
I: *Go and listen to it! After so many years you can decide whether you like*
it or not. You don't need the newspapers!

(Interview recorded August 3, 2005)

———

Among the older opera fans, professional critics are dismissed partly because
they are not harsh enough and, thus, must be dishonest, the grounds here
being that a well-tuned critical judgment would dismiss what is presented
nowadays onstage, and partly because they do not hold up the golden past
of the opera house for comparison. Julio makes this link explicit: "I don't
read any critic since my favorite critic died in 1988. He was a very honest
guy. He didn't like anything! People say, 'What a son of a bitch, he didn't like
anything,' and I say, well, there have to be many reasons why he didn't like
anything!"

The combination of benevolence with the accusation of corruption by
passionate fans derives from the conviction that people must learn what they
like by themselves. The rejection of the critics' mediation, then, means, not
that people are not on the lookout for advice as they embrace a moral/peda-
gogical dimension for consumption, but rather that knowledge is presented
as an achievement acquired through self-discipline and reverence to the
genre qua genre. Much like Weber's (1905/1930) guilty and anxious Calvinist
in his quest for the certitude of being among the chosen, opera fans model
the uncertainty of their judgment by organizing their music life as a disciplined practice in which one attends the opera many times for comparison's
sake and justifies attendance with references to "learning," "utility," and "a
more thorough understanding."

The capacity for learning is usually exemplified by how much you have
evolved throughout your life, from the first tastes in music (easier, less complex) to the later ones. The movement supposes hard intellectual work and
the conviction that, if you do not like what you are seeing, it is your fault, not
the opera's. Armando, a sports journalist at a local radio station, elaborates
on this: "You should take note of the capacity of people to grow. I have already listened to everything. I have de-formed myself, if you will; I can now
listen to anything because I've evolved. I remember how in the early 1990s

my wife told me she didn't like Debussy, and I said, Don't worry, we'll eventually get there." In this self-discipline, repetition is the way to carefully learn about a particular opera (hence the compulsion to attend the same opera at least twice), and accumulation is the way to pedagogically gain cumulative understanding about the qualities of opera in general. Thus, on one occasion, someone might go to focus on the singing, while, the next time, she promises herself to focus on the story and, the time after that, on the staging. At the same time, she always makes sure to return if there is a second cast performing so she does not miss the comparative element. Even so, passionate fans always manage to point to their shortcomings by saying that they "should" do more, qualifying each of their judgments and opinions with the phrase: "But I don't know anything about music." The cultivation of an operatic self implies labor; time is filled with exercises and practical tasks, resulting in the achievement of self-respect through multiple actions to correct and improve oneself.

While the enjoyment of more canonical composers like Verdi or Puccini is seen as effortless, to take pleasure in the work of modern or contemporary composers is the fruit of hard intellectual labor, along a continuum with the idea that, if you dislike something, it is because you do not understand it. *Bomarzo* by Ginastera, *Wozzeck* by Berg, and *Die tote Stadt* by Korngold are usually quoted by passionate fans as examples of works that are complex and maybe too avant-garde to produce pleasure. However, the reverence for these operas makes people attend them anyway, and some later apologize when they confess they actually dislike them. Andrea elaborates on this point: "There is stuff that you make an effort to listen to. They bring so much difficulty you arm yourself with everything you can. To me it's like intellectual work; it's just too hard. I might end up liking it, but it's not the same as with the others."

This tension between pedagogy and enjoyment achieves its limit with the modern works that "lack melody." The lack of melody in certain operas makes it too difficult for them to attract intellectual and emotional investment by operagoers, and, as a consequence, it is permissible to see them only once. *Bomarzo* (as we saw in chapter 3 above) is a particular work in which this tension can be seen at performances. Alicia follows up by commenting on this Ginastera opera: "I like all operas. To me there's nothing to change about opera. . . . I generally like the operas with melody, though, so the modern operas with modern music and no melody become kind of a burden to me." But it is Bianca who actually hits the nail on the head: "From the operas I've seen, *Bomarzo* didn't produce anything in me, didn't get to me at all. I thought it was interesting, I though the staging was risky, really avant-garde, but I guess I don't get modern music, whatever way you wanna call it."

parallels with abstract film / art?

Opera Sacra

As I have suggested throughout this chapter, passionate fans structure their experience after a belief in opera that they then affirm in conversations with (or against) others who also participate in the social world of opera. Against some, they emphasize their lack of passion; against others, they make of opera just any other thing; they berate instrumental uses and enthusiasms that they deem out of place; they reject as much the casual fan as the regular who partakes of it *casually*. The anger toward others who think differently about opera, the emotion awakened, not only by a music presentation, but also by their recollection of it, the noncirculatory character of the object of affection, all point toward the conception of the practice as sacred and of those who participate in its rites as set apart from others.

The literature on symbolic boundaries has shown how groups distinguish themselves from each other by appropriating certain practices or objects, classifying them as pure or impure, and establishing the proper etiquette for engaging in them.[22] In doing so, they tend to establish their worth and what makes them distinctive compared to others. Historical sociologists have shown how elites have drawn boundaries around the higher arts, making them sacred. Yet these sociological analyses have emphasized a distant, sober, civilized etiquette of behavior that neglects to consider that sacred conceptions of the good may be combined with ecstatic practices (see DiMaggio 1982a, 1982b, 1992; Levine 1988; and Beisel 1993). These sociological works couple the classificatory pair of high and low, not only with the opposition sacred/profane, but also with the binary sober/ecstatic.

On the other hand, this chapter has shown why the discussion of symbolic boundaries must be complemented by work that focuses, not only on its categorical components, but also on the actual practices. If we took the discursive apparatus of the audience members at face value, we would miss a big part of the story. We would be left with a highly refined cultural mandarin whom we would never suspect pushes others in the opera house. By looking at issues of sensuality, attachment, proximity, and bodily practices as well as discursive practices, I have complicated the idea of the classification of practices and objects as profane or sacred. I have shown how this case combines a cognitive/discursive understanding of the sacred that works, not through sober (as most of the literature would have it), but through ecstatic practices. This chapter shows how moments of intense engagement—or collective effervescence—are derived from a sacred representation of what people do and engage with, regardless of whether it is labeled and institutionalized as high or low culture.

That one-on-one relationship with music as sacred is organized in many ways. All share a common thread: the impossibility of converting what is said and done within the confines of the upper floors of an opera house into resources valid in other social realms. That is why passionate fans sometimes appear incongruent in how they balance the tension between emotion and self-restraint and in how they distinguish themselves from the other fans. They mobilize diverse scales of evaluation and cultural repertories to disqualify others. For instance, they employ a passionate and heroic understanding of self that distinguishes them from those downstairs and a discourse of aesthetic sophistication to separate them from the new members of the audience. They organize these traits under a moral economy of opera fandom. I dedicate the next chapter to dissecting this in a more elaborate manner, showing how passionate fans differentiate themselves, not from other kinds of fans, but from each other, by their diverse attempts to achieve transcendence through a devoted personal commitment to opera.

CHAPTER FIVE

Heroes, Pilgrims, Addicts, and Nostalgics

Repertories of Engagement in the Quest for Transcendence

Being One with Music (in the Company of Strangers)

Passionate fans strive hard to become one with the music and/or one with the artist as a gifted mediator. They close their eyes and silently focus, kneel as if they were praying, enclose their bodies by moving their chins closer to their chests, and try to move out of their sight anything that interrupts their one-on-one relationship with the music. Some of them do not watch all the time. Rather, they close their eyes and sit on the side, where there is no view of the stage, but where they claim they can focus more intently on the music. Some others, when it gets too crowded, just sit on the floor in the back, close their eyes (so as not to lose their concentration), hold their head with both hands, and listen until the end, when they finally stand up to see the artists take their bows.

The romantic understanding of opera listening I described in chapter 3 gets translated into two main strategies for becoming one with the music. The first makes the singer a mediator by focusing on his or her expressive capacity to communicate the composer's intentions, the meanings and effects we are supposed to gather from the music. The second puts the focus on the singer as his or her voice (and bodily presence) is enough to engender emotional and physical effects in the listeners. Audiences do not necessarily favor one strategy over the other; the two represent parallel repertories.

When fans named their favorite music fragments, those arias that "make their day," some, like Violeta or Julio, expressed the opinion that certain operas work regardless of the interpreters involved. "Puccini is like Mozart. It doesn't matter how badly you suck; you can't go wrong. You really have to do a lot of work to ruin *Tosca*." At the same time, there are titles that, while not always working regardless, promise good singing owing to their excruciating difficulty, regardless of whether Thomas Studebaker or a much more important singer like Siegfried Jerusalem is performing.[1] Those scattered few fans who are interested in contemporary operas and subscribe to the idea that the work of art is autonomous from the creative powers of the performer tend to comment more on the influences on and the structure of the music.

Verdi, Verdi, Verdi!

Rina and Irma have been attending the Colón for over fifty years. I met with them in Irma's small living room, and we had a whole afternoon together. This is one of the few questions I managed to pose since they mostly talked freely together for over three and a half hours:

CEB: *Do you have a favorite aria?*
   R: *I like a lot the arias from* Ballo. *But, no, I can't name one. I like everything. Everything moves me.*
   I: *Viva Verdi!!!!*
   R: *No, but also Puccini, and some other things, like Wagner. [In the background Irma continues: Verdi, Verdi, Verdi!]*
   I: *I like all of Verdi's arias.*
   R: *I like some fragments too; the end of the* Rosenkavalier *is wonderful.*
   I: *I like the tenor aria in* La gioconda. *Something that drives me absolutely crazy is in* Andrea Chenier, *the tenor and baritone duet. It drives me crazy!*

(Interview recorded August 3, 2005)

Interviewees named a few singers (Renée Fleming, Natalie Dessay), but Plácido Domingo stood out as the best example of what Alfredo and Irma dubbed "an artistic personality." He has the poise, voice, and charisma to command attention, yet, in his ability to communicate, he allows the music to be the main ingredient in the equation—and that produces maximum enjoyment. Diego named singers with a clear timbre, like José Carreras, or Juan

Diego Flórez, as being most able to become one with the work and, thus, help him become one with the music. Some few other singers (Pavarotti among the international stars and Darío Volonté among the Argentine nationals) have undoubtedly beautiful voices but are unable to be expressive enough to become something other than what they are—Pavarotti or Volonté singing a specific part. If you are not a fan of these particular singers, then the experience is ruined for you. It is not about technique or perfection for these fans; as long as favorite singers give them something, they can have failures and mistakes here and there.

If we think of the connoisseurs of Wagner, Puccini, Verdi, or Strauss—for whom singers are but a medium for their magical relationship with music (for better or worse, they are priests who invite the initiated to share the wonderful and intimate sacred ritual that happens through voice)—as examples of the first kind of engagement to music, then for the second type we find ourselves before the spectacular worship of the singer himself or herself, thereby losing the mediated relationship with music.[2]

Among the second group, we can easily name fans of Maria Callas as operagoers who fall in love with a voice of mythical character that in itself guarantees a mystical and lyric ecstasy, regardless of what is being sung. The infatuation with the Argentinean tenor José Cura invites us to recover the corporeal dimension of the spectacle of opera, its special relationship with a profane gaze.[3] The mention of his name usually caused a stir among the interviewees:

He's a disgrace. I have a review by a critic from the *New York Times* that asked why people applauded him. He always sings badly; too artificial, like through a tube. But he's really charismatic. (Néstor)

I don't like him, at all. His has an awful voice, he's too full of tricks. (Diego)

Nevertheless, most of the testimonies point to Cura having a great stage presence, emphasizing that he is a great actor. For a performance of Verdi's *Otello* at the Colón Opera House in 1999, he sang naked while rolling down a staircase called for in Beni Montressor's staging; hysterical screams preceded the euphoric applause that accompanied the *aria finale*. A quick assessment could label what happened as *technical difficulty*—that is, a man passionately sings notes that inflate his chest while he's lying on his back. But a second look allows us to assimilate the audience's high-pitched screams, similar to those lavished on rock stars but supposedly foreign to opera singers: the desire for a profane body that is not a medium for music but adored by

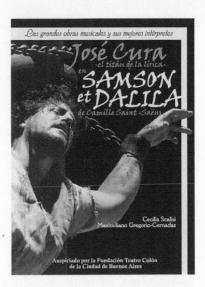

Las grandes obras musicales y sus mejores intérpretes

José Cura
-el titán de la lírica-
en
SAMSON
et DALILA
de Camille Saint -Saëns

Cecilia Scalisi
Maximiliano Gregorio-Cernadas

Auspiciado por la Fundación Teatro Colón
de la Ciudad de Buenos Aires

FIGURE 13. Poster advertising José Cura as Samson in 1997.

itself. Julio, the voice coach, asserts this interpretation: "He's full of artifice, of tricks. In smaller houses you should be able to listen to him better; but not in the Colón—the orchestra covered him. However, he had a peculiar magnetism onstage. He was bare-chested, showing off the hair, his body. He was using something else, and you couldn't stop following him" (see figure 13). Thus, the devotion shown by a connoisseur audience to artists often cataloged as mediocre by the music critics appears best explained by their powerful and distant physical presence.

A local tenor, Carlos Duarte, is the counterexample to Cura. His performance in the role of Manrico in *Trovatore* at La Plata during the 2006 season generated these comments from one fan-cum-critic in an online opera forum:

> The tenor Carlos Duarte is better appreciated in recordings than live. He has a beautiful voice and timbre that runs all throughout the hall. . . . He failed when confronting a role as particular as Manrico, a part in which his compatriot José Cura perfectly managed from an acting perspective. In this case, to see Manrico we have to close our eyes—which doesn't take merit from his voice. The costume director should have made him look more handsome and manly throughout the play; the belt crossing his waist didn't do him any good, pushing his gut out. This is probably a fight between fat singers and stage and costume artists as they ignore their particular needs.

Fans generalize this attitude when talking about other local and international singers. Pavarotti, again, is the favorite target for irate fans, frustrated with their inability to engage either with him or with the music in live performances. Franco said: "I like listening to him but not watching him. With him I have the sensation that singing an opera is the same thing as giving a recital. It's not just ugliness or clumsiness; it's like he's comfortable being so static. Since he's so important, it's like he's telling you, 'Here I am, deal with it.'" Guillermo recalls watching *Aida* on cable when he found himself slipping into a very bad mood: "I hate seeing him. You look at him dressed like he was, and there wasn't any way in hell he was coming from winning a war!"[4] Ernesto ties expression to internal and external beauty while discussing Pavarotti: "You see, beauty comes from the inside. The voice comes out as the expression from the inside. Unbelievable! That is why I don't like Pavarotti. Besides, he looks like a monster."

As we can see, opera is here mediated by the body of the singers and articulated by the fetishized divo and diva. They must be beautiful on the inside—like the true artist—but also on the outside. Violeta, for example, first praised the stage presence of the American bel canto specialist Jennifer Larmore, who has sung numerous times in Argentina: "She's divine! Beautiful people always look great onstage. Remember her in *L'italiana* [*in Algeri*]? She had those long gloves. They were divine. She looked like Marilyn Monroe." She then compared Larmore's poise to the presence of what she called a monstrous body, that of the rising local soprano Soledad de la Rosa (see figure 14). She is hardly alone in the assessment of the young singer. Other fans compared her impersonation of the mechanical doll Olympia in *Tales of Hoffmann* with "Chirolita," a famous Argentinean ventriloquist's puppet. Tito described her in *La traviata* as a "cork" (a colloquial expression for someone who is short and large bodied) and as a "wedding cake" (because of her layered, pale-pink dress). Another rising soprano, Carla Filipcic, while a much taller woman, has also been criticized for her combination of costumes, height, and weight; she was characterized, several times, as a tent.

Devotional Opera

The personalized admiration that makes a singer the cipher for the whole experience of opera provides us with a good occasion to observe the intensely committed, quasi-religious character of fan appreciation. During my fieldwork, the most extreme and literal example of this was a Mass for the Spanish-American soprano Victoria de los Ángeles, one year after her death in the United States. The Mass was organized by an association originally formed to preserve the memory and music of the late Spanish tenor Alfredo

FIGURE 14. Soledad de la Rosa, right, in *Lucia di Lammermoor*.

Kraus, a local favorite. Members papered the city's music venues, including the Colón, with leaflets and small posters, hoping to attract people to give a proper farewell to the soprano. This kind of gathering incorporates a dimension of sociability into an otherwise one-on-one practice with the artist that is achieved through collections of memorabilia and records.

––––––––––

"Her voice was a gift from God"

It's mid-April, and the weather is still nice, though a bit humid. I enter a small church close to a fancy downtown area where most of the hotels for foreigners are located. The street is dominated by bus traffic that makes for difficult walking on the tight sidewalks, but, as soon as I enter, the noise from outside ceases. There are over three hundred people distributed in fifteen lines, waiting anxiously for the beginning of the service to honor Victoria de los Ángeles, a Spanish-American soprano who died a year ago. She used to stay in the hotels nearby and attended Mass here, where she used to "pray to the white Virgin."

Among the crowd, there are some families and a few people younger than forty. Most of the people are old and dressed in frayed jackets and shoes that show they once belonged to the middle and upper middle classes. Little by little, it looks as though they are coming back to the starting point of their social trajectory.

Among the audience, I recognize a couple of critics and two or three musicians. Avid fans, those organized in a society to honor Alfredo Kraus, for instance, are here and helping out with seating arrangements and sound.

People are generally more relaxed than at the opera house and chat about family and friends, more than about opera or Victoria.

As a small chorus starts singing at the back of the second floor, the organizing committee, three men and two women, stand up next to the altar. After a couple of seconds, the whole auditorium is standing up.

"Let us pray for the resurrection of our Lord and of our friend, Victoria de los Ángeles." Some people follow the order and pray on their knees while others wait; one of the men in front starts reading a passage from St. Paul's letter to the Corinthians. He is replaced at the podium by the priest, and everyone stands. The voices have stopped singing, and only the organ pedal harmonizes in the background. "Who believes in me will live even when dead. . . ." The priest reads bits of the story of Lazarus but soon jumps into Genesis: "Man is the most noble fruit of God. . . . It reveals his capacity to create and the task of being a maker. . . . The artist is both the most human and the most divine of men as he gets from the divine artist a spark of his transcendent powers. . . . The more an artist is conscious of his gift, the more he looks up to God for understanding. . . . It has a peculiar relationship to beauty; the vocation our Lord calls talent *is a divine gift, and it is his task and obligation to develop it to put it at the service of the other and humanity. . . . She unites generations of admirers as she transmitted beauty in her art throughout eighty-one years dedicated to singing. We've been lucky to receive her at our house, our beloved Colón Opera, where she used to offer us as a gift never-ending songs outside the program. . . . I still remember the unbelievable amount of people who went to say a last good-bye to her."*

After a somber pause of almost ten seconds—no one made a noise—he concludes: "She was thankful for the art that God gave her by putting it at the service of each and every one of us. Through her beauty we arrived at God and his beauty. We ask you for the eternal rest of the soul of a soprano and a friend of all Argentineans: Victoria de los Ángeles. We hope she takes part in your angels' choir. Let's all pray together as a big family, a family of those who love beauty, singing, and music." The people from the organizing committee are first to line up for Communion. Half of the people from the church followed, as many of them were there, not for Communion, but to honor her.

When the Eucharist begins, the priest says: "Please, receive our gifts so our sister can be received by your son."

Fauré's Requiem *is sung live, with a violin soloist from the national symphony to bolster the accompaniment, and for a few moments everybody looks in awe in the opposite direction from the podium, at the rose window of the church. As music literally descends on us from above, the organizing committee reads a few last words: "Victoria looks at us from eternity; she thanks us and says, Good-bye, Argentinean friends." A tall old man, his hair white, his suit dark, holds hands with his partner and cries in silence. When the climax seems to have passed and the* Requiem *has ended, music starts coming out of the loudspeaker. It's Victoria herself singing the beginning of Gounod's "Ave Maria." It is from a live radio broadcast, and the voice fills the crisp air with the muffled sounds of an old recording. People don't seem to care, and they start clapping and shouting, "Bravo!"*

As I leave, I read the little printed thank-you note they gave us at the entrance; when I glance at the names of those involved in the celebration, I realize that, paradoxically, the name of the soprano for the Requiem *is not included. I wait at the door for one of the critics; he is visibly moved and asks me, "Wasn't it beautiful?"*

(Field notes taken April 15, 2005)

Celebrations like the one for de los Ángeles are not uncommon. Some years ago, a group of fans decided to place a plaque on one of the opera house walls in memory of the long-deceased soprano Claudia Muzio (not casually nicknamed "The Divine"). They hired a bronze sculptor, asked the opera house director for permission, and contacted a group of important people (writers, conductors, singers) to form a "group of notables." The latter were quite elderly, so the organizers were worried noone would participate, especially after they fought with the house's director because the plaque, instead of reading "To Claudia Muzio" as the director wanted, was inscribed "To the Divina Claudia." The organizers refused to change it, not because of the cost, but as a matter of principle. She, and only she, was "The Divine." In response, the Colón called the homage off.

All this unfolded at the same time that Joan Sutherland made her debut at the opera house, singing Violetta in *Traviata*. It was Muzio's favorite part! Fans considered Sutherland's debut offensive (especially when combined with the refusal of the plaque), and they went to the performance to boo her. The house director suspected that the booing was promoted by "Muzio's fanatics," so he decided to grant them permission to commemorate Muzio as they wished. They could not invite many people because of the short notice (although they invited Sutherland, as a joke), so they were quite surprised when they saw a full Golden Hall (a room seating over two hundred people that is used for chamber recitals and acts, characterized by the gold of its columns). They "had all come to hear her voice one more time at the Colón." Presiding over the fans was Muzio's number one admirer, a former house director who came walking in slowly with a cane (the hall is on the second floor, and you have to walk up two magnificent but very long marble staircases to make it there). He died—an interviewee told me—a few months after. A maestro gave a short introductory lecture, and they played some of Muzio's old recordings. One of the organizers read a few words before they uncovered the plaque (see figure 15).

The Elementary Forms of Opera Life

Sociologists have generally viewed opera as the epitome of an elitist and exclusive experience. They have defined it as high culture and focused on how participation in the world of high culture correlates with strategies to attain upward mobility or attempts to solidify group bonds among those who share other circles of affiliation. In all these definitions, high-culture consumption is subordinated to or dependent on a more encompassing series of social phenomena and presented as a resource to be exchanged for or converted into a different kind of capital: symbolic, social, or economic. But what happens when what is accumulated is not allowed to circulate, when we do not allow the things we love to be transformed over time or exchanged for other social products?

Sociologists and anthropologists, following the lead of Emile Durkheim and Marcel Mauss, remind us that what makes an object or a practice sacred is its nonnegotiable, totemic character (see, e.g., Durkheim and Mauss 1963; Durkheim 1965; Douglas 1966; Douglas and Isherwood 1979; Mauss 1950/1990; and Lamont and Fournier 1992). So what cannot be changed in the

FIGURE 15. A wall at the opera house full of commemorative plaques.
Photograph by the author.

Buenos Aires opera world? Opera has a limited canonical repertory of some eighty works that are performed on a regular basis. Opera houses in Buenos Aires are seasonal, which means that they change their programs on a yearly basis and mostly present completely new productions, unlike repertory houses such as the Metropolitan Opera where the same operas and productions are repeated year in and year out.[5] In Buenos Aires, even the most familiar operas are not often seen and are restaged each season they are presented (see table 1). For instance, while *La bohème* has been performed every season at the Metropolitan Opera since the work's American premiere in 1897, it has been performed just three times at the Colón (1987, 1995, 1999) over the last twenty years. Another staple of the Met seasons, *La traviata*, has been performed at the Colón just three times over the last thirty years (1981, 1984, 1999).[6]

Since changes in the libretto and the score are out of the question (we do not see many conductors doing Verdi with jazz-like syncopation), most of the innovation is left to the staging. In European houses, it is common to see adventurous and experimental staging: Muslim-themed versions of Mozart's *Idomeneo*, a *Magic Flute* with the cast costumed as astronauts, Wagnerian fantasies located in an insane asylum during the 1930s. Yet, for the passionate fans in Buenos Aires, every staging that is judged to be not "like the original"

TABLE 1. Seasons Performed per Title, 1980–2005

	Teatro Colón	Metropolitan Opera House
Bohème	5 (4)	24 (1)
Tosca	5 (4)	18 (1)
Aida	4 (3)	17 (2)
Traviata	3 (3)	24 (2)
Rigoletto	3 (3)	16 (2)
Barbiere	4 (4)	14 (1)

Note: New productions are given in parentheses.

gets booed and stirs controversy in online forums, at intermissions, and in preshow lines. In an opera world where turnover times are slow (even the most popular titles like *Traviata*, *Barbiere*, or *Bohème* are produced only every five or six years), fans long for performance that allow them to feel that they are seeing the opera properly, without any disrespectful deviations.

I have already presented two cases in which passionate fans were scandalized by the mise-en-scène: the 2003 production of Wagner's *The Flying Dutchman* and the 2005 *Barbiere*. To those we can add Wagner's *Die Walküre* in 2005 and Verdi's *Macbeth* in 1998. Fans added many titles from the off-circuit to this rather short list from the Colón, including a 2005 *Ballo in maschera* at the Avenida, a *Nozze di Figaro* at the Xirgu in 2004, a *Clemenza di Tito* at the Avenida in 2003, a *Rigoletto* at the Avenida in 2005, and a *Traviata* at La Plata in 2005. However, none of these cases generated as much scandal as a production of *Traviata* during the 2007 season by the French *regisseur* Eric Vignie.[7] The director, who models himself on Calixto Bieito,[8] had already staged *I vespri siciliani* at the Colón in 2006, changing the era of the work from the Anjou period to the mid-nineteenth century, and transforming a medieval episode into a minor chapter of the unification struggle in Italy. No one got as angry with him for the transformation of that title as passionate fans did when he shifted *Traviata* to Paris in the 1920s and turned Violetta into a street prostitute, styling her as the silent-era movie starlet Louise Brooks, and placing her in lesbian scenes with three other courtesans.[9] The production also included a dwarf in a bullfighter costume and the use of heavy drugs during the party scene at Flora's house.

Fans offer many reasons for their abhorrence (this is the only word that captures the intensity of the rejection and their feeling of being defiled by what happened onstage) of this particular production. Roberto, for example, referred to the attempts to modify the meaning of the work through stage direction as deviations that tarnished the original, or, as he called it, "the one and only, the one by Verdi." He called attention—as many other fans do—to the sources of inspiration for the libretto. Another audience member, Alfredo, referred to the fact that it was based on *La dame aux camellias* by Alexandre Dumas fils, a story as much about prostitution as it is about abnegation and redemption. Roberto pointed out that Verdi's wife inspired the part, so it was particularly distressful for him to see the Parisian courtesan who died for love reinterpreted as an everyday streetwalker because, "while Violeta didn't die a virgin, she didn't have syphilis." Other fans, like Diego, referred to the persistent and immutable character of the work, comparing it to a statement about *La bohème* that Diego attributed to Thomas Edison: "Men die and governments change, but the songs of *La bohème* will live eternally."

Fans accused stage directors of modifying the original work on a whim, in order to appear almost as coauthors of the opera. Diego was particularly mad at Vignie and called him "a late teenage transgressor," "full of haughty pride and egotistical," and invited him to "form a cooperative and show his staging to his uncles, aunts, and friends in some 'alternative' stage." He concluded by wondering, "Why doesn't he write his own work and stage it?" Susana attributed this disrespect to the director's ego: "These *regisseurs* want to be better remembered than the singers." Néstor has a rule of thumb for productions that modify an opera beyond the point of recognition: "If I see a picture of the staging and I don't recognize the work, I know the *regie* is bad."

Fans note two key objections to unrecognizable innovation. The first is that a capricious staging distracts from the enjoyment of the music by moving the focus away from the voice. Diego, for example, was angered by Vignie's comments to the newspaper *La Nación* that he was happy "the soprano wasn't worried about her voice" ("Más allá de cualquier dificultad" 2007). For him, this signals a complete lack of understanding of what opera is about since "we all want a soprano singing *Traviata* to be really worried about her voice." Alicia is even more explicit about the centrality of the voice: "Audiences go more than anything to hear voices. The public wants to listen to good singing and singers that sing according to the qualities demanded by the role; that's why they pay good money. Then they worry about whether they are great onstage or not. But the primordial element is the voice, and capricious staging usually distracts us unnecessarily from that." Carlos refers to a scene in *Traviata* that was ruined because, while the text said "questo colloquio non sappia la signora" (the lady should not know of this conversation), Alfredo had Violetta next to him onstage when, obviously, she was not supposed to be there. Other fans, like José Luis, complained about the staging of *Barbiere*, in which Almaviva and Rosina were already out in a 1950s, American-style street scene when they were supposed to be escaping her house.

The second objection is that a disregard for a work's identity or style dissociates a production from the "true" intentions of the composer.[10] Many interviewees claimed that several of their older friends and other regulars have abandoned the opera house owing to the modern staging and have chosen to take refuge in memories and records.

These examples call our attention to the meaning of scandals and how they are moments when some violation of the norm, always by a higher-status individual or group, is exposed and stimulates public outrage.[11] Outbursts of anger, such as over Vignie's stagings, are a way to restore, by dramatizing, the broken norms and lost order of the stage. The punishment of Vignie because of *Traviata* stems from the almost sacred quality conferred on one of the best-known opera titles. It is also an attempt to incarnate in the punished stage director all the transgressions that passionate fans feel they have been subjected to over the last few years by similarly provocative artists.[12] Explaining booing such a staging, Néstor told me: "It is the only chance that you have to express yourself if you've felt attacked because a distorted staging, like the one for *Die Walküre*[13] this season, has to be considered an attack on opera." As we can see evidenced in this statement, passionate fans' identification with opera and their understanding of it is complete.

Nevertheless, regardless of how angry they are, audience members wait until the end of the opera to boo. They "won't boo during the show"; they "don't want to ruin the music." For this purpose, both noisemakers in the audience and stage directors promoting risqué interpretations are included in the same category of opera polluter that interrupts the one-on-one connection to the music. As with Vignie, the out-of-place fans are taught a moral lesson. Collectively, at the same time as they reconstitute the transgressed norms, fans reaffirm the body of the community and their inclusion in it. In the individual sense, booing and violently silencing others helps move audience members from being angry to expressing anger. It means sensually overcoming moral outrage through booing.[14]

The Absence of Capital Exchange

Fans confine their antics to their fellow operagoers and to the space of the opera house. They do not try to exchange capital generated in the Colón in the outside social world (there is no networking, no durable ties). It is not transformed into symbolic capital (fans actually express shame and embarrassment when talking about their love of opera in the outside world), and it is certainly not converted into economic capital (only a few of the fans make a profession out of their love, translating it into employment or marketable assets).

In his description of the diverse material and symbolic goods over which social agents struggle, Bourdieu (1986, 1993) saves a special place for symbolic capital since it points directly to one of the three key elements that govern the fight for social power: social honor. Symbolic capital works on the basis of prestige or recognition, functioning as an authoritative embodiment of cultural value. Nevertheless, the fight for status and social honor, symbolized by the respect and recognition achieved, points to macrosocial structures (called *fields*) through which these exchanges are produced and to a cultural hierarchy in which most participants recognize the signs of distinction and recognition. Yet, if we were to apply this framework to opera fans and an understanding that what is at stake for them is a conversion of the capital accumulated through years of patient attendance and study, then we would arrive at a dead end. For the kind of honor these fans accumulate is hard to make meaningful beyond the boundaries of the upper floors, let alone the whole opera house.

Fans get rejected by the outside world for various reasons. Older fans are treated as crazy and snobbish, men in general are perceived as having "dubious" sexual preferences, and young women are imagined as boring and uninterested in marriage. More than stories of capital conversion, their tales tend to be about learning how to manage stigma—hiding their supposedly discreditable character by concealing those traits or a group identity—or about how they build a boundary between themselves and the outside world as a way of making something positive out of the outsider's rejection.[15]

Alfredo is the first one to signal how he hides his love for opera from strangers and outsiders: "I tell just a few people I go to the opera. You can't tell everybody; they look at you like you're crazy. They don't understand us. They don't have our same sensitivity. You have to divide people. If I would play soccer, there would be some people I would tell it to and some I wouldn't; it's like everything else." Bianca complains that even friends look at her funny because of her love of opera.

> They make fun of me. I have a group of girlfriends who are stuck in the idea that a woman in her early thirties, the only thing she has to look for is to look for a husband. But it's not only my friends. I feel it is generalized. People ask me, "Why do you go to the opera if you're thirty! You go to the opera when you're sixty and you're a snob, you're upper class, you are boring as hell, or if you wanna pretend to be something you're not." It's a weird sensation, people always try to cut you down [*te lo tira abajo*]. But definitely the worst are my friends who choose on a Saturday night to go listen to some asshole's sweet talk instead of listening to opera.

Néstor explains how he decides whom to share his love of opera with, employing the same soccer analogy used by Alfredo:

> I don't tell many people I go to the opera. They think it is too elitist. I try to explain to them, but it doesn't work. People just won't take a chance and come. I don't understand why. But I don't invite everybody. Since it's so important to me, I have to really know that the other person is attracted by it or shares my same sensitivity. But, if I find just a tiny bit of disrespect or no sensibility for opera, I don't even make the effort. It's like soccer. Though I work with physical activities, I don't like it at all. But, as much as I don't get offended if someone likes soccer or tennis and doesn't invite me, if I see someone who hasn't a disposition to go to classical music, I don't even bother telling him.

Diego has a strict definition of who is trustworthy enough to share his experience with: "I talk to one guy from my work. He was an actor, so he gets it. Those without any cultural curiosity, I don't make any effort to approach them. I don't waste gunpowder on carrion birds [*no gasto polvora en chimangos*].[16] Though I get so enthusiastic about opera, I feel like I have to invite everybody. I'm very careful about who I talk about it with. It's their loss, not mine."

The fact that their activity is concealed from others does not change the passionate fans' evaluation of self or of the opera as a meaningful and worthy activity. As we saw in the previous chapter, the others are disqualified in the fans' estimate because they are not intelligent enough to appreciate opera, because they are not spiritual or cultivated enough (which would shift the source of the problem from nature to nurture), or because they lack the proper respect for the art form. Yet, in their testimonies, fans seem to recognize the traits that outsiders ascribe to opera: that it is esoteric; that it is an activity out of the ordinary; and that it is for the elite. These outsiders who reject the fans also serve them (and us as observers) as mirror opposites of their idealized commitment, which involves respect, self-restraint, a special kind of sensibility, and knowledge plus equal parts passion and civilization.[17]

The Passion of the Opera Fan

While the previous chapter focused on how fans situate and differentiate themselves within the status tournament of the opera world, this chapter completes the task by showing how those differentiations are related to diverse individual strategies used to achieve self-transcendence through engagement with opera. By taking the metaphor *the love for* literally and using it as a template to produce a typology for practices of intense attachment, I explain how each of the types can be attributed to a specific dimension of the frame *love for* something. The types of orientations I will present—the hero, the addict, the nostalgic, and the pilgrim—are not distinctive positions in social space; rather, they are a repertoire variously drawn on by different actors. (Although they are presented as separate entities, in reality they sometimes coexist in the same person; they are part of the same *dispositif*, the term implying both institutional arrangements and subjective dispositions.)

The diverse styles of engagement are unified by a quest for transcendence, achieved through listening to opera. Passionate fans extend their engagement in four ways: the first emphasizes the moral economy of its organization and provides an opportunity for some to excel and transcend their everyday lives (heroes); the second centers on the highly personalized dissolution of the fans' selfhood because of a particular fragment of music that produces the sought-after effect (addicts); the third focuses on the past-centric character of the practice, where the self gets paradoxically transcended by its constant reaffirmation (the nostalgic); and the fourth is characterized by fans temporarily equating themselves with others with whom they are not familiar in striving for a moment when they can let themselves go (pilgrims).[18]

THE HERO

During the third week of the 2005 season, I asked a couple whether they were planning to see all the season's titles, including a somewhat contemporary Argentinean opera, *La zapatera prodigiosa*. They looked at each other, and one of them replied: "No. I can't stand *Zapatera*. I don't think we are coming. After so many years of attending everything, we have won the right not to come." He proceeded to explain that, insofar as there are a house orchestra, and house singers, and a house chorus, there is also a house audience—and they are part of it.

Their story demonstrates how the power of this kind of engagement comes from both a heroic ethic of self-sacrifice and moral obligation and a membership to the opera house, gained through that sacrifice, that grants rights and rewards. The demand for extreme attendance results in a moral economy of opera fandom that asks for personal sacrifices outside the opera house. The heroic style makes the opera world a realm of the extraordinary, one in opposition to the everyday routines the hero rejects. This particular world is the stage for extreme acts of courage, the quest for extraordinary goals, even for virtue and recognition, which contrasts with the lesser pursuit of everyday valuables.

I have heard lots of stories—about all-night ticket lines in which the places were certified by a notary, about winter weeks spent out in the cold, about expensive cabs taken five or six times in one night so as to come back and show that you are still on the line, and about sleeping in nearby cars. I witnessed a man in his fifties who had traveled 300 miles to see a performance and then drove back home the same night; a married woman who traveled almost 200 miles, bringing her children to the standing room, and then traveled back home again the same night; and another woman who would take two different buses from a small town 150 miles from the city because there was no direct connection but would still manage to attend two or three performances of each production. Yet the two times people told me I should wait on line for a performance (recitals by the international stars Juan Diego Flórez and Maria Guleghina) I woke up at 5:30 A.M. to get to the box office, only to find out I was the only one there. Nevertheless, that might very well be the nature of a heroic effort: that few effectively realize that it does not make it any less salient or valorized.[19] On the contrary, it helps transmit the collective mystique of participating in a specific kind of engagement; it becomes widely shared and constantly propounded. The moral economy and its language are embedded, almost like dead labor in the way opera was consumed by previous generations.[20]

Yet this language—which combines suffering, self-realization, and hero-ism—underscores the second feature of this engagement: the rewards, both symbolic and material, reaped for "giving your life to the Colón." Both kinds of rewards have to do with recognition. Symbolic recognition, for example, translates into becoming a member, claims of ownership over the opera house (once a month you actually own, through your subscription, a part of the opera house property, having it be "like your house" or even "like your mom's house," as Luis said), or becoming a recognizable name, as this example from Rina illustrates: "I ended up immersed in the Colón. It was like my house. It *was* my house. I was like an employee, but I still paid for a ticket. I wanted to have my own place, where nobody would bother me."

Caring relationships that develop are organized as fictitious kinship ties. Rina is a "mother" to Plácido Domingo—she has shown me some of her many pictures of and letters from him. She was also a "sister" to Flaviano Labo, a star of the 1960s at the Colón and Milan's Scala, and is now a "grandmother" to Bernarda Fink and Virginia Tola, Argentinean singers working abroad, especially when they come back to perform in Buenos Aires. Rina, who jokingly calls herself a "social assistant" for the opera house, is the most extreme case in a continuum that includes other practices, such as following singers whenever they perform, waiting for them as they come out from the opera house or their hotel, getting phone calls as soon as artists are in town, sitting at their restaurant table after the performance, picking them up to bring them to the hall, and getting pictures and recordings signed with special dedications (as seen in most of the houses of the interviewees). Other kinds of exchanges are more fleeting, less continuous, and harder to inscribe on any surface other than one's own memory. For instance, in 1967, the soprano Birgit Nilsson rewarded fans who followed her to the airport in a car caravan covered with Swedish flags by singing a folk song while standing on a chair.

The opera house is a third party that mediates the relationships of exchange. Instead of a deferred one-on-one relationship of gratification, the relationship established with the artist is mediated by fans' claims of "owning" the opera house and having the artists as their "guests." It is obvious, however, that the fans who claim to own the opera house are those who have sacrificed enough for it. This feeling of entitlement is evident as Andrea describes the emotion produced when she has artists as her guests:

> Sometimes, when it's the last performance, I get sad and remember a time when I entered and—don't ask me how—I ended up sitting on the floor of the aisle of the orchestra seating, the place was just too full. There was a black singer, and another guy that came from Africa, and another one from China, and the director was Russian, I think, and it was the last show, and they were saying good-bye, and I felt that incredible emotion to know that tomorrow they will all be gone in an airplane. The magic will be gone. All the people that got together to do a crazy thing, the two hundred, three hundred people are gone, and I just feel honored they've given it to me. That they just put it together for me, for the chair I own once a month at the opera house.

Roberto, who has attended for many years, reflected on the issue and on whether the house artists or the audience are the true owners of the Colón. After claims of ownership by the house artists, because of the long-standing conflict they were in with the city authorities during most of my fieldwork,[21] Roberto sent a general email to an opera forum stating: "Those who, like me, have forty years at the Colón, we've seen a never-ending amount of artists and authorities pass by. After they are done with their relationship to it, you never see them again. On the other hand, people like me, regulars, we just keep coming, both in good and in bad times, and we will keep doing so while authorities and artists just keep passing by." Much like the state employee or the secretary who sees boss after boss passing by, many of my interviewees and informants find their feelings of ownership strengthened by the permanence and the public character of the opera house.

Claims of ownership are enacted, not only with artists, but also with other, newer or more casual members of the audience. Older fans are attentive to newcomers, whom they try to engage in conversation while offering advice on how to place themselves to best listen and observe or whether they can get a seat. They are quick to point out the marvels of the building to international tourists and to explain the amount of vocal prowess they have witnessed. They are also quick to point out rules for casual fans, like the need to wear black tie for *gran abono* on Tuesday nights or the impossibility of sharing standing-room space with someone from the opposite sex except in the *paraíso*—a breach they are quick to bring to the attention of ushers—or the prohibition against taking pictures. In protecting their house, they are sometimes overzealous to the point of asking a permissive usher to remove a woman from the men-only floor or a man from the women-only floor.

A series of material rewards is tied to the symbolic ones. Habituation makes somebody "part of the landscape," as an usher put it, or "part of the inventory," as Rina's friend Irma referred to her. "They believe the house belongs to them," a former press secretary explained, as much as to guarantee being frequently included in guest lists for opening nights, knowing the house personnel to get preferential or free seating when available, or navigating the house's staff in order to get in for free even if the house has forbidden it.[22]

Organizers have taken advantage of this as fans and friends can also become a resource, especially to fill the seats on an opening night or for a midweek performance. Estimates of guests of the house for an opening night at the Avenida range from 50 to 150 (for a hall with a total capacity of 1,130 and orchestra seating for 454). While the number of complimentary admissions can be large on some nights (15 percent of the total hall and almost a third of the orchestra seats), it will never be large enough to hide a failure.[23] According to the organizers of the diverse opera companies that work there, some of the complimentary guests are critics, others are sponsors, others are future or potential sponsors, and still others are opera people. The more important the company, the more opera people are viewed as a burden ("people you just can't say no to!" as one organizer put it) and less as worthy word-of-mouth promoters. The more amateurish companies are closer to the fans and see opera people as an essential element of the enterprise to which producers are committing themselves. (Bela, one of the organizers, encompasses all of them under the category *friends of the house* [*amigos de la casa*].) The most organized of the new companies usually deny entry to opera people, whom they characterize as "burdensome" (*pesados, unos plomos*) or "hard to deal with," and frequently send them to the dress rehearsal. Press officers sometimes get mad at the ushers or the hall administrator, who let in some of the people who have been overtly denied entry. This happens, not only at the top floors, but also at the better seats.

There is a gray zone, especially for amateur critics who manage to convert habituation and frequency into preferential seating (leaving the upper floors for "critics'" seats at the orchestra level). Because of the changing character of the critical profession, it can be difficult for press officers to decide what works as a credential and what does not: Is this person writing for a newspaper or working as a correspondent for an international opera magazine or Web site? Or is it someone who claims to write for an obscure newsletter or has written reviews at some point but whose professional credentials rest on having been around the opera world for a long while? According to one organizer, she always finds the latter inside the hall, even when she does not have tickets to give them. The more recognized critics—some of whom work as organizers or press secretaries themselves—disqualify these amateur critics, who "do the same thing they would do or comment on in the gallery or *paraíso*, but with a microphone."

For some of the older fans, free tickets and preferential seating are not enough of a reward; the ultimate right to be won is the right not to come as you have proved yourself through intensive and extensive attendance and can, thus, attend only what you like or think will be appropriately performed. The declining quality of the circuit performances and the impetus for innovation in staging has caused many older fans to stop coming to the opera house. Much like the lover who has sacrificed all his or her life for a partner, when the affection is no longer reciprocated, the enthusiasm and commitment wane or are displaced, and the multiple trials and work the self has gone through to prove its worth come to a full stop.

While these audience members manage to invest themselves in the music world while being rewarded for an idealized commitment to a heroic ethic, others intensify this engagement to the point at which it offsets any possible rewards. These fans have become addicts.

THE ADDICT

The language of opera attendance resembles that of an addiction:

When my father took me to *La traviata*, I got hooked on it immediately. It was like doing drugs for the first time. (Eugenio)

Opera is a trip with no return. (Armando)

This is an addiction. The subscription is the first thing I worry about during the year. (Victoria)

I can be deprived of anything but opera. (Alicia)

At some point I'll have to stop, or I'll get sick. (Franco)

The amount of emotion that it produces in me, it's like nothing else. I have to go two, three times. It's like a disease I can't get rid of. (Andrea)

The French sociologist Antoine Hennion and his collaborators have already used the figure of addiction to conceptualize taste as an activity, referring mostly to record collectors. But they have not focused on the live-music lover as someone who has an intense engagement with an activity, develops a specific set of skills, and invests in an active discipline full of constraints and specialized knowledge that allows him to let himself go. Unlike Adorno's (1962) characterization of culture consumer, what is emphasized here is, not the stultifying character of the music consumption, but the high—actually resonating throughout the body—that opera produces through an overly informed practice. If we were to find an analogy from the world of drugs, it would be more like cocaine than Valium.

This particular style of intense affiliation results in the momentary dis-solution of the self as produced by a series of effects. The presence of others is absolutely secondary as the fix can be achieved by the extension of the opera experience to other media and formats that are more portable and individu-alized. Addicts express their engagement (*a*) through the intensification of the hero ethic, (*b*) by articulating what is abandoned for this active passion, (*c*) by expressing the physical consequences of the enjoyment, coded under a dual figure of sickness and cure, and (*d*) through the professionalization of their audience status, resulting in cultural "univorism."

These interviewees presented themselves as gaining nothing from their devotion to the world of opera other than the sheer moment of intensity. Some interviewees described to me how opera occupies so much of their lives that it organizes their yearly schedule. Others sadly confessed that they are lonely because they have invested so much of themselves in opera-related activities. One woman revealed that she remained in the Colón during a bomb threat in 2005, the day after the terrorist attack on the London Under-ground; she picked up the newspaper and turned first to the performance reviews. Another audience member complained that his body ached from standing at the opera house three or four times a week, and he noted that he was happy that there was not more opera to go to, that, if there were, "[his] body couldn't take it." Others described family quarrels over or separation from a partner who was excluded from their solitary pleasure.

The addiction is shaped as an active seduction. Addicts are convinced that opera's powers are mesmerizing, especially if one takes the proper steps to achieve "immediacy" (Hennion 1993, 2001), that is, preparing at home by listening to a recording of the work, reading the libretto or the score, following the radio discussions, attending the proper lectures and conferences (i.e., all the activities that allow us to decipher what there is to enjoy and how to partake in it), and then sitting in the same seat for every performance. Music, to the addict, is unavoidable; it guarantees more pleasure and interests than any other activity. One informant described to me how music distracts him from whatever he is doing, even sex, to the point that he has had to stop whatever he is doing and turn off his CD player in order to perform adequately.[24] This active seduction has a second part, proselytization, which makes people attempt to recruit others to participate (as individuals) in the same enjoyment—even though the recruitment of outsiders has proved to be a difficult enterprise for most of my interviewees and informants.

The physical character of music addiction often takes a dual form, combining being sick and feeling cured. Some interviewees described a profound sickness that invades them when they listen to something enjoyable. This sickness results in their being silent, shocked, and introverted for some time before they can actually begin to find pleasure in what has caused such an emotional impact. Some describe this as lasting some twenty to thirty seconds, during which time they get enraged by audience members who start clapping immediately ("Some music is so good it merits no applause!"). Others described a long, lonely walk home to lessen the impact of the music enough to make it delectable. Franco is one of the latter. As he describes it: "The pleasure is too much: it evolves into something nasty. It's like my body says I can't take it anymore. I never left an opera before the end, but I did have to walk instead of taking a cab, and, when I get home, I feel nauseous or something like that. It's like when you eat the chocolate you like the most and you reach a point where you have to stop because you just can't. When that sensation leaves, then the pleasure returns, but two or three hours must have passed by."

This painful process is part of the cure, the music high causing passionate fans to forget their everyday problems. It alleviates their anguish, gives them comfort when mourning, and makes them forget their current circumstances. Music is "something that can keep you company and away [from others] at the same time" (Armando). It is "better than going to therapy":

"Instead of spending money on therapy, I spend it on opera" (Rina). *Therapy* is a common trope, as we see in Alicia's defense of her continuing to travel the 200 miles to the opera house: "Some people spend money on therapy; they see a psychoanalyst. This is my therapy. With this I start flying and arrive home anew. When I used to work, the stress would kill me. But I arrive home from the opera house fresh as a little lettuce, happy, commenting on all the beautiful things I've seen. It has never come into my head to abandon it."[25]

The addiction literature emphasizes the active work of preparation required to achieve a high, in this case, a music high. Sometimes, however, this intense preparation is displaced by an even higher music fix: the moment of surprise. Many of my interviewees indicated that moments of surprise in an opera performance lead to the ultimate abandonment of the self, even more than crying at the end of *La bohème*, the love duet at the end of *The Flying Dutchman*, or humming "O mio babbino caro" or "La mamma morta." Since they are so overprepared for most operas, they spend much of the time during a performance thinking about the few moments during which they can achieve a high, or how much they prefer a particular CD version, or how much more interesting the last staging was, or how the soprano's voice is better suited to a different repertory. The surprise (a rarely performed or never-recorded opera, a contemporary work they have been wary of, a forgotten or long-overdue piece) allows them to "enjoy the show 100 percent, without worrying about any ghosts." This enjoyment sometimes leads them to out-of-town houses, where unusual titles like *Un giorno di regno* or Lully's *Armide* get staged, or makes them put up with sopranos who, while past their prime, are singing seldom-heard works like *Elisabetta, regina d'Inghilterra, Il pirata, Anna Bolena,* or *Maria Stuarda*. Or it might take them to a baroque opera staged at a factory in a way they would never put up with at the Colón.

Addicts take advantage of the new opportunities provided by the off-Colón circuit. As Franco summarizes it: "It's a great thing there is also the Avenida. If there were only the nine operas the Colón offers, we would die!" The off-circuit not only helps the heroes in shaping their sacrificial selves but also provides opportunities for the addicts to pursue their "treasure chase" (Fine 1998) for surprises beyond the exhumation of seldom-performed operas. When discussing surprises, the countertenor Franco Fagioli comes to mind since he jumped from the off-circuit to the European scene. At least seven of the fans I interviewed named him as someone they discovered through the secondary stages and companies. The fact that he is a countertenor, a seldom-heard voice, also plays into the surprising character of having found him outside the Colón. Fans also have favorites from this circuit that they seek out since they do not perform on the city's main stage.

Néstor provides an explanation of, not only how important the surprise is, but also how even the surprise follows the same self-disciplining mold that prescribes a series of activities in order to achieve immediacy and enjoyment. The search for surprises works, not against, but through an overinformed practice:

> I keep going to the Colón, despite its current quality, because I want to see new works. It's lots of fun when the Colón stages things that I don't know. *Lady Macbeth of Mtsensk, Jeanne d'Arc au bûcher, Dialogue of the Carmelites, Les Indes galantes.* Those are the operas I enjoy and do go to see again. The same thing with *Quichotte* this year. I loved it; it was the best by far, wonderful. . . . *Quichotte* sent me over the moon because I knew absolutely nothing about it. So to me it was like when Verdi premiered his work or when Wagner and Donizetti presented their operas in Prague, Budapest, or Paris. I didn't want to listen to anything at all; I was an absolute virgin; I didn't even read the story. I knew only the composer; that's it. And, when I saw the opera unfolding, I just loved it. Loved it! But the key was not to know anything.

This intense engagement, which professionalizes an audience member, results in cultural univorism. Authors of the American school of cultural production have shown how increasingly, in the United States and most of Western Europe, members of the upper class do not distinguish themselves by participating in a few esoteric cultural practices (they are not snobs anymore); rather, they distinguish themselves from lower-class audiences, which like only one cultural product, by the omnivorous and inclusive character of their consumption patterns (see, among many others, Bryson 1996, 1997; Peterson and Kern 1996; Van Eijck 2001; Lizardo 2005; and Zavisca 2005). Thus, given their social placement according to this literature, passionate fans at the Colón "misbehave." Most of them come from diverse factions of the middle class. Some are accountants, lawyers, dentists, physicians, high school teachers, and small-shop owners; others have already retired or are still working as freelance translators, schoolteachers, or public employees.[26] Yet, as all of them invest themselves in opera, they withdraw from other cultural practices, abandoning other kinds of music (including classical instrumental),[27] performing arts (theater or movies, a medium most informants used to be interested in but slowly started ignoring as they fell into opera), or the traditional beaux arts (like painting).

Yet, for some audience members, neither the preparation, nor the surprise, nor the complete abandonment of other media and forms is enough; they long for something else. These fans are the nostalgics.

Nostalgics remind you, not only of the time they saw Flagstad and Furtwängler, but also of the time they saw Muzio or Toscanini. This style of engagement is past-centric and derives from the intensification of a dimension of practice present in most people's lived experience.[28] It references a past that is always better than the present; it is shaped as a permanent jeremiad[29] that disqualifies most of what is currently offered at the opera house; it gets solved, not in the abandonment of the live experience for the recording experience, but in a permanent comparison and tension between these two ways of experiencing music. Though this pathos is constitutive of opera as a genre and a constant throughout opera history, in Buenos Aires it gets attached to specific historical moments and to a precise model of affiliation.[30]

Nostalgics behave in a paradoxical way. On the one hand, they reaffirm who they are by constant reference to a lost time. On the other, by doing so they transcend the current circumstances of their being, affirming the continuity in time, and attaching themselves, on a continuum from past to present, much more closely to the former than to the latter. People who enact this style of loving avoid going to the off-Colón opera circuit, and, every time they go to the Colón, they complain about the quality of what they hear. Their lament refers, not only to the golden age of opera, but also to the golden age of the country and the golden age of an audience composed of fully engaged and educated people. This transition is almost obvious since, for them, opera works as an embedded mode of sociability in which past performances refer immediately to all audiences with whom they shared that experience. To complement and reaffirm the superiority of what they heard live, they own extensive record collections, including vinyl records, bootlegs tapes, and transferred master tapes, but they also own collectibles and possess a repertory of anecdotes about the past that they are eager to share whenever the opportunity arises.

This continual reference to the past is not exclusive to older operagoers. As a dimension of practice, it appears in two ways among younger audiences (people in their late twenties to early forties who have attended for at most ten years): as a reference to the past as transmitted by the older members and as a reference point closer to their attendance but still in the past. Most people reference a moment between the 1950s and the 1960s (a moment that took advantage of the end of World War II, the migration of European musicians and audiences, and the relative richness of the country) that is captured in one informant's comment, "That's when they had two full casts to make the *Ring* cycle."[31] But a second golden age is located in a nebulous time when the opera house had more money and was more international. For some people, this time is the late 1970s; for some, it runs until the mid-1980s (when Caballé and Pavarotti, e.g., would still appear at the Colón) or the mid-1990s (when the exchange rate was favorable enough that the Colón could afford Freni, Ramey, Milnes, Mattila, and Domingo and the Argentinean international singers Cura, Alvarez, and Lima would still come back to sing). The economic crisis of 2001 forced the "nationalization" of seasons, with soloists recruited mostly from the secondary circuit, and erected the ultimate wall that distinguishes the present from what was a golden age. That season, the soloists for *The Rake's Progress* were the same two singers who would perform the parts at the Met in 2003. While in 2001 the likes of Renato Bruson, Neil Shicoff, Christopher Ventris, Giorgio Merighi, Frederica von Stade, Alain Fondary, Samuel Ramey, Paul Groves, June Anderson, Thomas Allen, Elizabeth Norberg-Schulz, and Giorgio Cebrian came to sing, from 2002 to 2005 Colón performers who also sang title roles at other first-rate opera houses were Olga Romanko (2002 and 2003), Jennifer Larmore (2003), Inés Salazar (2004), David Pittsinger (2005) and Antonio Siragusa (2005) (for a more complete listing, see table 2).

As we can see in figure 16, the opera house was as international in the 1990s as it was in the 1960s, featuring almost forty performers who also sang at the Met and at Bayreuth. Nevertheless, people refer much more to the 1960s as the golden age of opera in Buenos Aires. In most accounts, the 1990s is just a decade like any other, better than the contemporary moment, but nothing special. This reverence for the past requires, not experiential knowledge, but rather deference toward the older fans who offer experience and frames to codify it. As a consequence, one can find thirty-year-olds discussing whether Renata Tebaldi or Maria Callas is (discussions take place in present tense) a better soprano. In doing this, they perpetuate the belief that the post-World War II era was the pinnacle of the modern classical music and opera experience, more centered in the Italian repertory and Wagner and in big-volume voices as presented by immortal diva roles.

Though part of what I have just described can be explained by general mechanisms of memory (myth, in-group and generational patterns), there is something in particular about opera-induced nostalgia that distinguishes it from the longing found in other milieus: the availability of technological evidence to form a past-centered opinion, as evidenced in the many transfers,

TABLE 2. Title Roles Sung at the Colón by Singers
Who Also Appeared at the Met and Bayreuth

Year	Met Singers	Bayreuth Singers
1950	10	4
1953	11	3
1955	5	3
1960	21	6
1965	29	9
1970	23	3
1975	9	4
1980	15	7
1985	12	3
1990	10	1
1991	20	2
1992	22	1
1993	27	3
1994	28	5
1995	27	9
1996	24	5
1997	29	5
1998	29	7
1999	14	2
2000	11	2
2001	10	0
2002	1	0
2003	1	2
2004	0	0
2005	3	0

bootlegs, and CDs fans own. Access to a set, standard repertoire offers a somewhat disenchanting benchmark, dominated by a few singers against whom contemporary singers pale in comparison. Néstor, once again, provides a clear account: "But you shouldn't stage repertory plays when the audience has a measurement yardstick in their head. I don't want to see *Traviata* any more; I have three versions on CD, two on DVD. There is a moment when you either do it in a superlative, canonical way or can it." Contemporary singers face an audience that hears behind their shoulders the ghosts of performers past.

While sports fans can discuss for hours what the result of a tennis match between John Newcombe and Rafael Nadal might be or whether Leonel Messi is better than Pelé or Alfredo Di Stefano, they must speculate more; the continuous physical progress of athletes makes it difficult to compare

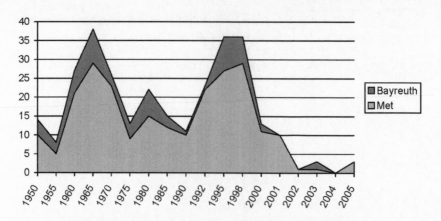

FIGURE 16. Internationalization index of opera seasons in Buenos
Aires, 1950–2005. Singers per season who also sung at the Met or in
Bayreuth (the high point of the graph for each year indicates the total
number of Buenos Aires singers at both the Met and Bayreuth).

the pace of a soccer, a football, or a tennis match today with one from the
1960s. On the other hand, opera fans can have head-to-head matches between singers past and present where the weight of evidence is standardized
by technology (and the lack of progress of the art form) and respected by
most. As such, their nostalgia is more analytically fueled than pure, enabled
by the reasonable confidence that there were at certain points in the past
singers who defined certain roles and were capable of handling a certain aria
or part with a certain level of technical or emotional skill.

The sociologist of culture, following the work of Benjamin (1969), would
expect the result of the disenchantment of the work of art—the result of mechanical reproduction—to be for the aura to be transferred or displaced into
the experience of the audience of a live opera. Nevertheless, in this particular
case, mechanical reproduction disenchants the present in such a way that the
production of a unique and authentic experience (the meaning of aura) rests
on the nostalgia for the live recordings of the past. Luis's distrust of studio
recordings is typical: "You never know when they've stopped, when they are
recording it straight up, when they are embellishing it. So sometimes the
singer is OK, some others he's not giving 100 percent, but you don't know it.
On the other hand, with live recordings you can tell from the stage whether
they are really singing well or not."

The live experience confirms the value of singers heard first on a record-
ing. For instance, when Juan Diego Flórez finally came to Buenos Aires,
Diego was exultant to discover that "he sounded exactly like listening to his
CD." Recordings work, not just as benchmarks, but also as yardsticks for the

confirmation of the validity of the performance. When Freni and Domingo came to Buenos Aires, fans were surprised, not only that they sounded like their recordings, but also that they did so night after night. Luis attended all seven of their performances and "was really surprised by the fact that the first show was as good as the seventh": "I can't distinguish one for reference purposes. Neither better nor worse, they were always great, something which I've only seen happening with other great singers."

While in other countries this type of nostalgia fulfills only an analytic function, in Argentina the impossibility of hosting current international stars makes it a central part of the jeremiad that laments the fact that golden voices from the past (or their equivalents) do not come to Buenos Aires anymore. The exact golden age referenced is not as important as the form that this engagement with music takes and the shared understanding that the present is always in decline. This is evidenced perfectly in Tito's description of a much older friend who has been coming to the opera for some sixty years (Tito himself has been coming for fifteen): "He started when he was really young. He saw Toscanini's debut conducting Beethoven's Fourth. That was the first time he [the friend] came to the Colón. After that, everything went downward."[32] In this sense, opera audiences are similar to those for classical music, where there is also a prevailing discourse about a postwar golden age and a state of decline.

Also central to this nostalgia is the notion that the golden age of opera in Argentina was also a more prosperous time. Not only could a larger number of international artists be engaged, but audiences were also more knowledgeable about the music and appropriate ways of consuming it. For instance, José Luis, one of my older informants, recently circulated a series of vignettes on "historic" operagoers in an opera forum (they will soon be compiled in a book). In those vignettes we see the audience being born out of the several waves of European immigration constituting the city's current population: Italian, Spanish, Central European, and Eastern European Jewish. Conversations with José Luis also revealed that Buenos Aires's Nazi past was important, too: "First came the Jews escaping the Germans and then the Germans escaping the courts." These various peoples brought with them European culture and an appropriate way of experiencing music, which involved intensive and extensive knowledge. By way of these vignettes, José Luis lamented that people do not read scores anymore or play an instrument at home. He celebrated autograph seekers, people who went to the airport to receive the singers, and well-informed, never-ending discussions that sometimes threatened to end in fistfights. He also celebrated the extravagant fan who called himself "Puccini"[33] and would thank people after a performance of *Tosca* or *Butterfly*. He longs, not only for the golden age of performances, but also for the more heroic, devoted, and educated time to which the romanticized and undefined origin of the current matrix of opera engagement can be traced, the time of the discovery of his idealized "first love."

¡"Ay, Ay, Ay, Ay, Ay" Feldman! A Vignette by José Luis Sáenz

We never knew where Feldman came from. Some thought he was Russian; some others said Ukrainian, Polish, even German. Somebody stated that he was born in Turkey and that he wandered through Ukraine, Poland, and Germany until he embarked for Argentina in 1929. What was certain was that as soon as he landed in Buenos Aires, even before finding a job or a house, he decided to stand at the back entrance of the Colón and in the standing-room section of the paraíso for every performance. He did so until the end of his life. He never missed a day, and once we stopped seeing him, we knew for sure he was dead.

He had gray hair, a hook nose, one blue eye, and one that was cloudy. He usually looked messy, with old, faded, dirty, and wrinkled clothing and a tie that pointed in the wrong direction, and his hands were always full of records, always wrapped in newspaper.

His collection of old records was famous. He had, or was able to acquire, what nobody else had or was able to get. He liked talking about them; he enumerated them in a detailed manner, with his imprecise Central European accent (strong and ineradicable, regardless of how long he had been in the country) and with an emphatic way of hammering the accentuation of the singer's name. He especially enjoyed the Russian names like Sobinoff, Smirnoff, Lemeshev, and Koslovsky, through which he copiously spit on his interlocutor. He liked to lend his records to a specialized radio show; he enjoyed talking badly afterward about the host of the show; he was a snake, he would say. But he kept lending them to him anyway.

He prefaced his criticisms about a singer with a lamenting, "Ay, ay, ay, ay, ay!" while he banged his forehead. He knew a lot about voices, both old and new singers. He was very demanding and could tear one of the night's singers to pieces. But soon afterward he would approach the same singer to ask for an autograph, igniting the fury of some unconditional fan who had just witnessed his ruthless criticism.

He was multilingual, able to speak in Russian with Gedda, in French with Crespin, in Italian with Taddei, in German with "la" Nilsson, and in English or Yiddish with Tucker.

He used to come to the opera house with his son, who had a hook nose like

him and the same messy hair, and was usually poorly dressed and groomed. The son also shared his father's opinions and was as fanatical as the old man. Old and new, they were two packages of the same product. The son managed to get a job as an extra onstage; or, better put, his father fought for him to get the job so that he could get fresh and direct gossip and show off his perfect information about how the rehearsals were going.

<hr />

THE PILGRIM

Recently, Craig Calhoun (2007) pointed to how productive a concept like that of liminality can be in elucidating relationship patterns within the opera house. Though he was referring to how a particular staging of a particular opera, *Le nozze di Figaro*, created a liminal space—outside everyday life yet close enough to engage with it critically in a way that would not have been possible with the spoken word alone—I want to extend his analysis and show how the concept of liminality helps us better illuminate relationships within the opera house.

The concept of liminality, as elaborated by the anthropologist Victor Turner, assumes the existence of a threshold beyond which specific practices are distinguished from the quotidian. The threshold is identified with the transitional state during initiation when people have neither abandoned their old ways completely nor embraced the new ones fully.

How does this concept help us understand the ways in which opera fanatics bond and the kinds of relationship they build once they have been initiated? Much like a religious pilgrimage, the practice of opera in which these fans partake erases the vagaries of the outside world and makes them embrace an imaginary *communitas*; their differential roles and status, duties and obligations, are cast aside, for a few moments, as all become one with the music. Pilgrimages have been defined as events at which people from diverse social backgrounds get together for the most diverse reasons and where etiquettes of personal intimacy are transformed for a set period of time; as a form of sociation that involves both a personal quest and a social organization that grants recognition to the individual journey, which is, nevertheless, noninstrumental to or independent of the individual's social standing once he or she returns home; as an out-of-time experience to which pilgrims attend in a highly individualized way, personalizing their belief and the motive of their quest; and as a place where, despite that highly individualized character, spiritual bonds among strangers emerge.[34]

In a similar fashion, the community of passionate fans does not institutionalize itself or coalesce into a permanent fixture of society; rather, it re-forms every time the lights are dimmed and the performance is about to start, when people are anxiously waiting on the steps, eager to show how they have learned to manage the unending details that make opera fully delectable, thus distinguishing themselves from the casual fans. Though particular fans engage with opera in diverse ways, preferring some singers or composers over others and music-centered over singer-centered works, claims of status fall away when confronted by the live experience of the work itself.[35] The key division is not from other committed fanatics, among whom small differences may exist—variation among the deserving members of the community is not turned into deviation—but from the casual or the "social" members of the audience.

The communality of fans is, not friendship, but the mutual recognition of a common understanding of the experience of opera. It dissolves as soon as the experience ends, only to re-form at the next performance. Contra recent findings in and generalizations from the sociological literature, cultural taste does not, in this case, evolve into a personal network extending beyond the opera house.[36] I entered fieldwork convinced that I was going to find people who had routines with friends from both within the opera world and outside of it—meeting for dinner, visiting each other, planning to attend performances together, and going out before or after. Yet my experience, both throughout interviews and participant observation, painted a different picture: one of a group of people who knew each other, were cordial, talked a lot about the performance, inquired about each other's families, and maybe shared an occasional phone conversation but who separated the rest of their social life from that part that involved the opera. This included people who had befriended others at the opera house many years ago and referred to them as friends, even though they had not seen or talked to them in over six months. It also includes people who have had the same subscription for years and converse with their neighbors (sharing a coffee during intermission) but who say good-bye after the last performance of the season and catch up with them again only when the season starts in April. Their sociability is dense but strictly confined to the Colón.

Franco gives us a clearer impression of how this works: "It's a pretty intimate thing, a communion between the opera house and the audience. I invite people from time to time, but actually love to come alone. It's an inside thing, intimate. I like to run into people I know, with whom I don't share any bonds outside of the house. I like those interactions with people you say hi to but don't really know much about their life. I rarely see those people outside the opera house at all."

This fleeting communality, established by the intimacy between fans and the object of their attachment, makes the experience of opera a liminal one, a ritual process that bonds fans as much with the scene as with others who attach themselves to it in a similar way, separating them from the everyday world, from other fans who cannot enter into the same engaged relationship and from their own everyday selves. Liminality, then, goes from being a moment—a passage or a transit from one state to the next—to becoming a permanent fixture, a particular dimension within the confines of the opera house, and, for some, a condition for enjoying opera to the fullest. In this sense, the experience of opera is not different from other forms of charismatic attachment, in which members of a particular group recognize each other as equal in relationship to that which provokes their attachment, even if this happens in a highly individualized way.

Seeking Transcendence

The styles of engagement that I have described are not rooted in performances for others. Rather, they are exercises in seeking transcendence. While in the previous chapter I emphasized how fans mobilize their expressive capacities in order to distinguish themselves from other audience members, in this chapter I focused on the diverse shapes of their intense personal engagement. Honor is not at stake, but transcendence is. It is, not a struggle over cultural membership or authority, but a story of how transcendence operates as a goal for many while at the same time organizing modes of engagement and the cosmology that underpins them.

The standing room works as a *dispositif* that integrates the many ways in which people engage with music. It constitutes the experience of music as a multifaceted one, yet it is anchored in certain categories and dispositions common to most of the passionate operagoers. These categories appear here nuanced or shaded as ideal types, but the ideal types are just dimensions of a way people engage with music in Buenos Aires. The range of variation, from heroes to addicts, has to do with social and personal trajectories: whether the fans have families or partners, whether they are committed to their work, whether they have other circles of affiliation. The heroes have something they temporarily surrender to; the addicts usually do not. The pilgrim is the less demanding style since it usually manages to complement the rest of a fan's life. While it is obvious that nostalgia is the style that usually colors the experience of older fans or those who have attended for a long time, it also frames the experience of younger people, with whom the older fans share an omnipresent romanticized and moralized past and a decadent present (both outside and inside the opera house); that they try to escape using opera while striving for transcendence points to the reproduction of an experience framed by values and commitments learned within the upper floors of the house. The general pattern of nostalgia is tied to local forms that stress the longing, not only for a better opera in general, but also for better times at the Colón and the country. This fact points to larger societal concerns and values and to how the outside filters the boundaries of the opera house, something I explore more fully in the next chapter.

PART III

FINALE

CHAPTER SIX

"They were playing in their shirtsleeves!"

Downfall, Memory Work, and High-Culture Nationalism

Singers, Picketers, and Strikers

It was May 13, 2005. This was the second month of my third fieldwork visit to Buenos Aires. I was in line for the opening night of *Don Quichotte* at the Colón, and, though only four weeks had passed since my arrival, there was a noticeable repetition in conversations: chatter tended to refer exclusively to the world of music performances. The line of fans, as much as other informal institutions of the opera world, seemed to be the locus and support of sociability, a process of pure sociation devoid of significant purposes. Fans did not bring their outside problems and obligations with them to the Colón. Work and family were mostly left behind in the subways, buses, and taxis. Political issues were rarely touched on, and the news of the day had no currency while they queued up.

Here and there, other issues would intervene, but nothing I have not already placed within the particular worldview of the passionate opera fan in Buenos Aires. For instance, during my second time on the line, a man (I would later learn it was Tito) was complaining about how bad soccer has been for Argentinean society, how it should be equated to drugs and thought of as a tool created by the English to stupefy and conquer the world. Another time, during the run of *Quichotte*, I discovered that a woman in her early sixties who was always first in line and would race me upstairs was not a model of heroism but actually the mother of one of the flamenco dancers hired for the occasion who wanted to "see her daughter making it at the Colón."

That is why I was thoroughly unprepared for and surprised by a four-minute diatribe that wove together, with the precision and the suspense of a literary short story, the pitch problems of a soprano in Avellaneda with the moral downfall of the country. The storyteller's name was Eduardo; he was an architect in his late fifties who narrated a highly complex tale that, after I became aware of its existence, would make itself visible everywhere. Afterward, much like the detective-historian proposed by the Italian historian Carlo Ginzburg (1986/1989), I started to inquire into some of the stories overheard on the lines, looking for traces or footprints of a larger, more comprehensible, yet less explicit narrative.[1]

Eduardo's story did not just make an easy connection between one series of phenomena and the other. It was not just the nostalgic narrative of a country that, having lost the power to attract the best singers, was not as good as it once was. His story started with his being so disheartened at how bad the soprano was in *Trovatore* at the Avellaneda that he decided to find solace at the Colón. Right before joining the line we shared, he had stood at the corner, next to 9 de Julio Avenue, only to notice how aged, untidy, and abandoned the building looked. Being an architect, he could not help but lament the semipermanent structure that had been built on the parking lot, between where he was then standing and the line. Though he knew it was preparation work for the renovation that would occur in a few months, to him it looked like "a blue army barrack" and also "smelled like one." While standing at the corner, he overheard a couple of tourists ask a policeman for the location of a famous local restaurant nearby. He was horrified by the officer's response, not only because he did not know the exact location, but also because he handled the situation so poorly. Eduardo emphasized how something like that would never happen in London or Paris. He had traveled and knew that police officers on the streets in those cities are prepared to handle any request. In his estimation, the policeman's lack of preparation was caused, not only by limited resources, but also by the corruption that had engulfed Argentina and the consequent lack of vocation felt by those in public service, thus making him pale in comparison to officers of the past. After making a quick detour to comment on the strike that was happening at the time at the National's Children Hospital and the harmful consequences of work stoppage among those who are supposedly guided only by their calling, his story would turn back to the Colón.

He had heard on a radio show that same day that conflicts between opera house employees and the city government, which had delayed opening night and forced a schedule of alternative shows, had escalated to the point that the workers were going to stop the evening's performance during the second act and announce that they were on strike. Though this did not happen, Eduardo's stream-of-consciousness story revealed, in a way I did not expect (and had not thought to push for before), the many links and mediations between opera attendance and the country's economic and political crisis, which has intensified since the late 1990s.[2]

After listing to Eduardo's rant (and a few days spent reconstructing his testimony and elaborating on it), I became more attuned to hearing—in the lines, on the upper floors, during intermissions, and in interviews—a narrative thread that conflated the house's decay (in patina and infrastructure) with the national crisis, as represented by the picketers, homeless people, and the hospital workers' and schoolteachers' strikes. Far from being just the lament of nostalgic passionate fans, the complaints pointed to the downfall of the Colón as a metaphor for the end of the white and bourgeois Argentina, and they followed Eduardo's initial tirade in terms of flow and structure. Much as their conversations about opera were slowly invaded by other issues, the forces of cultural degradation—incarnated in products such as *cumbia*, soccer, and trash television but also in larger processes such as corruption, a lack of vocation, and the politicization of all activities—had breached the gates of the Colón, letting the outside penetrate it.[3]

A Magic Citadel Crumbles

The historic insularity of the Colón, in comparison to other cultural institutions, can be better understood if we look to how little the opera house changed during the years of military rule, 1976–83. While a critical mass of historiographic work and intellectual analysis has shown how the military prosecuted, closed, and censored most cultural activities, altering the dynamics of fields as diverse as academic life, literature, popular music, and the film industry, there is nothing remarkable about this particular period at the Colón. This is meaningful as it contradicts what anyone would expect to have happened at the time and testifies to the power of the boundary that both separates the opera house from and links it to the outside.

The comparison between a text from the end of that period and a contemporary one can better illuminate how the bounded character of the experience became more porous. Once more, the writer Manuel Mujica Láinez gives a clear idea of how the experience of opera was perceived as taking place in a secluded space: "All that [i.e., the turmoil in the outside world] changes the Colón Theater into a magic citadel and a refuge for dreams in the center of Buenos Aires, a city shaken by political and economic passions, upset by the anxiety of time flowing and life passing in the impenetrable bosom of the theater, the paradox of endless time triumphs. . . . Happy place, enchanting and bewitching island" (1983, 13).

In contrast to that passage, which recognized the political and economic flux of the outside world but still emphasized the ability of the house to isolate itself, a more contemporary text by the journalist Margarita Pollini emphasizes the feeling of being in a ship adrift. Pollini writes:

> The first time I entered the hall of the Colón, I had a weird sensation: I was on a boat, a giant and luxurious cruise. I attribute this impression to the idea that the same hundreds of people are, as much as the passengers of a vessel, captivated for hours by the contemplation of the same horizon, without being able to descend for more than a few minutes to the multiple decks. . . . A bit of this is shared by those who feel the Colón like "an island."
>
> But the boat metaphor refers today to a very different aspect, and the island has ceased to exist. Our beloved house navigates in dense and tempestuous waters, without us being able to catch sight of a safe port. It's true that it is part of a convoy of ships that share the same luck, but its case is the most moving: there isn't any structure more monumental that gives at the same time a sensation of fragility as the Colón does. (2002, 255)

There is no more island shielding us from the crisis as the Colón suffers from the same ailments that affect the rest of society and the ship that it has become is slowly sinking, much like a few other institutions that have characterized Argentina's public life. The text continues, referring to what would be the necessary guidance to arrive at a safe harbor, pointing clearly to the turmoil and strife that have characterized the organizational history of the Colón in recent years. This disarray includes the lockout and suspension of the 2005 season, the closing of the house for renovations in 2007, the thirty-nine strikes called by a wide variety of unions that have caused schedule delays and cancellations, and the constant change of artistic directors—from 1995, when Sergio Rénan was the general and artistic director, until 2005, when Marcelo Lombardero took the reins, there were at least nine changes of authority.[4]

As we have seen in the previous chapters, opera functions as a self-enclosed world, with its own informal institutions, internal hierarchies, classifications, and modes of engagement. Nevertheless, the quasi-institutional character of the Colón's upper floors, which purports to regiment the life of the fan completely, rests in the promise of the experience within the opera house walls being completely different from the outside world. But what happens when opera stops being a boundary and a producer of different experiences than outside (at least for passionate fans), when what takes place on- and offstage is exactly the same, and when performances are so poor that they cannot produce those in-between moments for which fans strive? As we have seen in the intense and personalized way fans invest themselves in opera, the breach does not just destabilize the Colón generally, making things "not what they used to be." It disrupts one of the key parameters that passionate fans utilize to give an account of themselves: the extraordinary character of the experience of attending the Colón. As such, the destabilization of the fans' taken-for-granted world has deep, personal consequences.

How do fans cope with this breach? What forces do they identify as destabilizing the insularity of the Colón? What strategies do they use to try to link the world of the past with the current condition of opera productions? Have changes to the resources at the base of their worldview transformed their schemas of opera evaluation and appreciation? This chapter tackles those questions and continues with a brief theoretical overview considering the link between a particular social world and the dispositions of its inhabitants through concepts like *habitus* and *embodiment*. It then shows how the fans identify corruption, dirt, the hyperpoliticization of art (including its bureaucratization), and the consequent lack of vocation as forces invading the house and how a few passionate fans challenge nostalgic accounts and propose a competing repertory of evaluation, one based on the off-Colón circuit. Finally, it will point to the mnemonic strategies fans use to bring the past into the present and how their intense upper-floor sociability attempts to maintain a Colón-centered understanding of opera.

Breaches

Pierre Bourdieu has explained how, through embodiment, one acquires the appropriate classifications of identity underlying a particular social position.[5] Through embodiment, culture becomes second nature, as its conditions of acquisition are forgotten or repressed, and then becomes *doxa*—the taken-for-granted sense of reality. This second nature, the "social made body," is learned through what Bourdieu calls a *habitus*, an "acquired system of generative dispositions" (Bourdieu 1977, 95) within which individuals think that their preferences are obvious, natural. Individuals are not typically reflexive about such dispositions in the everyday world: "When habitus encounters a social world of which it is the product, it is like a 'fish in water': it does not feel the weight of the water and it takes the world about itself for granted. . . . It is because this world has produced me, because it has produced the categories of thought that I apply to it, that it appears to me as self-evident" (Bourdieu and Wacquant 1992, 127–28).

For Bourdieu, embodied abilities and schemas are the primary mechanisms through which the reproduction or the continuity of a practice and a social world in time is guaranteed. Imaginations, bodily sensations, a certain present, a particular past, and an expectable future are all connected to the ways we inhabit a particular world as particular agents in it.[6] The question is, then, how it is that this past-oriented practice, which negates the positive qualities of the present and reveals itself as blind to the future, can evaluate that same present, imagine the future, and reproduce itself, especially when the resources that have given rise to this particular interpretation of the world no longer exist. In a sense, I am exploring here the relation between habitat and habitus, between objective space and subjective representations in one specific universe (Auyero and Swistun 2007).[7] I am interested in understanding how passionate fans, who for years have been regularly exposed to an inferior environment (in terms of infrastructure and performance), think and feel about this declining world and still manage to invest intensely and extensively in it. How do they confront one of the two conditions under which the arbitrary qualities of practices get "denaturalized" (when the conditions of operation of the habitus are incongruent with the conditions of its acquisition)?[8]

The description of the forces that invade the house compels us to think about the relation between the opera world and the outside. Obviously, I am not trying to use this outside as a homogeneous entity—since there are many things outside the realm and scope of the opera world. Rather, I use it as an otherness defined by the fans themselves. As it is, the upper floors of the Colón stand in a double relation of symbiosis and opposition with the outside. They are a bulwark against the outside world, yet they are sometimes also a sieve, as we will see when I delineate the many faces of middle-class moral preoccupations about the decay of the country; sometimes opposing it, they strive for a transcendent kind of experience that is hard to find in everyday life.

Though I already spoke of the homeless at the door, the debris seen around the building, and the degraded character of some stagings, compared by fans to trash television, there are more forces that the fans recognize as menacing and, in their radical opposition, constitutive of their identity.[9] What are these forces, and how do they enter the Colón? In the next few pages, I describe, interpret, and analyze in depth the roles played by corruption, party politics, the lack of vocation, and dirt in undermining the separation between opera and its outside.

Chapter 4 discussed how passionate fans distinguish themselves by having a highly adversarial relationship with professional critics. They have two ways of confronting them: First, they link the critics indirectly to the maladies of the outside world by associating them with the new audience as they both share the lack of proper judgment. Second, they link them directly to one of the key features of the Argentinean downfall: corruption. While a previous chapter explored the former at length, I want to now focus on the latter.

Diego reiterates that he does not follow any particular reviewer, especially not those who write on the Colón:

> They give them an envelope with money [*les dan un sobre*]. It's obvious. The Colón always puts on "a five-star show." I mean, it's true that everyone is entitled to their own opinion, but to go from there to the fact that every time you attend you think it's fantastic. . . . It's so treacherous! The difference between what you see and what the critics see is insane. What really bugs me is, how could it be that ten years ago, when we had amazing casts, shows were reviewed as well as they are now, with third- and fourth-rate casts? What would happen if those casts ever come back? There won't be enough stars! They either get money or have lost their critical ear. On the other hand, in places that are not the Colón, they split hairs. For instance, with Adelaida Negri, they destroy her or look for the details. That makes it even more blatant.

Alfredo finds hard evidence of corruption in his firsthand knowledge of the critics. Having been a fan for so many years, he knows their faces and even talks to them: "I've known critics who would come in during the second act and then do the whole review and destroy the play, as if they had been there [for the whole thing]. No! Then how can you trust them? I think the reviewers are paid. I went to see *Trovatore* in Avellaneda, and it was a disaster and ended up with a fabulous review."

Juan Manuel finds continuity between the "lack of seriousness and preparation" of the critics and the accusations of corruption. "The reviews are not serious. Critics are unprepared. Other than Pola Suárez Ortubey [a musicologist who writes for *La Nación*, the main newspaper for the opera community], critics don't know about music. There are a few that came straight out of a horror movie. I understand, they probably get a little money [*les pasan un poquito de plata*] so they write a bit more or better and advertise the concert the payers are organizing."

Nevertheless, critics are not the only ones who are viewed as bringing corruption to the house; the authorities have also done so in diverse ways. They are usually perceived as alien agents, taking kickbacks from impresarios, or even as business associates of an artist's manager, reducing opportunities for local artists. This perception sometimes intensifies to the point where they are imagined as bounty hunters, just interested in making a profit, even if that means the closing of the Colón. On the first count, Luis warned me: "In an opera you are going to find some singers with a good level and a few others that are poor. There are singers from abroad that come because they are part of a package, meaning, you bring one but you have to hire all these others, too, four or five that are not that well-known. Usually, there is one that is really bad. It's as much due to corruption as it is to laziness. It's much easier to hire whomever when the money is not yours. . . . There are people who have the capacity to lobby because they know the authorities, but that makes it impossible for younger artists." As we can see, the indictment has three parts: (1) the authorities lack vocation, hence their careless spending; (2) they do whatever is necessary to make a profit; (3) this results in the corruption of the house's moral and artistic standards since, by taking part in spurious business with public money, they also diminish the artistic quality of the final product.[10]

This argument does not apply only to the Colón. The experience of La Plata's Argentino early in this decade, soon after its inauguration and before the exchange rate crisis, is viewed by some as symptomatic of this trend. Bela, for instance, relates the following story: "Inés Salazar, a Chilean soprano coming from La Scala and Covent Garden, told me that the biggest fee of her life was at the Argentino—$38,000 for one performance! They were paying four, five thousand to the secondary roles. Since the director was related to the secretary of culture, he had carte blanche to get the funding." The second part of his allocution takes us to an important feature of this configuration: the belief that corruption is protected by larger political alliances with officers who are absolutely uninterested in opera.

This protection results, not in straight-up kickbacks, but in extra sources of income provided by having more than one position on the payroll (this is known as *sobresueldo*). For instance, fans accused the then artistic director Renán, a *regisseur*, of hiring himself to stage productions when previous directors had been removed from their position for doing so. They pointed to his new house in an expensive and exclusive Uruguayan beach town as evidence of his enrichment. They also pointed to his second salary as an adviser to the Ministry of Foreign Affairs. Yet the scorn directed at Tito Capobianco was even harsher; he was accused of having three salaries, one as director, one as an adviser, and a third paid by the Foundation for "Rootlessness" since, in order to come to Buenos Aires, he had to leave his house in the United

States. Nevertheless, probably the worst reaction against him came because of an ad in the playbill for *Quichotte* in which a vineyard advertised a "special edition" wine, consisting of fifteen hundred bottles signed by Capobianco himself, for those who made a purchase with a specific credit card. The wine was very expensive and considered an insult to upper-deck fans, who felt that they were witnessing the crumbling of the opera house while its director was advertising an exclusive product targeted, presumably, to the kind of fans they despised, within an impoverished economic context.

Underneath these comments lies the conviction that, over the last few years, and regardless of the party in charge, the cultural direction of the music world has depended on the whim of political actors (most of the classical music and opera venues are publicly funded) who have been more interested in trying to gain economic advantage or secure power within their own political coalition. This divorce between the worlds of politics and music results in a conspiratorial vision of state officers as actively participating in the demise of opera for their own benefit. This can be best observed in the fans' outcry against the closing of two off-Colón venues (La Manufactura Papelera and Opera Buenos Aires) for code violations. One of the fans, very much worried about the progression, said, "First, they went against the first-line institutions, the Colón, the Argentino, and the provincial symphonies; now they are coming against the second-line institutions, the NGOs [nongovernment organizations] of culture, where people work like artisans to train young talent and give space and opportunities to youth to discover and measure their artistic conditions."

Other fans, like Roberto, reverse the order of the progression and see the closure of the Colón as a logical consequence of politicians' disinterest in culture. While he was by far the most agitated about it, other fans voiced concerns about the 2005 lockout at the Colón, but especially about the total closure for repairs in 2007, stating, "It was a good opportunity for them to test how little people are interested in opera and, using as an excuse the budgetary issues, close it for good."

PARTY POLITICS

As we have seen, the definition of politics strictly refers to the sphere of electoral activity and competition. As such, it is immediately equated with its most degraded versions: corruption, clientelism, and self-interest. Passionate fans aggressively denounce any political intervention. For them, art and politics should be absolutely divorced, though, in some variations of this sentiment, the subordination of politics to art (as when a president like Alvear made opera a central moral and civilizing force for the city inhabitants, securing municipal funds and mobilizing the legal authority to do so) should be commended.

The dissociation between opera and national politics is highlighted by the absence of presidents and other authorities at the opera house, emphasizing the perceived lack of culture and interest of those in charge (including the culture secretary), other than to put an economic or political spin on the situation. Susana points to the last time a president came to the Colón for something other than a presidential gala (which have lately involved nonclassical performances): "It was Alfonsín for an Independence Day gala, in 1985. He came to see *Traviata* with Marta Colalillo."[11] Others seriously debated the statement by the then city culture secretary—Gustavo López—in July 2005 that he did not understand why Buenos Aires Opera had to have two orchestras (the Philharmonic and the Opera House Orchestra) while the "Vienna Opera has only one orchestra." Fans answered by pointing to the smaller size of Vienna, the fact that it has two more state-supported opera houses, or that there are actually nine symphony orchestras in that city. Repeated messages on the online opera forum commented that López probably had enough advisers to fire to make up for a whole orchestra and pointed to his profound lack of knowledge about music, in particular, and high culture, in general. In fact, one of the fans circulated by e-mail the following prank survey for officers like López, using the hyphenated names of the composers Rimsky-Korsakov and Mendelssohn-Bartholdy and that of the Spaniard philosopher Ortega y Gasset as the source of confusion for the uneducated.

Survey circulated by e-mail to many fans:

Survey for Officers of the Culture Secretary and Related Agencies or Institutions Politically Designed
- Rimsky and Korsakov
  1. Were they two Russian dancers from the 1940s?
  2. Two Ukrainian wirewalkers from the Moscow circus?
- Ortega and Gasset
  1. Which one was French?
  2. Is it true they ended up enemies?
- Mendelssohn and Bartholdy
  1. Which one wrote the famous "wedding march"?
  2. Did Bartholdy write the lyrics?

The so-called lack of education of Argentinean officials was also highlighted by a comparison to the November 2005 strike at Venice's La Fenice Opera House. There, Mayor Massimo Cacciari, a philosopher who had collaborated with the contemporary composer Luigi Nono, interrupted the

"Slave's Chorus" during a performance of Verdi's *Nabucco* in order to protest against budgetary cuts by Italian president Silvio Berlusconi. Fans emphasized how incredible it was that an officer actually took responsibility and headed the protest. Such action was the opposite of what could be expected in Argentina, where politicians do not collaborate in writing music but some popular musicians (detested by the passionate fans, like the former governor of Tucumán and presidential hopeful "Palito" Ortega or "Piero," a folk-like musician who was the culture secretary of Buenos Aires State during the late 1990s), have participated actively in party politics.

Some passionate fans can recall far worse examples of the active intervention of politics into the classical music world. Diego, for instance, was very much surprised when, in 2005, while entering a performance of *Trovatore* in Avellaneda, he ran into eight trestles, four on each side, with posters and press clips proclaiming Evita and Perón's prowess. As in many other parts of Gran Buenos Aires, politics and high culture go together, and the sign of that political intervention in culture is always Peronist.[12] To make the relation even more obvious and dramatic, there was a stand-alone poster of Evita next to the hall entrance.

The intervention gets so personalized that some officers actually take to the stage. That was the case with Avellaneda's secretary of culture for a 2005 production of *Un giorno di regno*, and it was almost the case with the then governor of Buenos Aires Carlos Ruckauf for a 2000 *Oedipus Rex* at La Plata. Ruckauf was cast as the narrator but eventually bowed out of the production. The director of the play—the general director of the Argentino Opera at that time—said that his goal was to "link government acts with public culture, just as in ancient Greece" ("Le ofrecieron a Ruckauf" 2000).

Rina points to the consequences of such political intervention. She remembers how, when an important local conductor invited her to La Plata in 2004, she was surprised by the dressing room assigned to him:

> The mirror was on top of four drawers, and the table for the toilette was a cardboard box stained with coffee, grease, and ink. And I couldn't help but think, Is this a dressing room for a conductor? At a new theater? He later explained to me that there were numerous dressing rooms but they were all occupied by La Plata's municipal secretary of culture, who turned them into the party's offices. She's the grandniece of Evita. That's probably why, when I went to see Virginia Tola sing, I ran into a few banners that said: "Perón delivers; Evita dignifies." What is that doing inside an opera house? She invades everything and doesn't know anything about culture.

Fans see the invasion of music by politics—be it on the striking workers' side or on the officials' side, with the hiring of many extra employees—as demoralizing for both the artists and the audience members. Susana wonders how artists are supposed to resist "the Batallas, Capobiancos, Senanes [directors of the house during diverse contemporary periods], and whoever is in charge that day" and "answer to the spirit instilled in them."

LACK OF VOCATION

A week after he was announced as the new artistic director of the Colón, Marcelo Lombardero was interviewed by the newspaper *La Nación*. Among the many questions about the crisis of the opera house he was asked, one stood out: "Those who work at the Colón, do they feel like artists or public employees?" Passionate fans echoed this concern and the lack of boundaries of both spheres within the theater. For them, the artist in music workers is constantly undermined by the public dramatization of their attachment to a paid (and state-financed) job. The many strikes of 2005 resulted in *worker* becoming the key identification for the Colón musicians. They would play in their shirtsleeves, make a speech before tuning, put up a banner over the pit calling for the city authorities to bargain with them, and play the national anthem as a sign of protest before a few operas and concerts. While fans tried to be sympathetic, the lockout of that October was the final straw, pitting them manifestly against the protest. For fans like José Luis, the Colón had become "a public office with a stage."

Generally speaking, passionate fans resist seeing the artist as a worker. In their highly idealized representation, musicians are very special beings who give themselves to music without worrying about remuneration, just as fans do. While in no way do fans think musicians are not professionals and should not be paid for their job, the conviction that their lives should be about more than monetary reward rules out a strike or anything else that could stop a performance. Moreover, the replacement of one identity by the other—as they seem to be incompatible, according to the fans' repertory of evaluation—immediately transforms the musicians and other artists of the house into public employees, uninterested in taking any special risks, complacent in the security of a public career, boring and mediocre as a bureaucrat would be, and lacking the corresponding stimulus necessary for artistic creation and performance. This destroys the enchantment of the experience for some fans who, like Néstor, are "taken absolutely out of tune."

But this is not the only thing Néstor had to say:

I decided to stop seeing ballet, for instance. They are bad, but, even worse, they are fat! I can understand the union demands, but they end up being public employees. And a good dancer is no public employee! They should hire people and call for auditions every two or three years to have them revalidate what they did. If you're no good, you're out. Five more pounds, and you can't dance. If you are a musician, I'm sorry, otherwise they all end up like municipal employees; the concertmaster can't play; the dancers are fat, and the chorus is filled with old voices. It can't be! I'm very liberal, but the artistic institutions have nothing to do with municipal employees. I agree they should be paid better, but I don't hold with the idea that they have the right to be eighty years in a chair because they once entered Orchestra X. I have the right to get fed up and say I'm not going anymore.

Néstor is not alone. Fabiana complains vividly about what she feels when she goes to the Colón in these cases: "You get there, and you don't know if they are going to play or not. They sing the national anthem beforehand, they open the curtain, and you don't know what you're going to find. I don't feel like seeing *Quichotte* and having them singing the national anthem before it. I don't feel like singing the anthem! I don't wanna see people playing in shirtsleeves. They take me out of synch for what I'm actually going to see."

Older fans actually go a step beyond these criticisms and abhor the work conditions that prohibit never-ending late-night rehearsals; while they understand the rights of the musicians, they feel that, the more work rights they claim, the less they invest in the music as the final product. These fans, like Rina, go from the longing for the authoritarian maestros of the past to the disqualification of national (Volonté) and International (Flórez) stars. Her disenchantment with Volonté had to do with the fact that he declared that opera was work to him, that, as much as he was a truck driver before, he is now an opera singer: "To me, Volonté was over. An artist is an artist. The problem is that not everybody that sings well can be an artist." She then outlined the difference between a singer-worker and an artist in pursuit of a career. She lamented Flórez's performance his first night at the Colón, when he announced that he was sick, and predicted that he was not ready to "be an artist, like Plácido." She complained: "He was coming one day before so he could rehearse and sing. In order to do that you have to be perfect, and he ate sushi on the plane and got sick! If you're a serious guy, you don't do that. You don't have to become a monk, but . . ."

Rina's words echo how sociology has conceptualized the way charisma can be achieved (Weber 1946b). The charisma of an artist, the symbolic surplus that takes her a step beyond being *just* a musician, can sometimes be attained through ascetic-like ways. Their authority as such is unstable and based on a romantic representation that presents the musician as a highly subjective and special individual devoted only to cultivating his art. Their authority is based on the demand of admiration from the audience in virtue of her music mission. Musicians-cum-artists gain and maintain legitimacy by proving their strength in practice, being the owners of a personal gift outside everyday routine, highly at odds with the public employee identity, aiming to perform music miracles.

Sometimes preparation and asceticism are not enough, some fans demanding the ultimate commitment: death onstage. While Bela was moved by and loved the fact that the Italian conductor Giuseppe Sinopoli died onstage, it was Alicia who gave a thorough explanation of this. Referring to an older conductor she had recently seen perform, she said, "You know that conductors die onstage. They never retire; they keep going. Music is powerful; it's just too strong. It gives them vitality; it gives them life; it gives them mental lucidity. It gives them so much they just die." This description gives musicians, and conductors in particular, a prophetic character; they adopt a unitary purpose for their life.[13]

The abandonment of that unitary purpose is what makes older fans like José Luis feel that new artists are "made of plastic" in comparison with singers from the past. While the name of the tenor José Cura—again—figures extensively in the conversation, José Luis prefers not to focus just on him but to generalize. For him, the new singers might sing better, but they do not have artistry: "They don't know how to express. Works are full of intention, of phrasing. Sometimes singers are American, who don't know the language and something gets lost in the lack of nuance. There are no masters of expression; they never learn to value the text." He referred to seeing Tom Fox in *Die Walküre*, saying, "He's good and serious, but he is not Wotan compared to when Hotter grabbed the spear. We've heard so many great artists, but they don't make them anymore."[14]

DIRT

Dirt makes its appearance at the Colón under many guises and in many forms. It is the result of the lack of resources to keep things tidy, especially the infrastructure; it is the consequence of the bad allocation of those resources, which results in the main hall of the house not being maintained as well as it used to be, despite having a surplus of personnel; it travels from these more literal utilizations of the word *dirt* to the performances that are offered; it materializes in the "trash" culture of the outside.

Eduardito reflects sadly on the state of the house during one of the intermissions of the second performance of *Lucia*. Seated on a stair that goes nowhere, as it leads from the *tertulia* to the *paraíso*, which is closed for this performance, he describes what he sees: "There are holes in the wall, mixed cement on the floors, the seats are worn out, the facade is falling to pieces. Everything is dirty—the decorations on the boxes, the lamps, even the big chandelier. They have to do something, but where is the money?" Irma, on the other hand, is convinced that the issue is, not the money, but the many changes in the city authorities that have inflated the payroll, up to the point where "there are 290 people employed by the cleaning services, but half of them are probably not going": "How could they if the hall is always dirty! You have to think about it being the fault of politics, more than anything else, because each and every one of them hires their own people."

Dirt travels from outside the building into the hall but completes its movement when it becomes an adjective to describe what happens onstage. Daniel makes this transition explicit. For him, one of the ways the Colón can regain centrality is to "recuperate its historical standards, get its working mystique back and help you really enjoy the show." "What you get now," he continued, "is an impoverished or 'dirty' show, with an out-of-tune orchestra." The metaphoric and contagious qualities of dirt travel all the way to the instruments and the hands of the musicians and appear as the direct consequence of the lack of resources and the lack of vocation. While for the former the corresponding metaphor is *poor*, for the latter the word of choice is *dirty*. If we were to take an imaginary picture of the Colón as described, the dirt would extend, like a blob in a 1950s American horror movie, from the facade and the flyers on the doors to the inside of the house, staining stairs and walls, until it finally moves through the main hall all the way onto the stage and into the pit, where musicians hang banners demanding a salary raise and play out of tune in their shirtsleeves.

The British anthropologist Mary Douglas (1966) has reflected on the contagious quality of dirt and the moments in which these metaphors appear. In the case of the Colón, the pollution metaphor appears because there is no sanction for the interpenetration of music and politics. While passionate fans denounce the "invasion," the assault cannot be stopped because the boundaries that once kept the two systems apart have collapsed. Regardless, passionate fans ask performers to be magicians, special beings, the enablers and carriers of art. The moment artists break that pact and show how they are dependent on (poor) material conditions, the outside world enters the house, and the experience further loses its enchantment.

As with opera-appreciation classes and critics' articles, fans seek stories that confirm the experience, not subvert it. They are happy going to general rehearsals, learning about the weight issues singers might have, knowing how much they have trained to get where they are and how professionally dedicated they have to be to make it. Nevertheless, the moment the economic reality of the opera world rears its ugly head, they cry foul. It is not about discovering that the singers' gifts are honed by intense training but about the fact that discovering that the poor conditions of that training break the suspension of reality opera brings to their life. And by this I obviously do not mean that they believe in obese forty-year-old women playing timid, naive princesses, identify with the plot of *Otello*, or rest their hopes entirely in the genial personal character of the performers. Rather, I mean that what happens onstage cannot and should not reproduce the deteriorated living conditions that exist in the rest of the country. The suspension of disbelief has to do, then, not with the explicit recognition that there is a performance onstage, with its corresponding backstage, but with how, when the actual backstage appears degraded and rundown and mirrors the conditions of the poor country Argentina has become, it ruins the illusion of displaced grandeur the experience of opera has (had?) for the fans.

How do the Colón inhabitants make sense of these rundown surroundings? How much do they know about their collapsing habitat? As I have hinted, there is clearly no single, monolithic upper-floor point of view on the Colón's downfall, and its effects on opera evaluation vary. Perceptions range from outright denial to critical awareness, from doubts to deep-felt convictions. Let me now introduce each one of these positions.

2002

The economic and political crisis of 2001, which included five presidents in ten days, street riots, lootings, and the freezing of all bank deposits in dollars, resulted in a Colón season without any international stars. Only one international singer (Olga Romanko) was hired for what was an otherwise all-national roster of performers. As I noted in chapter 5, the last five seasons have been a period of intense deinternationalization of the house. On top of that, intense political battles over the last decade have revealed the precarious equilibrium between finance and music and undermined the artists' performances as they claimed their identities as workers, endangering the isolation of opera as constitutive of its experience and enjoyment. In this context, I bring back a question posed earlier in this chapter: How is it that this particular world gets reproduced when the conditions of production, or resources, do not correspond to the schemas passionate fans have to evaluate the experience? As William Sewell (1992, 13) states: "If schemas are to be sustained or reproduced over time, they must be validated by the accumulation of resources that their enactment engenders. Schemas not empowered or regenerated by resources would eventually be abandoned or forgotten."

The possibility of a disjunction between the schemas as internalized and the world in which those symbols operate opens up a space for the actors to reflect critically about the world. This reflection takes form in a debate about whether the Colón can regain its former standing (as an important and international opera house) or whether it should resign itself to its current state of affairs (and imagine itself as a secondary and provincial house, superseded by the off-Colón circuit). The axis of the debate is grounded, as could be expected from a peripheral country, in whether the opera house is recognized by the central metropolis.[15]

Several topics reflect how fans think about the worldwide importance of the Colón and the place of Argentinean opera in the world. The first one, a topic shared with pride by all the Colón's audience members, is that the house has the best acoustics in the world. In one of our many conversations, Julio brought up an article by a local newspaper that supposedly reproduced a survey of singers and music engineers conducted by the *New York Times* stating that the Colón had the best acoustics among international opera houses.

In line with praise for the architecture of the house (even if there are not many worthy singers or musicians to fill it) is the conviction that the building is also beautiful to the eye, that it is a unique hall combining the larger size of an American opera house with the grandeur of European architecture. For the fans, evidence rests, not just on their judgment, but also on the recognition by the many tourists who make the Colón a mandatory stop. During the 2006 season, the Colón authorities recognized the international character of the opera, in terms of audience composition, not performers, and started to charge tourists more for tickets.[16] Even if tourists do not attend performances, the house does a good business from the four guided tours it offers daily.

Yet there is a way in which fans manage to internationalize Argentinean opera. Just as I showed in chapter 3 with the opera-appreciation classes, the geography of opera gets transformed by extending the Colón to all the stages where Argentinean singers have triumphed, even when the Colón school has not produced those singers (as in the case of Marcelo Alvarez), when the house has openly rejected them (José Cura), or when they have not come to sing in it for a while (as with Luis Lima, who made most of his career abroad). Much as in soccer, where an impoverished local scene is always superseded by the triumphs of local players in the most important leagues in the world—mainly Spain and Italy—the success of high culture in Argentina is measured by displacing it into other geographies, in a claim that includes, not only singers, but also dancers like Julio Bocca, Hernán and Erica Cornejo, Paloma Herrera, Iñaqui Urlezaga, and Marianela Nuñez (principal dancers at the most important ballet companies in the world).[17] Rina best summarizes the situation, maintaining: "The Colón Theater is like Maradona,[18] [it] is our cultural presentation for the world. Where don't they know the Colón?"

Imagining the Colón extending overseas with every performer means following, not only successful singers from a previous generation, like Raul Giménez or Luis Lima, and stars of the present who seldom come to the country,[19] like Marcelo Alvarez or José Cura, but also the minor careers of performers abroad, like Virginia Tola, Darío Volonté, Franco Fagioli, and Fabiana Bravo, celebrating them whenever they come home, even if their moderate success can be measured only by the fact they sing on the secondary international circuit.[20]

Passionate fans not only collect stories of what singers who already have a career abroad are doing, through Argentinean newspapers and international Web sites and magazines; they also focus on the many international competitions for young singers organized by consecrated stars like Pavarotti or Plácido Domingo (Operalia) and report back on the fate of the many who try out. For many local singers, these competitions have been the springboard for a recognition that is nonexistent on the main stage of their own country.[21]

The anxiety of recognition also means that fans and critics repeatedly speculate about who will be the next great Argentinean singers to be taken abroad; during fieldwork, fans complained that the success of the young sopranos Filipcic and De la Rosa and the tenor Folger might result in them leaving the local opera scene. Fans, after having observed the likes of Alvarez, Tola, Cura, or Fagioli leave the country without performing at the Colón, quickly realized that whoever is going to be recognized outside the country and "not enjoyed enough" by them is likely not part of the established Colón roster but one of the youngsters on the secondary circuit.

The tension between the nationalistic and the cosmopolitan understandings of what happens onstage climaxes when fans debate whether an unknown foreign singer or a local figure should sing a principal part. That was the case when fans debated whether the local soprano Laura Rizzo would have been better than Leah Partridge and Eglise Gutierrez in the title role of *Lucia* in 2005. Since nationality was not enough of a justification, despite claims of her being "ours," some tried to establish the case for Rizzo by arguing that she had sung the role in 1999 or that she was a success singing Gilda in *Rigoletto* (2002). When that was not enough, since they were discussing the international character of opera in Buenos Aires, other fans pointed to her having sung the role of Olympia at Paris-Bercy. Nevertheless, older passionate fans dismissed most of the arguments easily: Rizzo had already sung the part, so why should the Colón, a seasonal, not a repertory, theater, repeat a singer? Also, Paris-Bercy is an amplified soccer stadium and, hence, does not qualify as a proved international venue. For these fans, the solution—which combines resignation and internationality—is to bring in young and unproved singers. Since it would be impossible to retain Natalie Dessay, Karita Mattila, or Renée Fleming, the best solution for the Colón would be to scout the international circuit looking for the stars of tomorrow, who would be impossible to bring back once they are actually consecrated.

The solution proposed by these fans, then, is to leave the stage of the Colón to young international prospects and advise singers like Rizzo to stick to the off-Colón circuit. These fans view the idea of advocating for local singers in primary roles as "a miserable nationalism" on the behalf of those who want to transform the Colón into a third leg of the off-circuit companies Juventus Lyrica and Buenos Aires Lírica and "make it into a provincial house, home for many local talents accompanied by a better orchestra than at the other opera houses."

While the fans who would rather have a strong scene led by the best national performers object to this description by the internationalist fans, they actually share the feeling about the continuity between the two circuits, and they challenge older fans by noting that passion (and even quality) is hard to find among artists in residence at the Colón or on the secondary circuit. In doing so, they displace the enjoyment that resulted from the isolation of the Colón to a new arena devoid of dirt, politics, and lack of vocation: the Avenida Theater.

"Singers are not interested in wasting a whole month here"

Younger fans—especially those who have made a profession out of their passion like Daniel, Bela, or Gustavo—criticize the nostalgic tone of the older fans. While they utilize the same categories to emphasize effort and artistic results, they seem to find the insularity missing from the Colón at the main company of the Avenida Opera House: Buenos Aires Lírica. The schemas of appreciation are differentially validated when put into action and are potentially subject to modification. While some fans find alternative strategies to turn a blind eye to the transformations of the resources available at the Colón, others take into account the same frame and displace it into a new situation that then challenges the previous definition and validation of the experience.

Luis demolishes most of the principles put forth about why the Colón is still important:

> Singers are not interested in wasting a whole month here. The Colón already lost its aura, and those who keep insisting that the Colón is one of the five key opera houses in the world are lying [*es todo un verso*]. Is not even among the [top] fifty! It's a big theater, beautiful indeed, the people who come are amazed by it, but the Colón isn't important [*no existe*]. In the international realm, it doesn't count. Nobody cares about coming. Here, people live off memories; we live saying that the Colón is the greatest. It's an empty shell. It's far away from being the greatest. They say it has the best acoustics in the world. So? The acoustics have to be filled up by great singers; acoustics alone don't make a theater great. Nobody wants to come. You don't make a résumé coming here like early in the twentieth century. Puccini used to ask how *Madame Butterfly* did at the Colón because that was a reflection of how it was going to work throughout the rest of the world. They did it with the same cast and conductor as in Italy.

Daniel adds that fans get bored at the Colón since the lack of a work mystique there makes for a routinized and unflattering final product. Connoisseurs, according to him, could never mistake the contemporary state of the house for what used to happen there during the 1960s and 1970s. Although the new companies might not get close to those historical standards and cannot engage international stars, there is an uncorrupted enthusiasm that renews the opera experience, imbuing it with passion once more. Other fans-cum-producers, like Bela, could not agree more, and the categories they bring up in conversation are the very same ones used to negatively characterize the Colón: enthusiasm, vocation, and organization.

These fans emphasize that, in a time when the Colón can no longer differentiate itself from other houses by the international stars it can afford to present (in fact, it shares many of its main principals with the off-circuit), the secondary circuit—which is not burdened by strikes and sudden cancellations or changes in the schedule or programming, where musicians and singers are always in costume, where ushers are attentive and the space, if not as magnificent, is as least clean—should be considered the center of opera in Buenos Aires. In doing so, they also challenge the centrality of certain traits of how opera has been characterized so far.

If what is emphasized is how, by being in charge of renewing, they are the actual continuators of this particular way of doing and understanding opera, an obvious candidate to take the fall is the glorified past that some fans—and music critics—utilize as a reference for evaluating the present. Nostalgic fans, who attend a performance already knowing they will not like it because they heard the same opera sung by a big voice of the past, are the main targets. They, along with other professionalized fans who have small radio shows, are considered the main culprits for the conservatism of this small but fanatical faction of the opera audience.

Gustavo gets bored with reminiscing about Callas, Caruso, and Gigli. He is also tired of Bergonzi or del Monaco fans and even of those who think that the main debate about international artists is between Domingo and Pavarotti or Carreras. His quarrel is not with the older fans as much as with the ones who, having never seen any of those singers perform live, still use them as a model for evaluation, ignoring more contemporary artists in discussions about the voices, the staging, and the acting. For him, a good question would be, Who is currently better at singing the French repertory—Roberto Alagna, Marcelo Alvarez, or Rolando Villazón?[22] He thinks that, for the good of opera and of their mental health, fans would be better off approaching a performance thinking that the best version of that opera is the one they will be attending. Otherwise, it would be wiser to stay home. He expressed that hope that, when he is eighty, he will not be thinking about the operas he saw in 2002.

His is a minority position among the passionate fans and one that shows how much of the repertory of evaluation is still present, even in a new scenario that supposedly challenges and undermines the previous one. Nevertheless, this position diverges in one key way: challenging the centrality of the past in the understanding of what constitutes a good opera. As I will demonstrate, most of the other passionate fans, who still make the Colón the center of their opera experience, use "memory work"; they employ a series of mnemonic strategies to evaluate what is going on at the Colón and elsewhere, applying the same repertory of evaluation to a very different situation.

Mnemonic Sopranos

What strategies do fans use to reisolate themselves? Through what means do they articulate representation and experience to look at opera in the same way, even when what they are seeing onstage diverges greatly from the standard they have known? As I have already discussed, bodies act as if they recognize certain sensations as meaningful according to specific cultural models. What I am trying to show at this point is how those same bodies keep acting "as if" even when there is a disjuncture between the world and the schemas needed to inhabit and interpret that particular world. In other words, I am looking at the powerful role of inertia as articulated by memory and how it keys a specific past into the present.[23]

Passionate fans see in some sopranos, and in the 2005 appointment of Marcelo Lombardero as the new director of the house, a potential reincarnation of the Old Colón (and an Old Europe) way of doing things, with work and passion at the service of art. While in one case it is mostly a reactive strategy (with the sopranos), the celebration of Lombardero, the son of a well-known soprano and a member of the house chorus, implies that they imagine a future that escapes the gloom of the present by essentially bringing back the past. I will come back to this point later in the section.

The soprano voice is favored for the reenactment and performance of community. Celebrations like the ones for Victoria de los Ángeles and Claudia Muzio described in the previous chapter are not uncommon. While other voices also stir debate, fans seem to equate the higher voice with the genre of opera itself. It is not strange, then, to find that one of the secondary opera venues where older fans congregate to hear young singers perform selections with piano accompaniment is actually the home of Adelaida Negri. One of Argentina's most important sopranos, she is now an active participant in the off-Colón scene; the years have taken a toll on her voice.[24] That *soprano* has become a synecdoche for *opera* is apparent in the name of the venue: Casa de la Opera (House of opera). The entrance is filled with pictures that remind us of her glorious yet not-so-distant past. The pictures are displayed from wall to wall, from ceiling to floor, forming a kind of baroque wallpaper reminiscent of royal houses from the seventeenth century (see figure 17). In them, we can see Adelaida with Pavarotti, singing *Aida* at the Colón, and we read her reviews from Boston, where the Met toured in 1983. We see her playing *Medea* in Bonn in 1987, as a black-and-white Butterfly in New York, and receiving numerous awards and standing next to major personalities of Argentinean culture (e.g., Olga Ferri, the foremost ballet teacher in the country) and those who fund it (e.g., Amalia Lacroze de Fortabat, one of the Colón's main donors and a former president of the National Endowment for the Arts).

She receives people in the entrance hall and has a smile for everybody. She is still very active professionally, as her company has been staging operas since 1997, always with her as the soloist in works that demand a powerful leading woman. Despite her age, people like Néstor still go to see her and respect her: "She gives herself out. I always say that, when she's onstage, it's like she never left the Metropolitan. Every little theater she is at, it is the Met for her; she's at full strength. If I know she is around, I always try to go."

FIGURE 17. The soprano Adelaida Negri at the entrance of Casa de la Opera.
Notice all the pictures of her on the wall.

Néstor's comments make one of the key inquiries of this chapter clearer by expressing how his representation of the present is modeled after certain traits of the past. Understanding the mechanisms of rememoration is a mandatory step, then, in appreciating how a community is formed, reproduced, and differentiated.[25] How is opera reproduced in Buenos Aires? How does a complex cultural form, international in scale but conducted in face-to-face fashion at the site, achieve historical continuity? To paraphrase Schutz (1967), what are the ways in which the present is presented as a cumulation of sediments of the past? And what are the basis, rites, and strategies of doing so? What are the resulting models, and what of the past is reproduced?

While testimonies point to the many differences between a golden past and a more-than-dubious present, there are many strategies through which the past is keyed in to the present. Memory works as a social frame that orients action, ascribing relations between two sets of cultural configurations, requiring the active participation of those involved in order to mobilize and transfigure one of the symbolic sets into the other.[26] For fans, the past is soprano-keyed into the present through relics and memorabilia.

RELICS AND MEMORABILIA

This is an obvious strategy since fans collect programs, signed photographs, and the like (including such ephemera as a napkin Mirella Freni used while dining at the favored after-Colón restaurant). As happened with the celebrations for Claudia Muzio and Victoria de los Ángeles, relics can involve mixed media and depart from the frozen, two-dimensional memento mori on Adelaida Negri's walls to include live reenactments.

ANALOGY

For instance, when the soprano Maria Guleghina came to the Colón for the first time in 2005, the occasion was framed by many fans as the kind of diva appearance common at the house during its golden ages (the 1950s, 1960s, 1970s, or 1990s, depending on whom you ask). They uttered statements like the following:

> This is the real First World! This, Juan Diego Flórez, you can really enjoy this. If you have an ear, you know what you are getting.

> She's the next Eva Marton or Montserrat Caballé [a Hungarian soprano and a Catalan soprano, respectively, who are also big and tall].

Now it is uncommon for big stars like her to come, but it used to be like this all the time.

It's been a while since this opera house has seen anything like this.

They made more normalizing requests, such as, "We have to ask Capobianco [then the house general manager] to bring her back. She has to do *Rigoletto*, even if we have to ask the senators to put up money!" And there were expressions of shared joy and happiness—the waving of hands and handkerchiefs and a deafening amount of *bravos* and *bravas*, prompting five encores—that let an outsider recognize that the standing-room-only audience celebrates with the same bodily repertory (including hugs) as a goal celebration at the soccer stadium.

Despite all this, most fans reflected on how the analogy was truncated since Guleghina's presence did not produce the factious behaviors of the past. A successful turning back of the clock would require another appearance by a star of the same caliber, to counterbalance the Russian soprano. The adjusting and flattening of time would be better achieved through a season in which some conflict between stars could be witnessed. During my fieldwork, interviewees referred to the factious divisions between those who admired Maria Callas and those who admired Renata Tebaldi or, later, Teresa Berganza. They referred to the complex interplay of the flags and handkerchiefs through which people communicated and fought over their attachment to sopranos like Renata Scotto or Joan Sutherland or how some threatened to boycott Sutherland's performances because of their love for Claudia Muzio. To have a fully working analogy, the element of conflict— which works much like solidarity as an integration principle—was missing.[27] As Fabiana told me: "One star is not enough!" The interest aroused by the budding Argentinean sopranos Carla Filipcic and Soledad de la Rosa can be interpreted under this conflict-cum-integration frame.

IMITATION OR REPLICATION

Unlike the analogy, which presupposes a displacement between the thing we have lost and that which substitutes for it, the replica or imitation implies the attempt to completely replace one with the other. A good example of this is Franco's longing for Maria Callas (who came to the country in the late 1940s, more than fifteen years before he was born), which has pushed him into following the career of two sopranos, one international—who faded into oblivion—and one local. While he never saw Callas live, the representation he has of her is already as mediated and stylized as her replacement, an Italian dramatic soprano named Tiziana Fabricini. She was the first singer to perform the role of Violetta in *Traviata* at La Scala after Callas's death, but she never managed to come to Argentina. "They said her *Traviata* was very much like Callas's, so I always send messages to radio shows asking about what happened to her. I followed her because I would love for Callas to come back, for someone to take the slug. You listen to those emulators, and you dream of finding someone larger than life, as people who saw her describe her. You live tied to a ghost. Maybe Tiziana was worthless, but it was worth the fantasy of bringing back Callas through her."

He did manage to follow the local soprano Patricia Gutierrez. "She was a lyric spinto soprano. She started great as a soloist but afterward went downhill. She made too many mistakes, took too many heavy roles, and lost brilliance. She was a great hope for lyric spintos; that is a really unusual voice, and she got too tempted. I saw her doing *Butterfly* and *Trovatore* at the Colón, *Giovanna d'Arco* in La Plata, and *Ernani* in Avellaneda. She is now in the Colón house chorus."

As these examples illustrate, strategies for replacement go beyond the dichotomy of live/recorded or national/international. The next example brings us closer to a classic subject of sociological inquiry: How is it that grace or gifts outside institutional routines are transmitted and made durable? While Fabricini and Gutierrez fall closer to examples of revelation[28] or the search based on specific qualities (they were rare lyric spintos, like Callas), the case of the young tenor Sergi Carreras is an example of hereditary charisma. He is the nephew of the world-famous tenor José Carreras, and, though an absolute unknown, he was brought to the Avenida by Adelaida Negri's company to perform the part of Don Alvaro in a May 2005 production of *La forza del destino*. He failed miserably, people booed him, and, after the first performance, he was replaced by a local singer.

REENACTMENT OF SPECIFIC PARTS

Adelaida Negri is, once again, the main example. Her performances of big soprano parts like Norma in *Norma* (2006), Leonora in *La forza del destino* (2005), Elisabetta in *Elisabetta, regina d'Inghilterra* (2004), Anna Bolena in *Anna Bolena* (2003), Maria Stuarda in *Maria Stuarda* (2002) recapture the golden past of international seasons but also satisfy the longing for an actual Argentinean star and the permanent presence of a big soprano voice. Like Néstor, Luis despises the nostalgic fans but still comes to see Adelaida for her strength onstage. "She doesn't have high notes anymore, but I can't stop coming; she's a star on the stage." Diego saw Adelaida singing *Aida* at the

Colón in 1992; he is a big fan and goes to see everything she does, though sometimes "the results are a disaster, like *Anna Bolena*": "It was at a really shitty theater, and the lighting was bad. You could not only hear—we all know her voice is so out of tune it gives you cramps—but see that she looked jaded, tired, aged."

As much as the results of this reenactment are close to a Marxian conception of repetition, where the reenactment of a symbolic configuration results more in farce than in tragedy,[29] they indicate what Buenos Aires's passionate fans are trying to replicate: the full closure of the community thanks to engagement with a performance based on reification and the fetishism of opera, a star soprano (or two, actually) whose voice is "magic" (not explained by training) and with whom one can identify, and a longing for big, dramatic parts as the staple of the repertory.

But the schemas of opera appreciation and evaluation are not just fed by the reincarnation of favored sopranos. They are also powered by the promise of a future that resembles the past, at least partially, and a sociability that proposes itself as the heroic model to be respected, moving the center of the evaluation of the experience from the stage to the stalls.

A Family Resemblance

The proactive character of memory was a factor in the appointment of Marcelo Lombardero and Guillermo Brizzio to two of the most important positions in the house: artistic director and *maestro de estudios*.[30] For some fans, the fact that they are both children of Argentinean singers who worked at the Colón during the 1950s and 1960s was a guarantee that they would bring back the mystique and passion necessary to produce engaging opera, if not the international character of it. By the end of my fieldwork, fans were hopeful that these musicians would be able to reproduce the golden age. They focused on how, being children of the Colón, they knew the "tricks of the house" and would be better able to change things from the inside. This was especially true for Lombardero, who, on top of being the son of a renowned local soprano, had studied at the Colón Art Institute and made a career in opera, starting in the chorus before moving on to leading roles and eventually becoming a stage director. Rina was happy with his appointment, not only because she respected his mother, but also "because he promised he would take the Colón back to being what it was when Maestros Kinski and Kleiber[31] were in charge." For fans like her, the promise of taking the Colón back to the Second World War means making it more European since it would at least bring back a work ethos that combined craft, vocation, and workmanship. This could result in more performances per title and in more committed and better overall performances from the diverse members of the house: singers, musicians, stagehands, costume designers, and even the cleaning staff.

Those values are perhaps best embodied in Rina's reference to Kinski. Roberto Kinski came to Buenos Aires for the first time in 1933, as an assistant to Maestro Fritz Busch. Far from being an international star, the Hungarian maestro was responsible for preparing singers for the diverse titles the house would offer—selecting casts, conducting the first reading of each title by the house orchestra, and scheduling rehearsals by the diverse artistic companies and singers. He also conducted operas and concerts and became the first conductor of the national symphony. Anecdotes about Kinski emphasize his workman-like qualities: punctuality, dedication beyond the usual work hours, and detailed knowledge of parts and scores. Such qualities are seen as necessary to rebuilding the house; rather than looking for a charismatic maestro who might solve all problems in one gesture, an egoless character could slowly reconstruct what has been undone by years of decline.

Lombardero himself announced that he wanted to "come back to the times of Kinski." Yet, aware of how much the conditions of production have been transformed over the years, he remarked how "for some things one is an artist but for others one is a public employee." He noted that he did not want to bring back authoritarian practices of the past, such as rehearsing until midnight and enforcing all-night shifts to get ready for a production, but instead sought a balance between the two identities, for, "when the rules are not clear, boundaries become too wide." For him, a main achievement would be to "leave the house in order and working, with internal and external prestige." These things would be done, not by hiring "an international roster of divos," but by "having a working chorus, orchestra, and singers who feel respected." The goal is for house artists to feel proud of belonging to it, for stage and costume workers to "be able to adapt, [to be] in love with their work." Otherwise, even though the Colón can afford to bring in some international figures here and there, "if we put them onstage with a bad orchestra, a mediocre chorus, and an absurd stage production, the result would be that of a provincial theater" (Chiaravalli 2005). His objective is to make a regular practice of those extraordinary productions the Colón now accomplishes only infrequently.

Lombardero's reflections illustrate the continuity of categories that I have been discussing so far (love, work, organization) and the abandonment of that which the Colón cannot do anymore to reproduce the isolation it once produced: the hiring of stars who would demand a big part of the house resources. His strategy includes a strengthening of the houses's core artistic elements as a basis for producing international prestige (hence the opposite of being a provincial theater). Yet, in doing so, he points to a national solution that, in a less obvious way, refers back to an international (i.e., from the Old Europe, as the characters emphasized are hardworking Hungarians, Germans, and Italians) way of doing things, an origin of the constellation of representations that make the Colón a meaningful and constitutive experience for passionate fans.

I do not want to confine the notion of family resemblance to a literal iteration, looking for kinship affiliations in comparisons of the present to the past. But I would like to point out how much passionate fans resemble those from the past by highlighting a few elements that help make sense of how the dispositions have survived changing conditions. Passionate fans, as we have seen, associate through a series of heroic narratives from the past that center on the audience and demonstrate how rich sociability used to be: the superior knowledge fans from the past possessed, the passionate debate they sustained, how they reacted to and engaged with a world of divas and stars (of "real artists"). As we can infer from this passage, it looks as if what is being reenacted is, not the Colón that experienced a golden past, a "glorious and international character," but rather a model of cultural affiliation in which heroism, intensive and extensive knowledge, and attendance are keys for audience members to model themselves as part of a community of passionate fans, regardless of how little of what happens onstage today resembles the type of performance that actually made sense for this model of engagement.

As the American anthropologist Charles Hirschkind (2001) states, exploring community resources, as embodied by the existing modes of practice and association, can help explain how a particular set of dispositions can outlive the material conditions that gave rise to it. Such continuity can be observed in the resources generated to help maintain particular traditions. While traditions are tweaked to make sense of the world, the forms of sociality continue and, with them, the ways through which people deliberate about and affiliate with certain practices. The fact that, as we have seen, the tertulia is a secluded space that offers few possibilities for circulation[32]— where people attend on an individual basis and not as part of a group of friends, a couple, or a family—makes for a particular kind of sociality, full of short-lived conversations based exclusively on the opera universe.[33]

This sociality among strangers is maintained through a deference to older fans, who sing the praises of the past and present themselves as living proof of what constitutes a life lived for opera. Much as the Chaco Toba tribe, native to Northeast Argentina, keeps seeing and talking about bushes in an area where intensive agricultural exploitation has produced grassland, farms, and ranches (Gordillo 2003), passionate fans keep seeing divos and divas and talk about all-night lines as if they are everyday occurrences (the last time an all-night line was seen was when Plácido Domingo came in 1998). They reminisce together, even if they are only in their late thirties, about "crazy" older fans like Puccini and about how great Birgit Nilsson was doing Wagner.[34]

Rebuilding the Levees?

Fans at the house differentiate themselves further than I have already discussed, although the distinctions have less to do with status or models of personal transcendence and engagement than with how to combat the collapse of the boundaries that once made the isolation of the opera house a constitutive feature of its enjoyment. Attempts to reestablish the closure of the house from the rest of the ailments that pervade society derive from diverse ideas that are anchored in competing definitions of *nationalism*. For some it is more nationalistic to have a scene with the best local performers; for others it better to strive toward making the Colón the best possible international house by finding those vocal gems from around the world who can fit the house's budget and capabilities. Even intermediate solutions, like the one offered by then new artistic director Lombardero, link the national and the international realms by guaranteeing that the revamping of the house's working mystique is modeled after the Old European values that originally helped produce extraordinary yet regularly engaging opera performances.

All the solutions share a categorical understanding of what has been broken and needs to be restored; to a certain extent, they all emphasize that, though some goals are possible (passion, work, vocation, and organization), it is impossible to regain one of the key features that shaped the isolation: the international stars. Nevertheless, fans engage with mnemonic practices to key certain parts of the experience of the past to the present. In that movement, memory shifts from being a model of evaluation based on the present to being a model for opera and society. Fans talked of the importance of reconstituting the boundaries against the outside, as if reactivating the experience of the Colón would also bring the country back from the long-term downward spiral into which they—along with many other middle-class people—think it has fallen. For some of the fans, the reorganization of the house would also represent a picture of what a better or higher mode of life would be, changing the direction of influence from the disruptive forces of society that have invaded the Colón to a generative working mystique that would then reorganize society. The chain that tied the house to its audience gets reproduced in both narratives, as the golden age of the opera is inextricably linked to the golden age of the audience (in knowledge and composition) and to the golden age of the building. While for a long time the grandeur of the Colón was an antidote for the gradual transformation of the rest of Argentinean society, passionate fans hope that its restoration can also be a step toward reestablishing an elusive golden age for the country.

CHAPTER SEVEN

"We've told you all about our life"

Conclusions and Implications

On Love

The title of this chapter comes from Irma's answer to my last question during our interview: "Is there anything that would help me better understand your relationship with music?" Her answer points to the homology between events in the life of opera fanatics (even those, like her, with children and grandchildren) and their commitment to the object of their affection. The presence of these kinds of reactions throughout my fieldwork and interviews made me center my inquiry on the affective character of long-term engagements. I did so by exploring how opera fanatics achieve an emotional attachment to a complex form, usually presented as an emblem of class and honor.

What I mean by *love* is nothing other than the intense personalized investment fans charge opera with, the object cathexis I referred to extensively in chapter 5. Authors as diverse as Simmel (1950), Geertz (1983), and Hennion (2007) have elucidated the shape and the content of this kind of attachment. Hennion (2007) did so by pointing out the "middle forms" of reflexivity, usually framed in the passive voice, that express a peculiar mode of being subject to something (especially in Romance languages) where things "are experienced" or "listened to." Simmel (1950) discusses the monogamous marriage as a social form in which the agent transcends herself through a decision that paradoxically negates her own autonomous character: giving herself away to someone (or, in this case, to some*thing*). This new figure subsumes, dissolves, cancels the individual and creates a new configuration, one linked to both parts from the get-go, impossible to divide. In both cases, we find a social form that is different from the mere sum of the individual and what she enjoys.

I want to follow Simmel's lead and explore how the creation of this paradoxical attachment is an active process, not a fixed entity. As I have discussed throughout this book, the emergence of a love of opera happens in diverse stages. Chapters 2 and 3 discussed the initiation stories of fans and emphasized two points—(1) the surprise felt by those who had not grown up with opera as a live or mediated presence in their lives and (2) the search for an understanding of what this new love produces—focusing mainly on how an embodied voice communicates with their own bodies. For most interviewees and informants, even those with a more refined, elaborate, and encyclopedic (we could say mediated) understanding of the experience, the effect that opera has on their bodies is central to explaining why passionate fans do what they do.

This point is not a minor one since it helps us position opera within a more inclusive category: *embodied practices*. I am obviously referring, not to all activities from this particular universe, but rather to the live experience of listening to a human singing voice in the company of others. While fans listen to recordings in search of particular bodily effects and moods, records also serve as a kind of index, providing a sense memory against which live embodied experiences can be measured. As such, their opera experience is located at an intersection that is particularly rich with sociological significance. Opera fans are not performers, so their intense engagement cannot be explained by categories of active practice that would explain loyalty to a performing endeavor, like being a musician (Becker 1963), a cook (Fine 1992), an auto mechanic (Harper 1987), a boxer (Wacquant 2003), a glassblower (O'Connor 2005), or a criminal (Katz 1988). However, they do retain the sensuous and embodied character of those practices while being more on the passive end of the experience category (Jay 2005). In that respect, opera can serve as a particularly fecund microuniverse in which to observe long-term engagements that are embodied in a more evident and extreme way than in other arenas of social life usually considered more important or fundamental, like political loyalties.

Chapter 3 looked at the mediating instances between neophytes and the practice, examining how opera is made a meaningful experience and how it is anchored in a particular place (the Colón Opera House) and time (an elusive golden age), while also presenting a model for affiliation: the maestro, whose intensive training gives him wide-ranging yet not esoteric knowledge.

Chapter 4 continued by showing how that model is but one among many competing in a local status tournament on the opera scene. Through the classifications learned, fans can elaborate on what happens both onstage and in their own physical beings, focusing on an intense experience of differentiation from others that results in a sense of identity.

In current debates about the social character of taste, we rarely see why people initially engage in a culturally esoteric practice—what their initial reaction to it is, what meanings they attach to the experience, or the stages they traverse to reach a level of knowledge and mastery that guarantees, at least for them, the most complete enjoyment (see Bourdieu and Passeron 1964/ 1979, 1977; Bourdieu 1984; Lamont 1992; and Lareau 2003). Thus, we fail to see the mediations (Hennion 1997; Heinich 2001) that occur between social structure and taste. The formalization of this process could lead to a more complete model of aesthetic attachment, one that considers the interaction of background and foreground factors. Such a model would focus, not just on the conversion of background factors into cultural practices, but also on (a) the initial circumstances that produced the coupling or uncoupling of these conditions, (b) the mediations that help transform the initial attraction into more elaborate and sustained attachment, and (c) the kinds of sociality into which novice fans are incorporated. It will allow us to observe not only how people are channeled into having opera as part of their menu for cultural consumption—the key question among sociologists studying taste— but also what they do with the cultural materials at hand and how much their activities as music appreciators are predicated on class, as a result of the organization of the group that receives them once they are fully socialized, or as a consequence of the work on the self they allow music to perform.

Insofar as I undertook a study of a specific social group, I do not universalize the individuals around whom the study revolves. It is in the practices themselves that a case for theoretical generalization can be made. Supplemental fieldwork on a small group of fans who travel to Europe (Verona, Salzburg, Paris, and Bayreuth) and New York shows the same commitment and activities organized under the love metaphor. While they point to another kind of opera, which has the international circuit as its pinnacle (even if that means meeting at the local movie theater to watch a live, high-definition satellite transmission from the Met), the love for opera organizes these fans' cultivation. Though some of them had early exposure to opera through their families, they did not fall in love with it until they managed to see a live performance by themselves. Their socialization also had a particular way of sustaining opera's impact on them, as did the moments when the emotion of a live performance was embodied and provoked physical reactions (crying, shouting, the need to take a long walk after a performance). As much as their poorer cousins go to free lectures, they have a private instructor who teaches them for a few months before their departure about what awaits for them in Europe; fans I have described throughout the book feel that they have graduated from certain kinds of music to more complex forms. Their activities are organized with the same pedagogical gradient that takes them to more obvious and simple choices (Italian opera at the Arena di Verona) and to more contemporary (the avant-garde staging at the Salzburg Festival) or ancient ones (Monteverdi's *Il ritorno d'Ulisse in patria*). Moreover, festivalgoers respect one another regardless of obvious differences in their degree of music cultivation (organizers distinguish among "simpler" and "sophisticated" festivalgoers but make the point to separate music sophistication from socioeconomic status and origin) and share a meal after every performance to comment on what they have seen. Fellowship arises, not only from their love for the same object, but also from the heroism expressed in their economic expenditures. When pressed for an explanation about where their love for opera comes from, even those who have always had more expensive seats in the boxes and on the orchestra levels note the link between Argentinean and European culture and point to the *paraíso* as the real and symbolic space where passion and knowledge meet; they also present themselves as equivalent in their love to the Francos, José Luises, and Rinas I have introduced at length.

This is hardly an Argentinean phenomenon since the symbolic economy of love parallels similar networks of signification and local activities elsewhere. A detailed review of each instance is beyond the scope of this book, but I would like to draw attention to the one perhaps best known by North American readers: the New York opera fanatic (see Mitchell 1998; Blier 1999; Melick 2003; Sollis 2006; and Leigh Scott 2009). Several journalistic accounts report the existence of such a breed at the Metropolitan Opera House in New York City. Music lovers wait in line all night for the few standing-room-only tickets the Met sells on the morning of performances; they reminisce about how long ago they met, celebrate the glorious past of self-described heroism they participated in and the stars they witnessed together; they become self-appointed standee culture historians and refer to the way immigrants from Italy populated the standing area as a mythical origin of the current experience. Some of them claim to come all the way from Boston just for a performance or to have gone back and forth to Chicago for one night to see Jon Vickers as *Otello*, while others save their special galas to come to the Met, even if it is just to be in line at 4:00 A.M. Narratives of personal discovery mark their stories of initiation; their early attraction to opera is described as "sudden and shocking as a thunderclap." Much like their *porteño* counter-parts, they refer to the direct sensory thrill and the preeminence of the voice over the orchestra (and the libretto). They also point to the primacy of their first experience over the expanded music materials they have laboriously explored during the years. They chastise current artists who "have lost their soul" and avoid taking risks, when compared to Carlo Bergonzi and Joan Sutherland. When asked to advance an explanation for their attachment, they become tautological and claim to be too passionate and irrational to be able to describe it.

Nothing represents all the fan tropes better than the radio show *Opera Fanatic*, which was broadcast by the FM radio station of Columbia University in New York from 1983 to 1995. The four-hour show included bootleg and live recordings with interviews with opera stars such as Alfredo Kraus, Franco Corelli, and Grace Bumbry and audience participation segments such as "Booing: True Confessions" and "Name That Voice." It combined idiot-savant extremism with the tendency to eccentric obsessiveness that critics and other audience members criticize in fans, bringing in Jackie Callas (Ma-ria's sister), allowing the opinionated host to shut down listeners who did not agree with him while celebrating the amateur spirit of those who provided him with recordings and "knew more than critics do," and fixing the opera canon during the postwar years (the host, Stefan Zucker, also promoted a forgotten singing technique that stretched the vocal range of tenors to three octaves or more and, thus, allowed them "to rival the castratos in virtuos-ity"). The show also published a magazine, deemed a mixture of *Opera News* and the *National Enquirer*, that had an article alleging that the American soprano Aprile Millo was the bastard daughter of John Fitzgerald Kennedy, promised previously unpublished photographs of castrati, included a center-fold of the turn-of-the-century tenor Victor Maurel wearing nothing but a fig leaf, and an interview in which Renata Tebaldi allegedly trashed Sutherland, Sills, and Cossotto.[1]

The host of the show, a tenor aficionado, also made the documentary *Opera Fanatic*, in which he followed divas from the 1940s and 1950s in an at-tempt to prove that contemporary singers have become "less personal, more mechanical, in some ways more proficient but colder": "Nobody sings with the variety of tone color these divas sung with." Following the fetishistic dic-tum of opera fanatics, he pointed to whether they sang with a "chest voice" as a marker to distinguish them from expressive singers of the idealized past.

Self-obsession and juicy anecdotes of opera *follia* have been reported in innumerable books. Rather than attempt to recount the many contexts and iterations of this phenomenon, I will reproduce a small part of the twenty-seven-page transcription of a conversation among amateurs at the entrance of the Opéra Garnier in Paris that could very well have happened at the Colón's doorsteps. The French psychoanalyst Michel Poizat documented the conversation as a key part of his search for an understanding of the ways in which the singing human voice generates attachment in opera lovers. In one paragraph, Guy, one of four "patients" Poizat interviewed, distills most of the topics this book has discussed:

> With me, my income is inversely proportional to the extent to which it's eaten away by opera! What with festivals, performances and recording, I spend on average, say . . . 800 francs a month on opera. I come to stand in line for tickets much less than I used to before 1980. At that time I was doing this about twice a week. Since 1980, I do it no more than about once a month . . . if that. This year I've come three times, four maybe, if you count *Tosca*. Otherwise I try to get seats at the last minute. I still try to see each performance at least once or twice, but there are things I only see once and even some I miss altogether. Whereas five or six years ago, I'd see every performance of a single production, now I'd say I make two or three, when the production is good. But inevitably I've become harder to please and much less . . . convinced by what I see nowadays in comparison with what I've seen in the past. (Poizat 1992, 13)

The Love For

The metaphor of love, which includes forms of precognition, recognition, socialization, career-like activities, moral obligations, and the erection of boundaries around our object of affection, is central to understanding how these fans use certain traits of their attachment to explain and craft themselves. As the anthropologist Charles Lindholm (1998, 244) has explained, love offers an experience of self-transformation, of personal choice, a meaningful future and sensual expansion. It operates as a metaphor of release as much as one of self-control. It produces selfhood through experiences akin to those of religious ecstasy. This direction of inquiry leads us into a sociology of affect and to the ways people perceive themselves as individuals, capable of certain feelings and tastes. Nurturing a specific taste is a guarantee of someone's uniqueness. Opera in Buenos Aires is an extreme example of this as people are secluded and concentrated in one room where this experience can be observed. But we could also think of other kinds of connoisseurs, such as foodies, wine lovers, movie buffs, sports fans, and passionate political activists. In consequence, a work of art (and cultural objects in general) can be thought of as a locus for personal and emotional investment or a medium for moral self-formation. The sociology of taste is too weak to explain the moments in which cultural objects orient life, give meaning, and allow people to lose themselves. Distinguishing it from a full-fledged sociology of passion is crucial. Doing so will allow us to understand that having a passion for a particular taste is more than expressing a preference (liking Italian better than Indian food, e.g.) and different from finding an object of attention for a preexisting psychological state: it is a particular kind of engagement with the world, both sensual and meaningful, that allows particular parts of the self to come to the fore, choosing particular lines of action and discarding others.[2] It implies a greater sense of engagement with the actor's self than plain cognition.

The love metaphor—the idea that, despite a lack of outside recognition, something we engage affectively with and charge with value becomes a building block of who we are—is better comprehended when it is extended and understood over time, when love becomes a bildungsroman, with stages at which the self matures as the individual becomes more heavily invested. The cultural historian Martin Jay (2005, 11) calls our attention to how, in German, the definition of *experience* has a dual character (*Erlebnis* and *Erfahrung*) that shows the movement from "having an experience" (as in a momentary rupture from the fabric of the quotidian, best explained by Simmel [1958] as "an adventure") to a journey that involves a *longue durée* understanding and is linked to the self as a narrative whole. Unlike the amateurs of Hennion (2007, 106), who are there just for the fleeting instances in which bodies and music articulate and "states emerge," the opera fans I uncovered attach one meaning of *experience* to the other, longing to make a moral career of those personalized highs that opera affords them, but blocked by a society that makes it impossible for them to have a real experience.

This study has also emphasized the internal variation within the practices of intense attachment themselves. The types that I have built up from the data emphasize the different dimensions of love they affiliate through. The pilgrim style indicates the suspension of status that happens in processes where people temporarily transcend themselves in front of the loved one; the hero commits, through a series of works and activities, to demonstrating the depth of his affection and worthiness; the addict moves from working feverishly to keep the flame alive to the repeated quest for an isolated opera experience that allows him or her to get high and achieve the ultimate dissolution of self; the nostalgic looks back to the first love and affiliates through constant comparison between the current experience and the idealized representation that hooked her the first time.

Stopping here would provide us with a complete yet superficial descrip-

TABLE 3. Structure of Variation in Styles of Loving

Hero	Addict	*Individual*
Nostalgic	Pilgrim	*Collective*
Long durée	*Immediate*	

Note: The X-axis indicates the movement from past to present, the Y-axis whether the attachment is individual or collective.

tion of the variations, without any understanding of what is behind them. The key, as I have shown throughout the book, and especially in chapter 5, is to understand which kind of work on the self each style affords and what dimensions combine to produce each type. The invariant structure behind them is based on a combination of two dimensions, one that goes from past to present and one that varies between collective and individual forms of affiliation. The hero would be a case of individual attachment based on the transcendence of everyday life, the chance to excel among like-minded people in a continuous activity that emanates from the past to the present. The addict would be a case of individual attachment in search of immediate effects and self-dissolution. The pilgrim engages through a collective that involves a transitory dissolution of the self rather than a long-term project (though, in opera, the purer case does not exist since rules of etiquette and romantic listening make for a highly individualized experience, even in a large crowd).[3] The nostalgic represents a case of permanence (in between transcendence and selfhood), although his or her efforts also transcend the reality of everyday life. Following Molotch (2003), nostalgia can also be considered a case of engagement through the collective as what is longed for is, not only the music, but also the people attached to it. The systematization of the variation would look like that displayed in table 3.

This model offers the potential for structural comparison, just as architectural blueprints can be used to reveal differences and similarities; we could analyze most practices of intense attachment through these four blueprints. This concept set offers the tools and enhances our capacity to sort out issues and generate questions. As Levine (1997) notes, it even provides us, for purposes of empirical description, with a categorial framework comprising indispensable statistical boxes. These types are not just found in an opera house. Examples of passionate practices abound in the social science and journalistic literature. Heroic fans of Manchester United follow the team around Europe, sacrificing the rhythm of their daily lives, and wreaking havoc along the way (Buford 1988). Nostalgic fans of Argentina's San Lorenzo protest endlessly during the matches that "soccer is not what it used to be, when players were so skillful they could play with dress coats, stick and hat" (Archetti 1999). Carnival purists explode when the venue of their celebration is moved into a strip and the contours of the practice get "disfigured," yet they still manage to dissolve their outside hierarchies among committed participants through singing (DaMatta 1979/1992). Nostalgic jazz (Marsalis 1988) and tango (Monjeau 1999; Archetti 2001) devotees battle against innovation by fixing a moment in time as representative of the music's essence, thereby anchoring their selves as well as the genres and combating any deviations from them. "Deadheads," devoted to the music of the Grateful Dead, toured the country following their favorite band and went on pilgrimage to commemorate the death of the founding member Jerry Garcia, later going on to see the innumerable Grateful Dead cover bands (Adams 1998). Fans of Guns n' Roses did the same thing (minus the death of their lead singer), getting their fix following the "best GNRS Tribute Band in the world" (Klosterman 2004). Surf enthusiasts on Long Island destroy cameras in the East Hamptons that give away the location of hidden beaches and, thus, attract too many neophytes (known to experienced surfers as *groms* or *kooks*) (Kilgannion 2008). Nostalgic Red Sox fans declare that they miss their heroic times of suffering now that they have finally won the World Series (Borer 2008).

Sports and music fans[4] are not the only ones who fit the description: comics collectors (and collectors in general) can also be viewed through this lens. Indeed, the comics-collecting market was called the *nostalgia market* at first (Wolk 2007), although its development as an insular world resulted in addicted fans who hit their local comics store every Wednesday, travel around looking for a missing issue or to attend conventions (Jindra 1994), spend large sums of money while living in otherwise impoverished conditions, and think of themselves as some kind of secret, embattled fellowship. Comics collectors long shared the stigmatization that opera fans report, which makes their accumulated capital hard to exchange for other social resources (Lopes 2006).[5]

Further development of the love-for framework, initiated by Simmel and advanced by contemporary authors like Hennion and DeNora, could help us more fully understand particular cases of heavily personalized investment, which tend to be dismissed with suffixes like -*mania*, -*philia*, and -*pathia* that demonstrate the impossibility of finding an explanation among the usual sociological suspects (status, networks, class reproduction). They force us to label practitioners with names that denote the nonreductive individuality and irrationality of their performance of taste, obliterating what is social about the affiliation they partake in.

Status

This study has meandered toward opposite shores, attracted by the two poles of cultural sociology: the relation of music to class and status and the meanings and kind of attachment music affords. At first, my research questions were aimed mostly at establishing the relation between social structure and music practices in a country where high culture was popularized early on, thanks to immigrants, civil society institutions, and state policies. I began by examining how people signified their middle-class status through art in a moment of extended political and economic crisis. Yet, the more I attended opera and listened to it, the more I realized that, while these questions can be answered, the relation does not follow a straight line; rather, it functions obliquely and through many mediations. Also, the more I became immersed in the field, the more I became aware of the embodiment, apprenticeship, and membership processes (Wacquant 2005) through which one becomes an opera fan; the specific kind of engagement with music that results was a key to my understanding of larger questions. As I made explicit in the last two chapters, class and status matter, not because passionate fans participate in a larger societal distinction game using opera as a tool or because class origin can help explain or predict the particular kind of attachment I have described, but rather because of the transcendent experience, reminiscent of a lavish spectacle and outside the framework of everyday Argentinean decline, that opera used to be able to provide music lovers.

The role of honor, in this case, is related, not to how much recognition fans can gather from peers outside the opera house or how much they can convert their lifestyle into other cumulative species, but rather to how they craft themselves as honorable people. Passionate fans develop themselves as worthy beings through a laborious, long-term engagement with opera. Fans conceive of opera as a meaningful activity that offers them a stage on which to enact certain values, feel in public, and express themselves as superior and highly refined beings among equals. To paraphrase Sennett (1977, 314), in a society where the imagery of *theatrum mundi* has been eroded by the absence of public life and everyday people are actors without an art, the opera house is one of the few places where people still engage in the public expression of emotion in the company of strangers, and they do so in an elaborate manner that presents passion as a playful activity, not just something one suffers from.[6]

As shown in chapter 4, the inside-status tournament in which fans participate to try and gauge cultural membership does not result in the expected social cohesion outside the opera house. It causes neither their horizontal integration nor their vertical differentiation from others (something that is a given in the sociological literature focusing on high culture and esoteric practices and that should, consequently, be explored in greater depth). As we can see in this case, the source of prestige rests on the recognition among the upper floors of the house of a residual cultural model that is also the basis for the fans' meaning and purpose.

The strategies that fans use for impression management do not lead to the display of a worthy self that possesses naturalized cultural abilities and dispositions, as Bourdieu (1984) would have it. Quite the contrary, they result in an exhibition of the industrious self-discipline and sacrifice that it takes to acquire those abilities. Though the staged self maintains the performing structure described by Goffman (1959), passionate fans make a theater out of the backstage. Unlike the classic analysis of confidence games by the Chicago school (Zorbaugh 1929; Cressey 1932) and some contemporaries (Grazian 2004), what impresses is, not what is hidden and effortless, but what is permanently revealed. In a certain way, passionate fans manage to invert what is expected from them a priori in the crafting of their public selves, following the formulations of both Goffman and Bourdieu.

Even though opera fanatics learn to love music alone, other relationships, whether friends or family, are key to calling their attention to the particular passages that can awake and sustain singular states, providing a springboard for the constant comparison and monitoring of their loving activity. The excitement produced by music must be explained; passionate fans find meaning (of a transcendent kind) in making sense of it. Being passionate about something allows fans to present what they perceive as their best selves, bringing their opera activities to the forefront, and confining what they see as less-interesting aspects of their lives (mostly their work, family, domestic, or erotic life—or lack thereof) to the background. By investing in opera, they are able to understand themselves as unique individuals, constituted as such by the cultivation and augmentation of their taste. The cathexis that opera produces and engages these fans in makes the art form a way of life, something around which to organize their lives.[7] As such, it becomes a constitutive experience, to a degree that the threat to opera as it should be is also a threat to their self-understanding as superior persons.[8]

As discussed in chapters 4 and 6, this study is a window into the durability of culture once the reproductive functions it fulfills are exhausted. While opera in Argentina was an integral tool for spiritual growth among the many European immigrant groups that arrived in the country from 1900 to 1930, and while it did go hand in hand with successful trajectories of upward mobility well into the late 1960s, most of the secondary literature shows that this is no longer the case; dominant conceptions of what distinguishes culture in Argentinean society have changed. Fans have emphasized that, when they reveal their passionate devotion to opera outside the opera house, they get rejected so often that they mostly hide the fact that they attend opera. We are witnessing here what Raymond Williams calls *residual* culture: a formerly dominant cultural configuration that has lost its power to institutionalize symbolic boundaries into social or economic ones but that nevertheless persists in certain areas. While it is true that, as the culture-as-status literature suggests, there is a process of differentiation from others, it does not automatically get transformed into verticality or power subjection.

There is a reason for this lack of recognition beyond the outdated concept of culture that passionate fans share or their lack of resources to transform a differentiating impetus into a vertical relationship. The way they affiliate, their model of cultural engagement, is far from the detached participation in cultural practices usually seen among those recognized as having mastered and naturalized the contents and forms in question. Rather, their attachment is predicated on the combination of a few civilized traits with an ethic of effort, passion, and experiential and emotional immersion. This point opens an avenue of exploration into how much the social prestige ascribed to certain practices is related to forms of engagement rather than actual content. It brings us back to the classifying and totalizing drive of Bourdieu (1984) but is more nuanced in showing how practices, cultural objects, and social groups are not correlated as one to one as he thought (i.e., a social position corresponds to a specific set of cultural products and a model for engaging with them) and how categories and models of engagement with a symbolic product are the result of processes within a localized realm of practice more than of preexisting positions in the social structure.

While going once a month to the opera (and other times to different venues and activities) is perceived by those on the outside as appropriate, restrained, and honorable behavior, participating in any activity three times a week (whether volunteering at an animal shelter, playing soccer or chess, or attending the opera) transforms the fans' self-image of love for into the madness and scorn of mania. As a new member of the audience explained to me: "They have to be insane. Otherwise, why would they pay to come and boo something?" Much like soccer fans who profess to love their team, attending practices, scrimmages, and matches week after week, yet insult the players and coaches, participants in this model of cultural affiliation build themselves up as loving, worthy selves through the very same mechanisms that undermine them in the eyes of outsiders. The competing legitimacies (or lack thereof) for this model of engagement point more to the segmented and localized character of cultural classifications than to a highly integrated system of legitimacies referenced by all.

To completely understand this story, we must realize that transcendence is at stake as much as honor. As I showed in chapter 5, transcendence is a goal for many while at the same time organizing modes of engagement and the cosmology that underpins them. Fans diverge along more than one axis, through categories that point, not necessarily toward a "positive . . . evaluation of honor" (Weber 1946a, 187), but toward what they can get from the experience, whether that be symbolic or material rewards within the confines of the upper floors, the possibility of longing for a fuller experience, or the prosecution of minimum pleasurable instances through intense study and self-discipline.

The distinctions invoked by passionate fans do not have much currency in the outside world as they are fabricated and operate only in the context of the Colón. Still, this entirely contrived social space does organize commitments, values, and orientations even outside the opera house. The Colón is a bracketed space with its own moral categories. These may be homologous with those outside, but, to a certain extent, the ordering defies social convention. This does not mean that we should jump into a carnivalesque understanding of the experience (Bakhtin 1984; Eco 1984; Darnton 1985; DaMatta 1979/1992). There are no subaltern groups bent on exacting revenge for the oppression they suffer in the outside world; rather, there are people who attempt to transcend the perceived maladies of the outside world through a very particular way of practicing opera. In doing so, they participate in a local world of shifting moral classifications, one that defies some of the outside ordering (especially with respect to members of the upper middle class) but respects others (the paternalistic miserabilism that they exhibit when talking about the popular fans). Interestingly enough, though most fans are from the lower middle class and the middle class, some also have the most expensive subscription tickets. Yet, when they participate in the life of the upper floors, their behavior is the opposite of that of the rich members of the audience.

That social life is not just a reflection of larger structural patterns, usually linked with power or domination, should not result in making of what happens in a local realm a creation ex nihilo of those who participate there. Rather, it should make clear how the situations we observe are linked to other realms of social life. As discussed in chapters 1 and 6, this points to a very specific historical process: the construction of the Colón as the key location for the expression of high culture's civilizing mission in Argentina, its occupation by a mixed and heterogeneous population, and its past isolation from the political and economic crises that have engulfed the country periodically. This past serves as the idealized model for the relation between opera and society, excluding certain events, practices, and activities from the opera world. The explanation for the presence of these intrusions rests on the brutal transformations that Argentinean society has undergone over the past thirty years and represents how impossible it is for fans to bracket the ailments that appear in their everyday lives from the extraordinary universe of the Colón. The disappearance of opera (and especially of the Colón) as they imagined it also means that the Argentina they have imagined—existing in an elusive golden past filled with noble politicians and a sense of service and vocation anchored in an extended European middle class—is but a dream. While they strive to escape from these social tensions and contradictions through their transcendental love of opera, the demise of the boundary that constitutes the experience as something outside the ordinary, linked in its isolation to better times, makes the pursuit seem increasingly futile.

Works

The British author Nick Hornby (2003, 5) wrote a book about his favorite songs.[9] In it, he states that he did not want to write about music memories. He notes that while he has a certain affection for music that triggers immediate remembrances—listening to the radio as a child, a summer job in the countryside, or an intimate act with an ex-girlfriend—music means nothing for him as music, only as memories. He describes how he is highly suspicious of people who like music because it transports them to thoughts of other people (like their family) or situations (like their honeymoon). For him, those people actually don't like music very much. He concludes by stating: "I wanted to mostly write what it was in these songs that made me love them, not what I brought to the songs." Let me paraphrase now and ask what opera affords that other practices do not and how it articulates what the fans bring with them. At the outset of this conclusion, I stated that I wanted to explain love as a process and an activity; in order to do so, it is mandatory to come full circle, to complete our understanding of the social world of the fans and their social classifications and how the works that produce the engagement are integrated. As object-centered sociologies (Molotch 2003; Latour 2005) have shown, objects are sustained by social practices as much as they help sustain engagements (see the work on Bach in Hennion and Fauquet [2001]).

Music does not exist or have meaning by itself. While this statement seems obvious now, it took a while for sociology to come to terms with the fact that the work itself has not been much analyzed, that it takes many forms and is isolated only by virtue of a collective act of definition (Becker 1999). Although music, by definition, has almost infinite affordances (Willis 1978; DeNora 2002), the breadth and variation of what opera affords is bounded by traditions, discourses, embodiments, and spatial and bodily practices.

The opera house works as an enclosed machine, with its own time and space. It is a circumscribed barrier against the outside world, sometimes permeable (the middle-class moral preoccupations about the decay of the country), sometimes impermeable (representing a striving for transcendent experience that is hard to find in everyday life). So while the respondents were from diverse factions of the middle class—with varying levels of educational achievement and different genders, ages, and sexual orientations—the experience of music sometimes appears monolithic.

There is still room for personal variation and internal differentiation since my study has focused primarily on the upper floors of the opera house, taking advantage of the secluded concentration of people for whom this practice is a way of life. While my description of opera as a system composed of agents, mediations, objects, practices, and discourses, navigated and worked by individuals as they become subjects, has led to a certain behavioral regularity, there is more to it. While acts of consumption are individual, the breadth of variation that music affords is fixed by its historic role as a practice in which people engage with moral intensity (opera has been the site of class, political, and national struggle; see Robinson [1986], Fulcher [1987], Arblaster [1997], Ahlquist [1997], Gerhard [1998], Stamatov [2002], Johnson [2008], Clancy [2005], and Johnson, Fulcher, and Ertman [2007]) and by the traditions of its organization as a practice, which in Argentina relates to its early popularity among immigrants and, later, to state policies. While people do let themselves go through music—as the individual-level literature would like it—the shape and framing of their experience would be impossible to understand if we did not look into the deep cultural representations, involving both the moral and the romantic characterization of the practice, that are mobilized each time they listen to opera.

Could these people find what they get from opera somewhere else? Can any other particular practice produce this kind of experience—an ecstatic state produced by music listening that leads to personal transcendence? Audience members learn how to immerse themselves in a sensual relationship with the music; they make the music work a part of themselves, appropriating it, trying to make it similar to themselves. An understanding of the process would be incomplete without an explanation of what is it that music does (or how it collaborates, lending itself to be utilized in a passionate way).

The process through which the subject almost becomes part of the music materials themselves is best understood by thinking of the key elements that are necessary to understand the opera fans' long-term commitment.

Is there any other complex practice that, in the same context, would provide the same combination of live bodily performances, moralized transcendent states, musicality, status claims, and intensive knowledge? Could any other object be the medium for their moral self-formation? The most obvious candidate, classical instrumental music, hides the body of the performer through many mechanisms: performers are seated sideways, with their backs to the audience or, as in the case of the pianist, looking into their instruments; there's homogeneity in the musicians' black clothing; applause is relegated to after the performance. On the basis of this, authors like Hennion (1997, 428) separate rock music from classical music as the former rejects the mediation of the live, embodied performance. On the other hand, tango, a local candidate, provides—as much as soccer (Archetti 1999; Garriga 2007) or *rock nacional* (Vila and Semán 1999)—for bodies and concerns about nationality. But status claims for tango fall short; the nature of the engagement is more centered on a dancing body or on lyrics (Archetti 1999, 2001; Monjeau 1999; Palomino 2007), and its visceral element caters almost exclusively to a masculine morality.

These comparisons bring us back to the actual work and how it produces engagement, providing an "experiential hook" (Willis 1978, 103) that draws people into opera, prompting them to dismiss other practices as uninteresting. The object/work is an active part of the explanation; as with dead labor, previous interpretations are already incorporated into the symbol in performance, interacting in affording or constraining meaning with the cultural configuration with which it enters into dialogue. The generalizations that I am making from this case make the object, not a part of what is explained, but an actual frame that also participates in the construction of meaning. What is explained is not the work, as something that would exist in itself or could actually be an original *then* put in circulation, but the engagement that it helps produce. The work is an active coparticipant in the practice. It is on the foreground of the action summoning agents to partake in it.

Unlike previous versions of the consumption/production dialectic—discussed mainly by cultural and literary studies scholars (Ingarden 1977/1989; Iser 1978; Jauss 1982; Radway 1984), who present cultural artifacts and objects as having dual meaning (either by themselves or in use) or no meaning at all (as literary critics like Stanley Fish [1982] or the followers of Durkheim would have it)—cultural products are always in use and already charged by a previous moment on the dialectic. Much as in Marx's theory of capital, cultural objects participate in a continuous cycle of valorization through circulation—a study like this just makes a synchronic cut and tries to show how the processes of valorization work for a specific case and moment—and the actual value of the product is not fully realized until it is consumed.[10]

Music sociology has gained momentum (Hennion 1993, 2001; Born 1995; Eyerman and Jamison 1998; DeNora 2000, 2003; Bull 2001; Grazian 2003; Atkinson 2006; Becker and Faulkner 2009; McCormick 2009) but still remains underdeveloped. This study of the Buenos Aires opera scene aspires to contribute to the collective endeavor of cultural sociologists, seeking to explain how people attach themselves to and engage with music by emphasizing the dimensions that constrain and afford meaning, building up from previous work and integrating levels of analysis. Comparative work will help us better understand, not only who listens to certain types of music, but also how and why. In doing so, we will have also responded to the key problem José Luis had with the frames and tools sociologist have used to inquire about why people attend opera (and other activities considered high culture). He asked me: "Why is it that you sociologists always ask about if I go to the opera to be seen, to meet people, to see my friends, to achieve a better professional status, but always fail to ask me if I go because I like it or, better, because I love it?"

NOTES

PREFACE

1. Originally from Colombia, *cumbia* has been well-known and appreciated in Argentina for a long time, but it gained nationwide scope and attention when it became popular among the lower-class people in the main urban centers in the 1990s. The basic rhythm structure is 4/4. Owing to its origins, both African and native New World influences can be felt in *cumbia*.
2. For the 2001 performance of *Tosca*, sung by Darío Volonté, the state government sent twenty-four buses full of people from the Colón parking lot to La Plata.

INTRODUCTION

1. The German composer Richard Wagner called opera *Gesamtkunstwerk*, or "total work of art." For him, opera was a synthesis of all other arts as it united music, drama, visual arts, and stagecraft on an unprecedented scale.
2. The tide might be slowly changing, however, as recent books by Atkinson (2006), Johnson, Fulcher, and Ertman (2007), and Johnson (2008) bring opera back into sociological scrutiny.
3. On these points, see Adorno (1962, 1994), DiMaggio (1982a, 1982b, 1992), and Gramsci (1951), respectively.
4. As Adorno (1992, 20) has said, opera was movies before movies.
5. Social theory has dealt with love in many ways: relating it to domination (Foucault 1972, 1978; Benjamin 1988); using it as the paradigmatic example to bridge the dichotomous distinction between meanings and interests in the modern world (Zelizer 2005; Illouz 2007); using it to explain how *longue durée* macroprocesses have affected the intimate sphere and mating etiquette and patterns (Elias 1978/1994); showing how it works as a cultural frame that shapes behaviors and expectations, but is not coherent and unitary, and is used according to circumstances

—— 195 ——

(Swidler, 2001); using it to define the aesthetic realm as the cultural arena where we charge forms with value or affection (Geertz 1983); using it to scrutinize how the *romantic love complex* distorted American thinking on the topics of love and marriage (Goode 1959); using it to explore the changing meaning of sex and affection (Seidman 1991); and using it to discuss the rationality of practices deemed irrational (Heimer and Stinchcombe 1980).

6. I should make note here of the work by Sigmund Freud (1920/2003, 1930/2005) and Herbert Marcuse (1955) that traced the role of eros as a creative force. In Freud's work, eros was also referred to in terms of libido, libidinal energy, or love, as the life instinct innate in all humans. It is the desire to create life and favors productivity and construction. Here, eros is characterized as the tendency toward cohesion and unity, whereas the death drive is the tendency toward destruction. Even with the recognition of the existence of this powerful force, Freud and Marcuse also dealt with the struggle between this drive to pleasure and its repression. The conflict was postulated by Freud in *Civilization and Its Discontents* (1930/2005) as the struggle between human instincts and the repression brought on by the socially tuned conscience. Freud claimed that the biological clash between eros and civilization is inevitable and results in the history of man being one of his repression. Even if one of the main purposes of civilization is to bind men libidinally to one another, love and civilization eventually come into conflict with one another. Civilization itself, thus, is conflicted, the product of antagonistic drives and impulses. For Marcuse, Freud's mistake was to see the repression of drives, not as a historically situated phenomenon resulting from particular (and, therefore, mutable) social conditions, but as an absolute given indispensable to the growth of civilization. Marcuse's main argument appears to be that capitalist society suppresses sexuality and, thereby, perpetuates and creates neuroses. His utopian sketch of eros makes of it a culture builder and the reconciliation of reason and instinct, and, as such, he diverges from Freud, who makes of cultural practices the civilized sublimation of those erotic drives.

7. I follow here Taylor's (1989) definition of *transcendence*. For Taylor, transcendence gives us a sense of reality and of the good as something beyond the immediate world around us. Moreover, his discussion of self-transcendence supposes going beyond mere self-interest (as the metaphor of capital exchange would have it) and more limited notions of the self, involving the process of self-formation and transformation I want to emphasize throughout this book.

8. For an understanding of cultural-capital theory and its early uses in American sociology, see Lamont and Lareau (1988).

9. On production, see Arian (1972), Hirsch (1972, 2000), Peterson and Berger (1975), Crane (1987, 1992, 1997), DeNora (1991), Lopes (1992, 2002), Towse (1993), Peterson (1997), Anand (2000), Dowd, Liddle, Lupo, and Borden (2002), and Dowd (2004). On distribution and evaluation, see Sarfatti-Larson (1993), Platner (1996), Peterson and Berger (1996), Shrum (1996), Fine (2003, 2004), Anand and Peterson (2004), Lena (2004), and Rossman (2004). On consumption, see Peterson and Simkus (1992), Bryson (1996, 1997), Peterson and Kern (1996), and Van Eijck (2001).

10. Though Becker recognizes the indeterminate character of the work of art as the main contribution of sociology to the study of the arts, he also lays out the work-

ing premise that, in principle, works of art are never truly finished but have a long history comprised of different stages that can be viewed as "the work." The many mediations that shape decisions of what is the work of art are, for him, the subject of the sociology of the arts and, as seen in this case, what audiences lash up to.

11. For a good review and criticism of this literature, see Robinson (2002).

12. Classical sociology has explored the link between objective and subjective culture. See, e.g., the work of Simmel (1911, 1916) and the typology of music listening coined by T. W. Adorno (1962), which combined forms of affiliation with the materiality the music afforded. Unlike Adorno, however, I am not interested in the diverse ways in which particular patterns relate to other social series, like social class. Rather, I am looking for the variation within a very particular kind of listener, one that would constitute only one position among the many Adorno proposed—and among the many that exist empirically at the Colón and in general. For a contemporary typology of music listeners, see McCormick (2009), which explores the internal variation among listeners in music competitions, showing the active work that goes into being an informed member of an audience and how the audience works collectively as a public sphere.

13. For a brief overview of this literature, see Buford (1988), Hornby (1992), Jenkins (1992), Jindra (1994), Harrington and Bielby (1995), Adams (1998), Fine (1998), Archetti (1999), Bennett and Dawe (2001), Parks (2002), Lopes (2006), Borer (2008), and Wolk (2007).

14. The exception being Pearson (2007).

15. The problems are more extreme in the journalistic literature on self-obsession, where, once the usual sociological suspects (class, gender, in-group socialization, the moral economy of the crowd, age) are exhausted (and the phenomenon in question is not fully explained), what is left in terms of key analytic devices are psychological reductionism and claims of almost pathological irrationality—though, as in the case of the 1997 American film adaptation of Nick Hornby's *Fever Pitch* (1992), you can grow and mature out of it.

16. Dilthey's *Verstehen* (see, e.g., Dilthey 1988) seems to be the conceptual frame more suited for this kind of comprehensive understanding. In it, the ethnographic authority is based on sharing a common experience, an experience that is constituted and reconstituted in a common sphere and works as the frame of reference against which all texts, events, facts, and their interpretations are compared.

17. From classic theorists like Simmel (1950) to more contemporary approaches (Said 1996), the figure of the stranger, or the one who positions himself relatively outside the inside, has been granted a special epistemological status.

CHAPTER ONE

1. The importance of the opera house was such that, when people liked the quality of other endeavors, be it tango, soccer, or even boxing, they would sing: "Al Colón, al Colón!" (To the Colón, to the Colón).

2. It is unclear how much money this would be nowadays. According to certain sources, it would be close to US$19 million; according to others—basing their estimate on the U.S. consumer index—it would be around US$7 million.

3. A *porteño* is someone from Buenos Aires.

4. That did not mean that the city was left without opera, however; a series of other theaters attracted the audience members that frequented and the artists that used to appear at the Colón.

5. We can state, following Gorelik (1998), that this is the period when the whole city was planned under the dual-matrix park grid. This particular matrix generated population growth and the integrative and equalitarian inclusion of migrants as citizens.

6. Two other Paris-inspired diagonals were built years later. They also start at the Plaza de Mayo and cross the Obelisk in the north and the Avenida de Mayo in the south. The diagonal going north ends at the square surrounded by the Palace of Justice and the Colón. They are the only part of Buenos Aires that reproduces the sense of proportion and perspective of the rue de Rivoli.

7. The Colón was originally going to be located at the current site of the National Congress.

8. This list (de la Guardia and Herrera 1933, 9) included former presidents (Juarez Celman), traditional last names from independence days (Dorrego), families who had made their fortune with cattle (Anchorena, Pacheco), merchants who got rich through exports and transportation (Mihanovich), and the architects in charge of the project (Tamburini and Dormal).

9. José Pacheco y Anchorena, Enrique Arana, Julio Peña, Elisa F. de Juarez Celman, Manuel Cobo, Luis Linck, Alfredo Demarchi, Enrique Flynn, Juan José Romero, Pablo Amespil, Santiago Barrabino, Pio Perrone, Rosa A. de Tornquist, Enriqueta L. de Dorrego, Sara C. Resta, Mercedes O. de Anchorena, Nicolas Mihanovich, A. Tamburini, and twenty other subscribers.

10. Pueyrredon, e.g., is the name of one of the first general directors of the country, while Mitre and Roca were the last names of two of the most important modernizing presidents.

11. This tradition has continued, with some adjustments. Nowadays, the president and the city mayor reserve the central boxes of the lower-balcony level, which are utilized at the discretion of the house authorities.

12. Protocol demanded that the president sit in the central balcony with his ministers and the city mayor. To his right would be his wife and her guests, to his left the wife of the mayor and a few other distinguished female guests. During the first intermission, the president and his retinue would pay their respects to the ladies. During the second intermission, a drink would be served, and the president and the other government officials could walk freely and mingle with the rest of the guests in the orchestra seats and balconies. No one would leave the performance until the president had done so himself.

13. These were the first two presidents elected democratically in modern Argentina. Their attendance shows how, even after the electoral reform of 1912, popularly elected presidents still followed the protocol established by the liberal elite.

14. The United States sent its ambassador but also, and more importantly, a fleet of four ships to parade next to the recently finished Puerto Nuevo.

15. The opera was composed by the Italian conductor Ettore Panizza, who divided his allegiance between the Met and the Colón.

16. On May 18, 1999, the tenor Darío Volonté (a veteran of the Falklands War) was compelled to give an encore of the aria. According to most newspapers, it was the first time in history that an aria was repeated during the most expensive and elegant subscription series (*gran abono*), which is black tie only; its audience is usually perceived as the least effusive of all the series audiences.

17. The new version premiered at the gala on July 9, 1945, in front of Military President Farrell and the then labor secretary Juan Domingo Perón.

18. The frenzy meant that, by the beginning of the twentieth century, opera made it to the northernmost part of the country; both in Salta and in La Rioja, theaters had opera. The enumeration continues with houses in Santa Fe, Cordoba, Santiago del Estero, and Tucuman, all of which were inaugurated during the first fifteen years of the century.

19. In Buenos Aires, the Teatro de la Opera opened in 1872, and, during the twenty years the Colón was closed, it ruled the opera activity of the city. The Politeama, a bit smaller and more modest in scope, opened in 1879. Two smaller theaters, the Nacional and the Odeon, which combined opera and other spectacles, opened in 1882 and 1892, respectively. The small Argentino also opened its doors in 1892. In 1907, the Coliseo opened and, with a seating capacity of 2,550, sought to match the power of the Colón. A provincial census of Buenos Aires State counted twenty-four theaters, many of which included opera in their seasons.

20. The Colón presented Pareto, Perini, and Anselmi (who also sung the national anthem) and the international stars Titta Ruffo and Vitale; the Opera cast included Clasenti, Smirnov, Stracciari, and Mardones; and, last but not least, the Coliseo had a roster that included Bevignani, Constantino, Galeffi, and Maestro Barone. This was a most extreme case of the ongoing battle between two opera cartels that had, e.g., fought over the rights to premiere *Otello* in 1888 and *Tosca* in 1902.

21. Aside from Buenos Aires, no other Argentinean city matched Rosario, the country's other big port, which had three opera houses. Opera activity in Rosario in the 1910s was comparable with that in Buenos Aires as it was fed by the same troupe of impresarios that managed the Colón, the Coliseo, and the Politeama. It included international stars like Caruso, Galli-Curci, Tetrazzini, and the Titta Ruffo–Maria Barrientos pairing. As Margaret Cohen (2002, 23) emphasizes, the role of "the waterways of Modernity" is crucial to understanding the patterns through which modern European culture traveled, changed, and reproduced itself throughout the globe. Opera in Argentina is an obvious case of this as the circuit was organized by impresarios following the possibilities of maritime and riverine travel, from Rio to Montevideo and from the Uruguayan capital to Buenos Aires and then Rosario.

22. Ramón L. Falcón was in charge of the repression of the May 1 celebrations that culminated in eight deaths and over a hundred injuries. Falcón had a curious relationship to opera, too. According to Salessi (2000, 139), he was worried about the ridicule suffered by police officers and other civil servants at the opera house since the lyric theater was "a school of mores, because of the moral influence it imposes over the popular masses."

23. In a peculiar way, this is another sign of the cosmopolitan character of Buenos Aires as other anarchist attacks during the late nineteenth century and first few

years of the twentieth had killed the president of the United States, William McKinley, the president of France, Sadi Carnot, the empress Elizabeth of Austria, the Italian king Humberto Primo, and the Russian czar Alexander II.

24. The *paraíso*, the *tertulia*, and the *cazuela* are the top floors of the opera house. All three have seats at the front and a standing area at the back. The *paraíso* allows both men and women to stand together (it can accommodate up to three hundred people), while the *tertulia* and the *cazuela*, following an old tradition, have a strict gender separation in the standing area (which in each can accommodate up to one hundred people). Early in the twentieth century, only women would sit in the *tertulia* seats. These three areas (plus the *galería*, a small section of the *paraíso*) are the cheapest in the house. Seats are five times cheaper than seats in the orchestra and the lower balconies and boxes, and standing tickets are twenty to twenty-five times cheaper.

25. The Colón has been a favorite stage for planned political assassinations. For instance, in 1948, an opposition group led by Cipriano Reyes tried to kill the then-president Perón and his wife, Evita, during the Columbus Day gala.

26. The book is considered one of the first and most important examples of *gauchesca*, a genre embraced by the nationalist elite at the end of the nineteenth century that uses what was thought to be the dialect of the gaucho. Prieto (1988) has shown how *gauchesca* texts were for the elite a way of affirming their own legitimacy and rejecting the disquieting presence of foreigners, a nostalgic device for the displaced creole population that rebelled against new urban forms, and a visible and immediate way of assimilating for the newly arrived.

27. The extension of this model of analysis to other cities—e.g., Milan (Santoro 2000) and Manchester (Storey 2006)—attempts to uncover a pattern in the development of the production and consumption of opera as high art and provides us with a basis for comparison.

28. It was common among opera houses around the world to mount productions that were sung in translation. However, while the other big non-European opera house, New York's Met, premiered *Tannhäuser* in German in November 1884, it took Buenos Aires almost forty more years to break away from the hegemony of Italian.

29. According to Gramsci (1951), the popular character of opera is what caused the absence of serial romance novels like those found in France and England during the late nineteenth century and the early twentieth.

30. All this information comes from Dillon and Sala (1997).

31. There is also evidence of parallel attendance growth within the Jewish population. Looking at the *cazuela* roster, we find last names like Pawlosky and Schudt.

32. As I have already hinted, this heterogeneity is undoubtedly related to the European (especially Spanish and Italian) ancestry of a considerable part of Argentina's urban population. As Cinel (1982), Massey (1998), and Moya (1998) have shown, Argentina was behind only the United States and ahead of Australia, Canada, and Brazil in the number of immigrants received during this time, and the Buenos Aires population was totally transformed by this immigration influx. According to Moya (1998, 46), the total number of immigrants received by Argentina between 1820 and 1932 was 6,501,000, which, including their second- and third-generation descendants, resulted in almost 78.5 percent of the population at the end of that era. Italian arrivals ac-

counted for 45 percent of the total, Spaniards for 33 percent (with 54 percent of them coming from Galicia), and Eastern European Jews for a little more than 3 percent.

33. The area included all the spaces and arenas for sociability provided by the local organizations (libraries, cooperatives, sport clubs) and the surrounding common parks and plazas.

34. Interestingly enough, the first radio transmission in Argentina was of an opera performance. On August 28, 1920, four radio enthusiasts transmitted *Parsifal*, conducted by Felix Weingartner, from the Coliseo.

35. The July 9, 1949, gala, at which Maria Callas sang for Perón and Evita, is an example of how protocol was followed to the last detail. Perón was received at the entrance of the house by the city mayor and the Colón's director. He was then escorted by the chief of the presidential guard amid a double row of grenadiers. Evita was not next to him, as women and men had not sat together on these occasions since the opening gala in 1908. Instead, she sat with the wives of the ministers in the right *avant-scène* box. During intermission, he went to the Salón Dorado (Golden hall) for a toast. Callas was then an unknown singer, and the newspapers of the time seldom make a point of her being there, emphasizing rather the presence of the local singer Delia Rigal. See, e.g., *Clarín*, July 10, 1949.

36. Peronism related to classical music in a different way than it did to other elite cultural practices, trying to appropriate its highly symbolic character. It never confronted the inherent qualities of opera; it tried only to broaden access to it to include as many people as possible, in terms of both its production and its consumption. Its goal was to make high-culture goods accessible to everyone without changing the social and economic structure of society.

37. The ratio goes all the way to one hundred to one if we take the standing-room tickets into account. Prices today range from US$1.50 for standing tickets to US$125 for *gran abono* orchestra seating.

38. In 2001, after investors took large sums of capital out of the country, people fearing the worst began withdrawing large sums of money from their bank accounts, turning pesos into dollars, and sending them abroad. The government then enacted a set of measures that froze all bank accounts for twelve months. Because of this allowance limit, many Argentines became enraged and took to the streets of important cities. President de la Rúa declared a state of emergency, but this only worsened the situation, precipitating the violent protests of December 20 and 21 in the Plaza de Mayo during which demonstrators clashed with police. The confrontation ended with several dead and precipitated the fall of the government. De la Rúa eventually resigned, and a political crisis ensued. The president of the Senate took office but quickly resigned, followed by the president of the Chamber of Deputies. The Legislative Assembly convened with the goal of creating a more legitimate interim government. It finally appointed Adolfo Rodriguez Saá, then the governor of San Luis, who also resigned after defaulting on the US$93 billion public debt the country had accumulated.

39. Figures are taken from the city budget.

40. In comparison, the Madrid Real Opera House has a US$60 million budget and a state subsidy of 65 percent. The Milan Scala has become a mixed foundation, and the state participation is only 15 percent. All these institutions, as well as the Paris

Opéra, self-finance a third of their budgets with ticket and subscription sales. The Bavarian State Opera finances half of its budget with the income it produces. The Colón, on the other hand, produces only 16 percent of what would be necessary to finance itself. The Colón's foundation, which deals with private sponsors and patrons, provides 2 percent through advertisements in the program and house rentals to corporate patrons. On the other extreme of the continuum, the Metropolitan Opera gets no state subsidies, other than renting the hall to Lincoln Center for US$1 million, and finances itself with tickets and subscriptions (41 percent) and donations by private patrons (59 percent).

41. These are numbers extracted from a 2002 internal report by the house authorities (who were in charge from 2000 to 2004). I could not get other numbers released despite many interviews and phone conversations with house officers over the years.

42. Some authors, like Sanguinetti (2002) and Pollini (2002), contend that the house stands 1,000 people. Benmayor (1990) puts the number at 1,500. The city, on its official Web site, places it at 700. Looking at the floor plans, and consulting with the box office, I would suggest 620 as a more realistic number: 300 go to the *paraíso*, 100 to the *tertulia*, another 100 to the *cazuela*, and 120 stand behind the orchestra seats. Still, for an average audience of 2,000 per performance, the percentage holding standing tickets (almost a third) is quite high.

43. In comparison, the Metropolitan Opera House has only 175 standing places. La Scala had 160–200, recently replaced by 139 seats at the standing-room price. The San Francisco Opera has 200 standing places, while the Opéra Bastille has only 62. A comparable house is the Vienna State Opera, which has space for 567 standees, including 124 behind the orchestra seats. The Chicago Lyric does not offer any standing-room tickets.

44. There were twenty-two performances of eight operas at Avellaneda (seats 560 people), twenty-four performances of seven operas in La Plata (where the Argentino seats 2,200), and forty-nine performances of thirteen operas at the Avenida (1,250). The remaining thirty-nine performances of twenty-six operas were offered at other diverse stages, which house 200–600 people.

45. Enzo Valenti Ferro was one of the central figures of the Argentinean opera world for much of the second half of the twentieth century, and his influence can be felt even after his death (in 2009 at ninety-seven). He started the Wagnerian Music Association, a German-oriented concert society, presided over the Critic's Association, and was the general manager of the Colón for twelve years during two different time periods. In 1986, he created the Colón's Chamber Opera Company. His many books provide a comprehensive understanding of the history of opera performances in the city.

CHAPTER TWO

1. Bourdieu (1984, 17), e.g., cites attending classical-music concerts or playing an instrument as practices that suggest a higher class because of the "rarity of the conditions under which the corresponding dispositions are acquired." Those conditions include a familiarity with high culture not learned in educational institutions but transmitted and naturalized in the immediate family circle.

2. A second strategy, which has become increasingly prevalent among contemporary ethnographic endeavors—entering an apprenticeship (O'Connor 2005; Wacquant 2005), physically immersing oneself in the social world, following the steps of the natives, acquiring their skills and understanding body and soul, passing through diverse rites until becoming a full member of the community—was outside my range of possibilities. Coming from a family of musicians, I am already a part of the music world, and, if anything, the challenge was, not to domesticate the exotic while embodying it, but to find the distinctive qualities of a world that seemed second nature to me.

3. The date of the performance was June 1948. Another fan I interviewed also remembers that performance, but as the first opera that she ever heard on the radio.

4. Until 1971, these high schools certified their graduates to teach elementary school.

5. Alicia was not alone in her quest for recognition. León, who got very sick during my fieldwork in 2005, called me twice, the first time to apologize for having to cancel the interview we had set up because he was hospitalized, the second time to ask me whether I wanted to interview him anyway. We chatted on the phone about his life as an opera fan for forty-five minutes.

6. *Upper-middle-class* means that they own more than one property and at least one car, travel abroad frequently, and have a credit card and a steady source of income.

7. Alfredo has spent his whole life working for the Argentinean tax collection agency. He did not go to college in order to become an accountant; he completed a six-year high school program to earn his *perito mercantil*, which certifies him to do accounting.

8. The educational structure in Argentina is different than that in the United States. In Argentina, one can achieve a degree in law, architecture, or medicine through a six-year *licenciatura* program.

9. Among the most representative studies are Feijoo (1993, 1995), Barbeito and Lo Vuolo (1995), Minujin (1995), and Wortman (2003).

10. They use the marketing categories ABC1, C2, D1, D3, and E to refer to these groups. These categories combine the educational level of the head of household, his or her occupation, the possession of durable goods like homes, cars, televisions, and air conditioners, access to credit cards, etc. (*Plan estratégico* 2006).

11. The same sources calculate that, in 1996, e.g., the middle class made up 49 percent of the city population vs. 30 percent in 2002.

12. They have completed their university studies, own at least one car, and work as independent professionals or in managerial positions.

13. They have completed elementary and high school, but most of them either did not attend or dropped out of college. There is a 60 percent chance that they own a car, and they either are specialized workers, own a small business, or hold an intermediate position in a public office.

14. They have completed elementary and high school, but only a fifth of them attended college. Only 40 percent of them own a car, and they either own a shop without any staff or work as semiskilled workers or nonhierarchical personnel.

15. They dropped out of high school, are nonqualified workers, and are employed only temporarily or at the lowest levels in either the public or the private sector.

16. I have tried for four years to conduct a survey of the house population. Unfortunately, I have never been able to do so owing to a general lack of interest and

cooperation, a complicated and bureaucratic organizational chart, and constant staffing changes in positions of power.

17. These numbers come from a report composed by the Equis Group after surveying the Avenida's audience from July 24 to August 3, 2003, during performances of *La bohème*. The opera company's executive director, María Jaunarena, has been generous, not only in sharing these data with me, but also in letting me know that the high numbers in the lower echelons might have been due to the popularity of the opera, which makes it more accessible to nonhabitual audiences.

18. This should not come as a surprise as the median age was sixty, which was also the case for my interviewees.

19. Among the interviewees, there were at least seven who studied piano when they were young, two men who studied violin, and five women who took ballet lessons.

20. With almost 400,000 Jewish inhabitants, Argentina has the third largest Jewish population in the Americas, behind the United States and Canada, and the sixth largest in the world. Of those 400,000, 244,000 reside in the Gran Buenos Aires area and 156,000 in the city of Buenos Aires. Jewish *porteños* make up 6 percent of the city's total population (*Estudio de población judía* 2004).

21. Over the last twenty-five years, the north-south division of the city has been reinforced; 75 percent of foreign direct investment is located in the downtown-north corridor (Cicolella 1999). This division is continually strengthened through the suburbanization process that occurs with the construction of highways and the simultaneous change in the radial growth pattern as settlements no longer follow the railroad tracks, partly owing to the end of indirect subsidies given to homeowners after the privatization of public lines (Torres 1993). This results in new suburbanization that avoids the poverty ring and the traditional suburbs (Torres 2001).

22. From 1939 to 1959, the price of public transportation multiplied by five while the cost of living multiplied by over thirty (Torres 1998).

23. While in 1947 property ownership in Gran Buenos Aires was approximately 27 percent, in 1960 it was 58 percent and in 1967 67 percent (Torres 1993).

24. The expansion of all public services, like water or electricity, followed the same pattern: starting in the core of the city and slowly radiating to the outskirts. The suburbs beyond the city borders have their own municipal authorities, and their public services depend on the Buenos Aires State government.

25. The Argentinean historian Eduardo Hourcade (1999) has shown how one of the consequences of the occupation of the land and the organization of colonies was the importing of a European sense of sociability. Cities like Punta Alta, Dolores, Azul, and San Nicolás developed as either ports or trading posts and had a significant influx of European migrants. Most of these towns are small, ranging nowadays from twenty to sixty thousand inhabitants, and most are located within a 160-mile radius of Buenos Aires, although Villalonga (Franco's hometown) is a smaller rural colony close to Punta Alta, 450 miles to the south.

26. The preferred metaphors are *explosion*, *impact*, and *shock*. I will elaborate more on the embodied character of opera activity later in chapter 4.

27. Daniela, Alicia, Antonio, Esteban, Guillermo, Roberto, Diana, José Luis, and Gustavo are currently married or part of a couple. Andrea, Irma, and Germán were

married for a long time and were either widowed or got divorced, but all of them have children from those relationships.

28. Although Germán was a civil engineer, he spent much of his time as a radio producer, traveling around the country looking for pieces for his show.

29. Behind Bourdieu's understanding of cultural reproduction, there is a highly centralized power that punishes every deviation as an infraction. While that might work for France, in Argentina the most interesting literary works of the early and mid-twentieth century came from those middle-class factions that had the utmost respect for and interest in European high culture but felt free to reconfigure it and play with it, like a *bricoleur*, up to the point of producing original works. For an analysis of the relationship between the petit bourgeoisie and high culture during diverse periods of Argentinean culture, see García Canclini (1979), Prieto (1988), Sarlo (1988, 1991), Gutierrez and Romero (1995), and Altamirano (1997).

30. I use the word *amateur* in the French sense, popularized by Hennion (2000), of "lover, appreciator, fan."

CHAPTER THREE

1. Piscitelli sang the main female part, Maria, of Verdi's *Simon Boccanegra* in 2003.

2. Anderson and Piscitelli both sang the leading role in the opera. Anderson had four dates, but Piscitelli, her understudy, managed to eclipse her in her two performances. The falling rate of the peso against the dollar would make Piscitelli a far more frequent presence at the Colón than Anderson.

3. She was Elisabeth de Valois in the 2004 season.

4. Leona Mitchell sang the role of Amelia in the Colón production of 1994, the last time it had been performed.

5. She was actually referring to the 1995 performance, which included the Finnish soprano Karita Mattila, the renowned baritone José van Dam, and the bass Ferruccio Furlanetto.

6. In 2005, some members of the opera house orchestra circulated a petition in support of hiring some of the older fans as tour guides.

7. Sociology has dealt with this nascent state in many ways. Weber made of these moments the unstable foundation for a charismatic attachment to an authority figure; Durkheim attributed the genesis of value formation and commitment to collective effervescence. More contemporary approaches, like those of Alberoni (1983), Giddens (1992), and Joas (2000, 2007), have focused on the phenomenological character of these experiences, though they mostly refer to religious or emotional experiences, and not to aesthetic ones, as intense moments of self-transcendence and self-formation that then get routinized or institutionalized.

8. For an example from the literature on opera, see Levin (1994). For sociological examples, see Gamson (1994), Grindstaff (2002), Grazian (2004, 2007), and Atkinson (2006).

9. This was the case with Massenet's *Don Quichotte* and Verdi's *I Lombardi*, both of which premiered in Argentina at the Colón during the 2005 season.

10. The Argentino is La Plata's main opera house, the second most important in the country.

11. Johnson (1995) traces the beginning of romantic listening to the late nineteenth century. It involved a new way of listening that not only involved a private understanding of listening as something closed off from community and inaccessible to language but also implied new rules of etiquette and the physical transformation of the theaters and concert halls. The result was a new experience: deeper, more personal, and more powerful.

12. In order to understand fully how initiation instances simplify complex cultural forms, see Turner (1967, 1974).

13. Delia Rigal sang the title role for the four performances mounted during the 1952 season. She was a local favorite and shared the bill the only time Maria Callas came to sing *Aida* in 1949.

14. Here, I am adapting Katz's (1999) discussion of road rage as an embodiment and dramatization of the anger caused by being cut off from the car and the road.

15. In one of his classes on verismo, Arce also used instrumental interludes as an opportunity to speak about the opera and its meanings.

16. An example of this with a male voice is Edgardo and Raimondo's final aria in *Lucia*.

17. It is important to consider here the complexity of opera as a cultural form in comparison to other, nonmusic forms or more codified music materials (like those from Broadway musicals, where the end is clear in a belt-'em-out number kind of way). Learning where to clap is the result of getting acquainted with and habituated to the nuances of the material. Unlike other instances of performer-audience interaction, e.g., political speeches in public rallies (Atkinson 1984; Heritage and Greatbatch 1986), in which the speaker uses a repertory of tones, tropes, and rhetorical figures to indicate to the audience where and when to clap, opera arias, with tricky changes of volume and pace, make coordinated clapping quite complicated. Claims of status lay in knowing, not only where and when to show appreciation, but also when not to, making sure not to mess up the aesthetic ensemble. As Phil Smith commented (personal communication): nobody wants to be the only person clapping.

18. The horseshoe shape of the hall has a curve 75 meters long (some 246 feet); its minor diameter is 29.25 meters (some 96 feet); its biggest diameter is 32.65 meters (107 feet). It is 92 feet high, and the stage is 16 meters (52 feet) wide and 8 meters (26 feet) high.

19. I write this in the passive voice since, as Hennion (2007) reminds us, these forms of attachment are presented by those engaged in them as something actively suffered, to which the person attaches himself or herself while surrendering to it in an almost passive way.

20. This is another point at which this model complements Becker's. Since Becker was discussing the initiation into a deviant practice, it would have been odd to find formalized initiation situations.

CHAPTER FOUR

1. For a thorough presentation and analysis of diverse cases of cultural practices in which upper-middle-class people participate, see Wortman (2003).

2. For a more general assessment of the use of this metaphor as a model for cultural analysis, see Geertz (1983).

3. Wayne Koestenbaum (1993) made the same point when pointing out that music turns language into "songuish" liquid. He wrote: "I don't care about understanding; I want to be pleased by the Songuish Part. I care about an opera's words only because music has garlanded them. I love the words 'Ma il viso mio su luis risplanderá,' from Boito's libretto to Verdi's *Falstaff*, because music has touched them" (185).

4. A system that categorizes singers by certain voice types, or *Fächer* (sg. *Fach*), in order to match singers with roles that are best suited for them. It tries to categorize voices by vocal weight and color.

5. Despite being a lyric soprano, Renata Tebaldi was renowned for a supposed fiery rivalry with Maria Callas. Their quarrel started during the early 1950s, when Callas was Tebaldi's understudy at Milan's Scala for the title role in *Aida*. The rivalry between the sopranos caused shouting matches at performances, the fans of the one loudly voicing their support and causing an equally loud response from the fans of the other. The culmination of this rivalry came in an article in *Time* magazine where Callas was quoted as saying that comparing herself to Tebaldi was like comparing champagne with Coca-Cola. On September 16, 1968, the much-publicized feud came to an end when Callas went backstage after a performance of *Adriana Lecouvreur* to congratulate her rival for a job well done. The two sopranos, in front of photographers, posed and embraced. Until her death in 1977, Callas would have nothing but kind words to say about her former nemesis. Tebaldi sung at the Colón in 1953, Callas in 1949.

6. Ethnomethodologists like Harold Garfinkel (1964) refer to and have used breaching experiments to study social interaction. These are experiments designed to observe how people react to the breach of implicit social rules or norms.

7. At the Colón, this is usually the lateral second and third rows of the *tertulia*, which have a less-than-partial view of the stage; the same thing happens with the lateral *galería* section and with some lateral back seats in the *cazuela* and the *paraíso* and also at any spot that has a column in front of it.

8. They cost the same, 5 pesos (roughly US$1.60), four times less than a movie ticket and three times less than the cheapest standing-room-only ticket to a first-division soccer game.

9. The plot of the opera revolves around the main character—the Dutchman—who is captive aboard a phantom ship and doomed to travel with it forever. This 1987 staging had not been performed since 1992. Every other time it has been performed it has been a new production. In comparison, the Met has played its 1989–90 production in four other seasons.

10. *Barbiere*, an opera performed almost yearly until the late 1940s, had been seen only three times after 1962 (1969, 1991, 1997). In comparison, the Met performed its 1981–82 new production in thirteen seasons until 2004–5.

11. During the early 1980s, it was common for fans from the top floor to throw eggs at the performances they did not like. On one occasion, the 1981 *Traviata*, they painted the eggs black so that they could not be traced back to them and launched them right before the soprano, who was punished for being politically protected, could sing "Addio al passato."

12. For a thorough description and analysis of how sports fans and pop lovers usually act, see Gans (1974/1999), Elias and Dunning (1986), Bufford (1990), Archetti (1992), Gamson (1994), Hennion (1997), and Illouz (2003).

13. For a thorough discussion of music and bodies, see Alford and Szantos (1996), DeNora (2000, 2002, 2003), and Hutcheon and Hutcheon (2000).

14. In doing this, I follow the work of Alfred Schutz (1967), who discussed in detail the relation between the typifications we use and the provinces of meaning we build to make sense of the world we inhabit.

15. The metaphor is more than appropriate since the editorial team that produces the print publication has been historically in charge of publishing the cultural foodie magazine *Cuisine et vins*.

16. Veltri conducted many operas at the Metropolitan Opera, La Scala, Covent Garden, and, of course, the Colón and was the artistic director of the opera house from 1996 until his death on December 18, 1997, as well as of the Liceu Theater of Barcelona.

17. As explained in chapter 1, the Marconi Theater was a house focused mostly on the Italian repertory and Italian operetta. It opened in 1903 and staged its last performance in 1960. It catered to the local Italian community, mostly to working-class and lower-middle-class patrons.

18. *Chicken house* was the name given to the audience on the top floors of the opera houses in Buenos Aires. While the name originated in Italian houses like the Marconi, which usually fenced off the loudest and most aggressive fans so that they could not throw food at the performers, it is still used to refer to the *paraíso* audience.

19. This is the name of the river that divides the city from the southern and western sections of the larger metropolitan region.

20. Despite possible appearances, this circuit is not like the community circuit in the United States. All the performances at the Avenida and the Roma that I attended were part of cycles that were reviewed in national newspapers (especially *La Nación* and *La Prensa*, which have the most extensive coverage of music life in Buenos Aires).

21. Offenbach's *Tales of Hoffmann* has four parts for soprano (Olympia, Antonia, Giulietta, and Stella). The parts are a vocal and acting tour de force since they are very different (although Stella is a minor part when compared to the other three). Being able to sing all four parts—or at least the three soloists' roles—is considered a sign of greatness. At the Colón, this accomplishment has been achieved only twice, in 1921 (Ninon Vallin) and 1980 (Faye Robinson).

22. Especially in the version advanced by Michèle Lamont (see Lamont 1992, 2000; and Lamont and Molnar 2002).

CHAPTER FIVE

1. The sopranos that alternated in the main female roles during the 2005 season at the Colón were the Cuban singer Eglise Gutierrez and the American Leah Partridge, hardly famous voices. They both participate actively on the secondary international opera circuit, singing at provincial houses in Italy and the United States.

2. Max Weber (1978, 1997) offers a similar interpretation in his writings on religion.

3. José Cura was a protégé of Plácido Domingo's. He debuted at the Metropolitan Opera in New York City in 1999, sharing a cast with his mentor in the double bill *Cavalleria/Pagliacci*.

4. Pavarotti was playing Radames, the captain of the guard. In the scene Guillermo was talking about, Radames is coming back victorious from Ethiopia, bringing with him the defeated as prisoners.

5. The Met averages four new productions per season (the average of titles presented per season is twenty-three). A caveat is in order, however: the new productions are usually premieres or seldom-performed operas. The most-performed titles get renewed rarely (one new production for *Traviata* every ten years by the cinematic naturalist director Franco Zeffirelli; a new production in 2006–7 after twenty-five years and fourteen seasons for *Barbiere*; a 1981–82 production of *Bohème* that has been presented twenty-three times).

6. The other operas among the ten most performed in the history of the Colón are *Tosca* (four times in the last fifteen years), *Aida* (last produced in 1996), *Barbiere*, *Rigoletto* (three times since 1973), *Madame Butterfly* (five times in the last twenty-five years), Massenet's *Manon* (twenty-three times since 1910 but only four times in the last fifty years), *Il trovatore* (three times since 1990 and one of the most recently performed operas), and *Lucia* (five times in the last thirty years).

7. He was at the time the director of the Opera at Lausanne.

8. Calixto Bieito is a young Spanish stage director usually considered the enfant terrible of European opera for his radical reinterpretations of classic operas. He first gained notoriety with his production of Verdi's *Un ballo in maschera* for Barcelona's Liceu in 2001. He set the first scene of the opera on a split-level set; on the top half, the primary action of the scene (involving the king and his loyal subjects) played out. The conspirators were ranged along the bottom half of the stage, sitting on toilets with their pants around their ankles. More recently, his production of Mozart's *The Abduction from the Seraglio*, for the Komische Oper in Berlin, caused a big stir. He decided that the opera was about prostitution and the slave trade, so he made Bassa Selim the lord of a brothel rather than a harem and kept Constanza on a leash in a cage. He also hired actual sex workers to be onstage. Osmin sings the first aria naked in the shower, giving his genitals a good scrub. Later, he urinates in a glass and forces Blonde to drink it. Then, while Constanza sings "Marten aller Arten," he hacks up a prostitute with a knife, finally offering the soprano a pair of bloodied, severed nipples.

9. The critic Paul Bardin reasons that the almost unknown character of *I vespri* is the main reason why people did not get as crazy as they did with *Traviata*. People seem to think they know *Traviata* since they have seen endless versions of it, but the 2006 production was only the second time *I vespri* had been performed in Buenos Aires. The previous time had been in 1970.

10. However, not every work must stick to "the time period in which it was originally situated," "the spirit of the work," "the intentions of the author," "the work it was based on," or "the moment at which it was composed." The limits of innovation have to do with a double variation that rises from the same axis. One kind of variation distinguishes major from minor forms of opera (opera seria vs. opera buffa).

The second kind distinguishes some authors from others on a hierarchical scale that seems to reflect the musicological canon: Wagner, e.g., is considered untouchable, while some lesser-known Italian composers, and the lesser-known works of some better-known Italian composers, are deemed appropriate for variations in staging. For a musicological discussion of this canon, see Kerman (1956/1988). On how the canon came to be and became a site for political contestation, see Lindenberger (1984).

11. The sociologist Ari Adut (2004, 2005) has studied the mechanisms of scandal. The logic behind scandal is usually based on popular justice, where, by socially shaming the higher-status individual, the collective attempts to reclaim the monopoly of evaluation and reestablish the social (or, in this case, artistic) norms that were loosened by actors like the punished group or individual.

12. Adut (2005) himself includes examples of artistic scandals. He calls them *provocative scandals* since the transgression is publicized to a normative audience by the offender—usually by the public execution of the transgression.

13. The opera had been performed only three times since 1967, and most of my informants and interviewees still remembered the revered 1981 production, restaged in 1996. Among the contested topics of the 2005 staging were a giant plasma television in Valhalla and Fricka's second-act entrance in a roller-coaster car instead of a ram-drawn chariot. In comparison, the Met's last new production dates from the 1986–87 season and has been presented for ten more seasons.

14. Obviously, these are not the only people at the opera house. There are others who deploy their moral superiority by refusing to boo, even if they dislike the performance, to show their respect for the people who staged or performed it. Since they are usually on the same floors of the opera house as the booers, we are witnessing a competing understanding of community. There are also people who are disinvested enough not to boo, clap, or shush others and who consider those doing so "crazy."

15. For a full understanding of how stigma management works, see Goffman (1963).

16. This is a highly colloquial expression, derived from the rural countryside in the nineteenth century, meaning that you are not going to overextend yourself for something unworthy.

17. This is a point signaled by authors as diverse as Becker (1973), Foucault (1979, 2003), and Elias (1978/1994).

18. While I follow closely the work of Antoine Hennion in this section of the chapter, he and his collaborators have considered only the addict as the blueprint for practices of attachment or affiliation. In comparison, this chapter tries to show a further differentiation even within practices of intense aesthetic attachment.

19. For a more complete discussion of the hero ethic, see Weber (1975, 378).

20. While the obvious reference behind this would be to Marx and the passages in which he discussed the organic composition of capital, a few sociologists, like Jepperson and Swidler (1994), have adopted the distinction between dead and live forms of culture, with the former embodied in the infrastructure of institutions (i.e., resources and commitments) and easier to measure and capture since it requires less symbolic maintenance or ritual reinforcement than the latter.

21. The last title of the 2005 season, *Turandot*, was canceled and several performances

of *Capriccio, Lucia,* and *Die Walküre* were rescheduled, which meant that many of the originally programmed performers had to be replaced. City authorities closed the opera house in November.

22. Audience members are especially keen to befriend ushers. Some audience members become friends with the ushers outside the opera house context and rely on them to act as guides inside the opera house. One of the first times I called an informant, I left a message using my first name and saying that I was from the opera house; he was convinced that I was one of his usher friends.

23. The more organized and successful company would give me a hard time about getting in for free, while some of the others, especially after a poor opening night, would call me to offer, not just one, but two or three tickets for the next performance.

24. Bull (2004), following Adorno and Horkheimer (1972) and Taussig (1992), has discussed how the modern aesthetic understanding of pleasure is built on the sublimation of its erotic character and based on its aural quality.

25. The framing of music as therapy appears obvious for Buenos Aires, where psychoanalysis has been a cultural force for the last seventy years, so much so as to be a part of insurance plans or to shape the provision of services for the poor population through what has been called *the Lacanian Ward* (see Plotkin 2001, 2003; and Lakoff 2006).

26. A survey of the Juventus Lyrica audience at the Avenida shows that 12 percent are schoolteachers, which reinforces the relation between opera and pedagogical practice.

27. This is something that the sociological literature, with its emphasis on homogenizing the taste for classical music and the taste for opera, has failed to differentiate. The analysis of Bourdieu (1984) is an exception, carefully pointing as it does to intraclass distinctions as they are deployed, through homologies, between the field of productions and the positions in the social space.

28. While past-centric, this is an actual way of loving opera in the present. Unlike the topos of melancholy, which emphasizes a love for a never-fulfilling object, however, the desire is fulfilled, in the tension between the performances at the Colón or the Avenida and the intense and mediated activities outside the live circuit, like record listening at home, buying old bootleg versions at specialized houses like Piscitelli, participating in forums and discussions on radio shows, having listening sessions with old friends from the opera house, or attending DVD viewing sessions in private homes or cultural centers. The love of opera is never abandoned. What is abandoned sometimes, however, is the performance of such love at the live circuit.

29. A jeremiad is an act of self-flagellation in which the value of what does not exist anymore gets affirmed (Walzer 1988). The more committed to denouncing the person is, the bigger the sense of vocation, of mission.

30. To a certain extent, we can trace this trope as far back as the seventeenth century, when the dramas by Metastasio were produced as a reaction to the Venetian opera genre advocated by Monteverdi, which was perceived as decadent. For an analysis of this, see Roland (1991). I owe special thanks to Tom Ertman for both the observation and the reference.

31. The *Ring* cycle comprises *Das Rheingold, Die Walküre, Siegfried*, and *Götterdäm-merung*. Contra to accounts by many informants and interviewees, including some of the younger ones, the complete *Ring* cycle was performed in Buenos Aires at times as disparate as 1931, 1935, 1947, 1962, and 1967. And never in the house's history did a Wagnerian opera have two full casts for the principal roles. The 1947 production of *Die Walküre* was the closest, with a full second cast for every role but Wotan and Sieglinde.

32. The concert Tito refers to took place in 1941, the piece in question was actually Beethoven's Ninth, and the appearance was far from the conductor's Buenos Aires debut, which took place in 1903. In fact, Toscanini had appeared in the city many times in the intervening years, and his son, Giorgio, died there in 1906.

33. Several interviewees and informers told me stories about him. He would dress in a golden bow tie for the Puccini opera performances and in a silver one for a Verdi opera, to indicate the minor status of the latter. He would also bring flowers for the women on the opening night of any of Puccini's operas.

34. The sociology of religion has dealt with modern and medieval pilgrimages thoroughly. For a review of the literature, see Sumption (1975), Lukatis (1989), Osterrieth (1989), Pace (1989), and Zapponi (2007).

35. In this sense, the experience of opera is not different, e.g., from other forms of charismatic attachment, like the ones produced by radical politics. See, e.g., the work of Michael Walzer (1965).

36. For the most representative works among this literature, see Mark (1998) and Lizardo (2006).

CHAPTER SIX

1. Carlo Ginzburg (1986/1989) suggests a way of conceptualizing the changing ideas about enigmas and solutions in the late nineteenth century. He defines the epistemological model of *symptomatology*, examples of which he finds in Morelli's art connoisseurship, Freud's psychoanalysis, and Sherlock Holmes's detection methods. In this conjectural model, "marginal and irrelevant details . . . provide the key to a deeper reality, inaccessible by other methods" (87). The efficacy of such a key depends on the assumption of depth and on the existence of a conduit between the surface and the hidden recesses: "Reality is opaque; but there are certain points—clues, symptoms—which allow us to decipher it" (109).

2. While in many conversations colleagues suggested that I explore the relation between the country's recent crisis and the passion of the fans, I did not want to establish it by myself, linking two series of phenomena, as the first wave of sociologists of art have done (Heinich 2001), establishing that here is art, there is society, and, therefore, these must be the connections between the two. Following Hennion (1993), I thought that it was necessary to show the mediation that would articulate them, not as the neutral channels though which predetermined social forces operate, but rather as intermediaries with effectivities of their own that define the practice and the subject as it goes along. I was also interested, not in imposing my own definition of the situation on the self-understanding of the agents, but rather in looking for how they build the link, making the two cultural configurations

(opera attendance and the country's demise) one. If these fans did became more involved in the opera world after the crisis, then we should find that they get outside recognition for it, they started attending after 2001, or they have experienced an economic reversal that has left them only putative claims to status. As I have shown in chapters 2 and 5, none of these statements is true.

3. National decline is a persistent theme among middle-class Argentineans, refracted in various spheres. Socioeconomic decline, e.g., is seen as a slow process of degradation that is contrasted with an elusive golden age, exhausted—depending on whom asks—during the 1930s, the 1940s, or the 1970s (see Semán 2006; and de Santos 2009).

4. Kive Staiff was the director between 1996 and 1997 (Miguel Angel Veltri was the artistic director until his death in December 1997). Luis Osejevich took over in 1998—with the, contemporary composer Gerardo Gandini as the music director—only to be replaced in 1999 by the critic Juan Carlos Montero, who was himself replaced in 2000 by Rénan. Rénan lasted only that season, and the stage director Emilio Basaldua was named director during the 2001 season. Basaldua resigned in 2002 and was replaced by the critic and composer Gabriel Senanes, who lasted until 2004, when, after publicly denouncing the city government culture secretary and the house employees from the legal section who "conspired against him," he was ousted. Tito Capobianco came back to the country to assume the directorship after seventeen years as the, director of Pittsburgh Opera, but he lasted only a year and a half. After a brief moment in 2005, when the house's director of finance (Leandro Iglesisas) served as acting director, Marcelo Lombardero, a singer and *regisseur* born and bred in the house, became the artistic director. The institutional instability of the opera house pales, however, in comparison to the five presidents the country had in a ten-day period at the end of 2001. I suffered the constant instability firsthand as I had to contact a new set of authorities every time I visited Buenos Aires to conduct fieldwork and attempted to obtain authorization for a survey of the house audience.

5. A competing, less precise, less embodied, but a bit more imaginative epistemological configuration is advanced by Raymond Williams (1977), who utilizes concepts such as *formation* and *structure of feeling* to refer to these informal settings and to think in diffuse forms of ideology, sensibility, and consciousness. The key concept for him is that of experience, as something cognitively, rhetorically, bodily, and emotionally lived.

6. As Katz and Csordas (2003, 9) remind us: "No one just lives within the limited boundaries of face-to-face or immediately situated action. Ironically, 'symbolic interaction' developed by marshalling research within those boundaries, even though its philosophical father, George Herbert Mead, was deeply involved in the effort to capture the past-acknowledging and future-casting time horizons of social action as it is immediately lived. . . . The present exists only in dialectical relation to a past that it invokes and a future that calls out its details."

7. Auyero and Swistun studied the poisonous world of the flammable shantytown and how people go around making sense of their lead-loaded environment.

8. The second condition is when there is a crisis that results in the habitus not producing the results with which it is historically associated.

9. As Ernesto Laclau (1991) has suggested, any entity is both defined and limited by objects of alterity. Moreover, external figures, when constituted as menacing, help define and shape the limits of an identity.

10. A couple of fans referred to this when they saw the larger size of the new playbill and immediately reflected: "It's bigger so they can put more ads and Capobianco can make more money."

11. Raul Alfonsín was president of Argentina from December 10, 1983, to July 9, 1989. He was the first democratically elected president after many years of military government. His government sponsored the Trial of the Juntas, prosecuting some of the top members of the previous military regime for crimes committed during the Dirty War.

12. For reference, see Auyero (2001) and Benzecry (2006).

13. I am still using Weber's *Sociology of Religion* categories to make this assertion.

14. Tom Fox is an American singer who played Wotan, the main baritone role in both *Die Walküre* and *Das Rheingold* at the Colón in 2005. José Luis refers for comparative purposes to Hans Hotter, who sang the part of Wotan in both operas at Buenos Aires in 1962. In 1952, Hotter began his twelve-year association with Bayreuth, and, for the rest of the 1950s and 1960s, he was generally regarded as the world's leading Wagnerian bass-baritone, particularly associated with the role of Wotan. He also sang at Covent Garden, Munich, the Met, and the Vienna State Opera.

15. Scholars have diverged in conceptualizing the relation between nation, periphery, and metropolis. Frederic Jameson (1986), e.g., imagines a relation of absolute overdetermination in which every act of creation in a peripheral context is an allegory about the nation. Pierre Bourdieu (1994) has made the metropolitan field for a specific discipline into an instance of recognition and consecration for creators and performers in secondary nations. The Argentinean literary critic Beatriz Sarlo (1988) has coined the term *peripheral modernity* to discuss how central cultural elements are reconfigured in countries like Argentina but how there is always a tension between that appropriation and the original that looks to Europe for recognition. The hybridization model that the Argentinean anthropologist Eduardo Archetti (1999) elaborated to explain the triumph of polo, soccer, and tango abroad showed how a national style is elaborated in the rearticulation of modern and central elements that are producers of difference and nationality, with instances of recognition in the circulation and success of the creators and performers abroad. Juan Corradi (1997) further elaborates on this model, showing how so-called local practices are transformed in circulation back and forth with the metropolis, granting local consecration to national practices and performers better or first recognized abroad. As Sarlo (1993) shows, e.g., the success of Borges among the left-wing writers grouped in the *Contorno* magazine can be explained by this model since it was not until Sartre's *Le temps modernes* consecrated him that they started reading him differently.

16. The change in price structure was actually presented as a discount for Argentinean citizens (with the appropriate ID).

17. Bocca, the Cornejos, and Herrera dance with the American Ballet Theater; Nuñez and Urlezaga are with the Royal Ballet of London.

18. Diego Maradona is a retired Argentinean soccer player best remembered for leading the country to win the FIFA (International Federation of Associated Football) World Cup in 1986 and to the final match in 1990. In 2005, he beat Pelé in a survey by FIFA as the best player of all time. He won the Italian league and the European Club championship with Napoli, a small team.

19. José Cura came to Buenos Aires in 1999 and 2007; Alvarez performed there just once, in 1997, early on in his international career.

20. Among the opera houses where they can usually be heard are Cagliari, the Los Angeles Opera, the National Opera in Washington, DC, the Real Theater in Madrid, Barcelona's Liceu, Trieste, Genoa, the Bonn Opera, the Zurich Opera, the Teatro Regio in Torino, the Teatro Regio in Parma, Naples' San Carlo Opera House, the Opera Orchestra of New York, the Pittsburgh Opera, and the New York City Opera. Volonté sang *Tosca* at La Scala once, in 2000, and Bravo was a part of the Met roster for *Aida*. Other singers who recently came back to Argentina include the likes of Gustavo Porta ("the guy from Córdoba who triumphed in Europe"), Dario Schmunck (who left the Colón for Germany and was received as a success in the 2005 *Lucia*), Eduardo Chama, and Luciano Miotto (who, though acting in a secondary role in Avellaneda, brought in a few enthusiasts who wanted to "see that guy who sings in Florence").

21. Fabiana Bravo and Marcelo Alvarez triumphed at the Pavarotti Competition, while Cura (and Cecilia Diaz, a mezzo-soprano whose career has happened mostly at the local level) won Operalia in 1994. Virginia Tola won the audience award at Operalia 2000 and the 1999 Queen Sonja International Music Competition (Oslo). Fagioli won the 2003 Neue Stimmen (New voices) competition in Germany.

22. All three have entered the international scene during the last ten to twenty years and are under forty-five.

23. The present that I am describing here is based on a past model for the experience, using Geertz's (1973) distinction between a model of experience (as in the process of judging the actually existing reality) and a model for the experience (as in the architectural principles behind it). For a critical review of the concept, see Sewell (1997).

24. She has not sung at the Colón since 1998, when she appeared as Lady Macbeth in Verdi's *Macbeth*. She did not sing with the first cast but in the alternate representation usually reserved for local artists.

25. Diverse social theorists have scrutinized the collective character of remembering (Halbawcs 1925/1952), asked about the genres of commemoration (Wagner Pacifici and Schwartz 1991), shown how remembering is a social construction anchored in the present (Anderson 1983), made explicit the factious interest behind mnemonic narratives (Hobsbawm and Ranger 1983), examined the uses of the process of commemoration to reconcile opposite visions of the past (Olick and Levy 1997), posited collective memory as a frame to organize present experience (Schwartz 1996), and revealed how much the past is shaped by the present but also frames the current categories of appreciation and understanding (Zerubavel 1996). In discussions of remembrance among smaller and larger groups, the role of ceremonies (following a Durkheimian understanding of the social body) has been emphasized, and the

transition from one volume and density to the next (as in the changing scale from village to nations) has been made evident by the use of larger, more encompassing and abstract cultural forms.

26. Sociologists and anthropologists have elaborated thoroughly how culture works as a frame and the ways in which certain interpretations are mobilized. For further discussion, see Geertz (1973), Goffman (1974), Griswold (1987a, 1987b), and Schwartz (1996).

27. Simmel (1955) explains how conflict either produces or modifies communities of interest, unifications, and organizations.

28. Weber (1978, 247) talks of revelation when the legitimacy of the new leader depends on legalized forms of selection. In Tiziana Fabricini's case, she was chosen by the La Scala music director Ricardo Mutti to perform *Traviata* for the first time after Maria Callas. The other singer plucked to channel Giuseppe Di Stefano was Roberto Alagna, who went on to a successful international career. If we were to find a successor for Callas through designation (Weber 1978, 248), it would be Montserrat Caballé—the Catalan soprano deemed her successor—although her looks are opposite to the paradox Callas incarnated, a fragile body with a strong voice.

29. The whole quote, which can be found on the opening paragraph of the essay on Louis Bonaparte, is: "Hegel remarks somewhere that all great, world-historical facts and personages occur, as it were, twice. He has forgotten to add: the first time as tragedy, the second as farce" (Marx 1852/1978, 594).

30. *Maestro de estudios* would be a position in between what Europeans call a *Kapellmeister* and a *repetiteur*.

31. Erich Kleiber was the father of the internationally known maestro Carlos Kleiber.

32. If you are standing up, you cannot move to the sides, you cannot go upstairs (as the *paraíso* has a different entrance), and you cannot go downstairs (as the boxes and the orchestra seats have a different entrance and the standing section of the *cazuela* is for women only). You are damned to be social among the strangers who surround you. This sociability is easier to reproduce in the *tertulia* than in the *paraíso*, where people do attend in groups formed outside the opera house.

33. I am, to a certain extent, turning Bourdieu and Sewell on their heads with this question. Both theorists consider such discrepancies to be a source, not of social continuity, but of social change, yet the passionate fans draw on a lost past to reproduce, more or less, an attitude toward opera born in that past but persisting through and in present-day action and discourse. Instead of finding an almost automatic adjustment between circumstances, disposition, and practice, what we have learned from the empirical analysis is that the community resources, the in-group sociability and its isolation from competing interpretations, are all key factors in mediating the production of adjustment or discrepancy between resources and practice. While in other cases—Auyero and Swistun (2008)—the perceptions of those involved in the world are caused by a concerted "labor of confusion" by outside actors, in this case it is the actors themselves who are blind to the transformations. This confirms insights advanced by anthropologists like Hirschkind (2001) and Gordillo (2003), adding an extra mediation to the relation between schemas

and resources that calls to attention the role groups play in maintaining the productive power of representations.

34. Nilsson appeared in 1955, 1956, 1962, 1965, 1967, and 1971 and for a secondary role in 1979.

CHAPTER SEVEN

1. Another iteration of this "fan culture" is Wayne Koestenbaum's book *The Queen's Throat*, which documents the author's obsession with opera divas. Koestenbaum provides us with a recollection of opera trivia and discussion, reflecting on the capricious and opinionated character of diva fandom, and presenting the many treasures he collected as part of his career as an amateur. The book presents an experience that is easily recognizable in comparison with this book and other stories of passion for opera.

2. For a thorough discussion of this, see Mahler (2008).

3. Practices other than opera might help us understand the purest version of this type. Soccer fandom, e.g., is a key place to observe the sense of collective immersion, the giving up of one's own individual being.

4. Studies of fandom have usually referred to these two kinds of practices and seldom to classical music and opera (other than the work by Hennion), hence the heavy concentration of scholarship among sports studies and pop culture studies scholars (Schimmel, Harrington, and Bielby 2007).

5. Much like opera addicts, mushroom collectors exchange treasure tales, war stories, and fish stories (the one that got away) while defining the limits of what they do against professional mycologists (Fine 1998).

6. This is a key point since Sennett is very specific about showing how, during the nineteenth century, the private sphere becomes the appropriate space for intimate expression and the display of passion while impersonal public life becomes something to escape, either through self-confinement in a community of similar people, the ability to transcend through narcissistic impulses, or the submission to a strong, charismatic personality.

7. Freud (1959) and Bourdieu (1994, 1997, 1998) have both used the term *cathexis* to describe the intense libidinal investment in an object or a practice. While the father of modern psychoanalysis described the attachment as one that is substituted or fantasized through the object for other persons, Bourdieu focuses mostly on how the libidinal energy is socially channeled through different fields and transformed into field-specific *illusio*. For a thorough discussion of the tensions in Bourdieu's late writings between a cognitive understanding of social action (through schemas, classification systems, and habitus) and one full of psychoanalytic metaphors, see Widick (2003).

8. Both the crying when reminiscing and the poise gained by the interviewees when talking about the first opera they saw have to do with their lack of recognition outside the opera house and their intense interest in having their story told, so much so that some did not want me to leave after over three hours of conversation. As the anthropologist Nancy Schepper-Hughes (1992, 28) says in a very different context: "I think of the subjects of these books for whom anthropology is not a hostile gaze

but rather an opportunity to tell a part of their life story." To paraphrase Pierre Bourdieu (1999, 615), the joy in their expression, the sense of relief, and the density and intensity of their speech all point to the interview as an occasion to explain themselves in the fullest sense of those terms.

9. While mainstream sociology has been disdainful of these kinds of questions, popular culture has been going hard at them during the last decade or so. Movies like *High Fidelity, As Good As It Gets, The Other Side of the Bed, Moulin Rouge,* or *Same Old Song* and pop literature like the aforementioned Nick Hornby's *Songbook,* Bret Easton Ellis's *American Psycho,* or Alain de Botton's *On Love* have used music as material that conforms the frames of reference that organize experience, cognitive maps to educate actors on which actions to take. In them, music allows biographical problems to be expressed, what *has* to appear when words are not enough, a technology of the self.

10. This kind of understanding about symbolic circulation makes signs an activity or a process. Much as in Peirce (see Bernstein 1980), social semiosis, the relation of the sign to its object, becomes the object of the new interpretant, which assumes the position of a sign in a new triad.

REFERENCES

Abel, Sam. 1996. *Opera in the Flesh*. Boulder, CO: Westview.

Adams, Rebecca. 1998. "Inciting Sociological Thought by Studying the Deadhead Community: Engaging Publics in Dialogue." *Social Forces* 77, no. 1:1–25.

Adorno, Theodor W. 1949/1973. *Philosophy of Modern Music*. New York: Seabury.

———. 1962. *Introduction to the Sociology of Music*. New York: Sage.

———. 1981. *In Search of Wagner*. New York: Seabury.

———. 1985. "On the Fetish Character in Music and the Regression of Listening." In *The Essential Frankfurt Reader*, ed. Andrew Arato and Eike Gebhardt, 270–99. New York: Continuum.

———. 1963/1992. *Quasi una Fantasia: Essays on Modern Music*. London: Verso.

———. 1994. "Bourgeois Opera." In *Opera through Other Eyes*, ed. D. Levin, 25–44. Stanford, CA: Stanford University Press.

Adorno, Theodor W., and Max Horkheimer. 1972. *Dialectic of Enlightenment*. New York: Continuum.

Adut, Ari. 2004. "Scandal as Norm Entrepreneurship Strategy: Corruption and the French Investigating Magistrate." *Theory and Society* 33, no. 5:529–78.

———. 2005. "A Theory of Scandal: Victorians, Homosexuality and the Fall of Oscar Wilde." *American Journal of Sociology* 111, no. 1:213–48.

Aguilar, Gonzalo. 2003. "The National Opera: A Migrant Genre of Imperial Expansion." *Journal of Latin American Cultural Studies* 12, no. 1:83–94.

Ahlquist, Karen. 1997. *Democracy at the Opera*. Urbana: University of Illinois Press.

Alberoni, Francesco. 1983. *Falling in Love*. New York: Random House.

Alexander, Jeffrey, and Philip Smith. 1998. "Cultural Sociology or Sociology of Culture: Towards a Strong Program for Sociology's Second Wind." *Sociologie et sociétés* 30, no. 1:107–16.

Alfabetismo y educación en Argentina. 2004. Buenos Aires: Censo Nacional de Población y Vivienda.

Alford, Robert, and Andras Szantos. 1996. "Orpheus Wounded: The Experience of Pain in the Professional Worlds of the Piano." *Theory and Society* 25, no. 1:1–44.

Altamirano, Carlos. 1997. "La pequeña burguesía, una clase en el purgatorio." *Prismas* 1:105–25.

Anand, N. 2000. "Defocalizing the Organization: Richard A. Peterson's Sociology of Organizations." *Poetics: Journal of Empirical Research on Culture, Media, and the Arts* 28, nos. 2–3:173–84.

Anderson, Benedict. 1983. *Imagined Communities: Reflections on the Origin and Spread of Nationalism.* London: Verso.

Appadurai, Arjun. 1987. *The Social Life of Things: Commodities in Cultural Perspective.* Cambridge: Cambridge University Press.

Arblaster, Anthony. 1997. *Viva la Libertà! Politics in Opera.* London: Verso.

Archetti, Eduardo. 1992. "Argentinean Football: A Ritual of Violence?" *The International Journal of the History of Sport* 9, no. 2:209–35.

———. 1999. "Hibridación, pertenencia y localidad en la construcción de una cocina nacional." *Trabajo y sociedad* 2:12–26.

———. 2000. *Masculinities: Football, Polo and the Tango in Argentina.* London: Berg.

———. 2001. *El potrero, la pista y el ring: Las patrias del deporte argentino.* Buenos Aires: Fondo de Cultura Económica.

Arian, Edward. 1972. *Bach, Beethoven and Bureaucracy: The Case of the Philadelphia Orchestra.* University: University of Alabama Press.

Aronowitz, Stanley. 1993. *Roll over Beethoven: The Return of Cultural Strife.* Middletown, CT: Wesleyan University Press.

Atkinson, Max. 1984. *Our Masters' Voices: The Language and Body Language of Politics.* London: Methuen.

———. 2006. *Everyday Arias: An Operatic Ethnography.* London: AltaMira.

Auyero, Javier. 2001. *Poor People's Politics: Peronist Survival Networks and the Legacy of Evita.* Durham: Duke University Press.

———. 2006. "Celebratory Stories and Their Troubles." *Contemporary Sociology* 35, no. 1:5–6.

———. 2007. *Routine Politics and Violence in Argentina.* Cambridge: Cambridge University Press.

Auyero, Javier, and Debora Swistun. 2007. "Confused Because Exposed: Towards an Ethnography of Environmental Suffering." *Ethnography* 8, no. 2:123–44.

———. 2008. "The Social Production of Toxic Uncertainty." *American Sociological Review* 73, no. 3:357–79.

Baily, Samuel. 1985. "Patrones de residencia de los italianos en Buenos Aires y Nueva York: 1880–1914." *Estudios migratorios latinoamericanos* 1:8–47.

Bakhtin, Mikhail. 1984. *Estética de la creación verbal.* Madrid: Siglo XXI.

Barbeito, Alberto, and Miguel Lo Vuolo. 1995. *La modernización excluyente.* Buenos Aires: Unicef-Losada.

Becker, Howard. 1953. "Becoming a Marihuana User." *American Journal of Sociology* 59, no. 2:235–42.

———. 1961. *Boys in White*. Chicago: University of Chicago Press.

———. 1963. *Outsiders*. New York: Free Press.

———. 1973. "Art as Collective Action." *American Sociological Review* 39, no. 6:767–76.

———. 1978. "Arts and Crafts." *American Journal of Sociology* 83, no. 4:863–89.

———. 1982. *Art Worlds*. Berkeley and Los Angeles: University of California Press.

———. 1995. "The Power of Inertia." *Qualitative Sociology* 18, no. 3:301–9.

———. 1998. *Tricks of the Trade: How to Think about Your Research While You're Doing It*. Chicago: University of Chicago Press.

———. 1999. "The Work Itself." Paper presented at the conference "L'oeuvre elle-même," Grenoble.

Becker, Howard, and Rob Faulkner. 2009. *Do You Know? The Jazz Repertoire in Action*. Chicago: University of Chicago Press.

Beisel, Nicola. 1993. "Morals versus Art: Censorship, the Politics of Interpretation, and the Victorian Nude." *American Sociological Review* 58, no. 1:145–62.

Benjamin, Jessica. 1988. *The Bonds of Love: Psychoanalysis, Feminism and the Problem of Domination*. New York: Pantheon.

Benjamin, Walter. 1969. "The Work of Art in the Age of Mechanical Reproduction." In *Illuminations*, ed. Hannah Arendt, 217–52. New York: Schocken.

Benmayor, Lily. 1990. *Nuestro Teatro Colón*. Buenos Aires: Ediciones Arte & Turismo.

Bennett, Andy, and Kevin Dawe, eds. 2001. *Guitar Cultures*. Oxford: Berg.

Benzecry, Claudio E. 2006. "Curtain Rising, Baton Falling: The Politics of Musical Conducting in Contemporary Argentina." *Theory and Society* 35, no. 3:445–79.

———. 2007. "Beauty at the Gallery: Sentimental Education and Operatic Community in Contemporary Buenos Aires." In *Practicing Culture*, ed. Craig Calhoun and Richard Sennett, 171–92. London: Routledge.

Blau, Judith. 1983. "High Culture as Mass Culture." In *Performers and Performances*, ed. Jack Kamermann and Rossana Martorella, 1–37. South Handley: Bergin & Garvey.

———. 1988. *The Shape of Culture*. Cambridge: Cambridge University Press.

Blier, Steven. 1999. "The Fan Club." *Opera News* 64, no. 3 (September): 5–8.

Borer, Michael. 2008. *Faithful to Feinway*. New York: New York University Press.

Born, Georgina. 1995. *Rationalizing Culture*. Berkeley and Los Angeles: University of California Press.

Bourdieu, Pierre. 1977. *Outline of a Theory of Practice*. Cambridge: Cambridge University Press.

———. 1984. *Distinction*. Cambridge, MA: Harvard University Press.

———. 1986. "The Forms of Capital." In *Handbook of Theory and Research for the Sociology of Education*, ed. John G. Richardson, 241–58. New York: Greenwood.

———. 1990. *The Logic of Practice*. Stanford, CA: Stanford University Press.

———. 1992. *The Rules of Art*. Stanford, CA: Stanford University Press.

———. 1993. *The Field of Cultural Production*. Oxford: Polity.

———. 1994. *Sociology in Question*. London: Sage.

———. 1997. *Pascalian Meditations*. Stanford, CA: Stanford University Press.

———. 1998. *State Nobility*. London: Polity.

———. 1999. *The Weight of the World*. Stanford, CA: Stanford University Press.

Bourdieu, Pierre, and Jean-Claude Passeron. 1964/1979. *The Inheritors: French Students and Their Relation to Culture*. Translated by Richard Nice. Chicago: University of Chicago Press.

———. 1977. *Reproduction in Education, Society and Culture*. Beverly Hills, CA: Sage.

Bourdieu, Pierre, and Loïc J. D. Wacquant. 1992. *An Invitation to Reflexive Sociology*. Chicago: University of Chicago Press.

Brunner, Joaquín. 1992. *América Latina: Cultura y modernidad*. México: Grijalbo.

Bryson, Bethany. 1996. "'Anything but Heavy Metal': Symbolic Exclusion and Musical Dislikes." *American Sociological Review* 61, no. 5:884–99.

———. 1997. "What about Univores? Musical Dislikes and Group-Based Identity Construction among Americans with Low Levels of Education." *Poetics: Journal of Empirical Research on Culture, Media, and the Arts* 25, nos. 2–3:141–56.

Buch, Esteban. 2003. *The Bomarzo Affair: Opera, perversion y dictadura*. Buenos Aires: Adriana Hidalgo.

Buford, Bill. 1988. *Among the Thugs*. London: Trafalgar Square.

Bull, Michael. 2001. *Sounding Out the City*. London: Berg.

———. 2004. "Thinking about Sound, Proximity and Distance in Western Experience. The Case of Odysseus's Walkman." In *Hearing Cultures: Essays on Sound, Listening and Modernity*, ed. Veit Erlmann, 198–220. London: Berg.

Burucúa, José Emilio. 2002. *Corderos y elefantes*. Buenos Aires: Buenos Aires University Press.

Caamaño, Roberto. 1970. *Historia del Teatro Colón*. 2 vols. Buenos Aires: Editorial del Teatro.

Calhoun, Craig. 2007. Foreword to *Opera and Society in Italy and France from Monteverdi to Bourdieu*, by Victoria Johnson, Jane Fulcher and Thomas Ertman, xxi–xxviii. Cambridge: Cambridge University Press.

Cambaceres, Eugenio. 1885/1980. *Sin rumbo*. Buenos Aires: CEAL.

Chartier, Roger. 1994. *The Order of Books*. Stanford, CA: Stanford University Press.

———. 1998. *Escribir las prácticas*. Buenos Aires: Manantial.

Chiaravalli, Verónica. "A veces el Colón parece un ministerio." *La nación*, October 9, 2005.

Cicolella, Pablo. 1999. "Globalización y dualización en la región metropolitana de Buenos Aires." *EURE* (Pontificia Universidad Católica de Chile) 25, no. 76:5–27.

Cinel, Dino. 1982. *From Italy to San Francisco*. Stanford, CA: Stanford University Press.

Ciria, Alberto. 1980. *Peronismo y antiperonismo*. Buenos Aires: Centro Editor de América Latina.

Clancy, Brian Carl. 2005. "An Architectural History of Grand Opera Houses." Ph.D. diss., Rutgers University.

Clifford, James. 1988. *The Predicament of Culture: Twentieth-Century Ethnography, Literature, and Art*. Cambridge, MA: Harvard University Press.

———. 1992. "Traveling Cultures." In *Cultural Studies*, ed. Lawrence Grossberg, Cary Nelson, and Paula Treichler, 96–117. New York: Routledge.

Cohen, Margaret. 2002. *The Literary Channel*. Princeton, NJ: Princeton University Press.

Corradi, Juan. 1997. "How Many to Tango?" In *Outsider Art: Contesting Boundaries in Contemporary Culture*, ed. Vera Zolberg and Maya Cherbo, 194–214. New York: Cambridge University Press.

Crane, Diana. 1987. *The Transformation of the Avant Garde*. Chicago: University of Chicago Press.

———. 1992. "High Culture versus Popular Culture Revisited." In *Cultivating Differences: Symbolic Boundaries and the Making of Inequality*, ed. Michèle Lamont and Marcel Fournieur, vii–xiv. Chicago: University of Chicago Press.

———. 1997. "Globalization, Organizational Size and Innovation in the French Luxury Fashion Industry: Production of Culture Theory Revisited." *Poetics: Journal of Empirical Research on Culture, Media, and the Arts* 25, no. 6:393–414.

Cressey, Paul Goalby. 1932. *The Taxi Dance Hall*. Chicago: University of Chicago Press.

Csordas, Thomas J. 1990. "Embodiment as a Paradigm for Anthropology." *Ethos* 18, no. 1:5–47.

DaMatta, Roberto. 1979/1992. *Carnivals, Rogues and Heroes: An Interpretation of the Brazilian Dilemma*. Translated by John Drury. Notre Dame, IN: Notre Dame University Press.

Darnton, Robert. 1985. *The Great Cat Massacre and Other Episodes in French Cultural History*. New York: Vintage.

Davis, Natalie Zemon. 1977. *Society and Culture in Early Modern France*. Stanford, CA: Stanford University Press.

de Certeau, Michel. 1984. *The Practice of Everyday Life*. Berkeley and Los Angeles: University of California Press.

de la Guardia, Ernesto, and Roberto Herrera. 1933. *El arte lírico en el Teatro Colón (con motivo de sus bodas de plata)*. Buenos Aires: Zea & Tejero.

De la Torre, Lidia. 1983. "La ciudad residual." In *Buenos Aires: Historia de cuatro siglos*, ed. José Luis Romero, 1:325–38. Buenos Aires: Abril.

Del Campo, Estanislao. 1940. *Fausto (Impresiones del gaucho Anastasio el Pollo en la representación de esta opera)*. Buenos Aires: Biblioteca Nacional.

DeNora, Tia. 1991. "Musical Patronage and Social Change in Beethoven's Vienna." *American Journal of Sociology* 97, no. 2:310–46.

———. 2000. *Music in Everyday Life*. New York: Cambridge University Press.

———. 2002. "Music into Action: Performing Gender on the Viennese Concert Stage, 1790–1810." *Poetics: Journal of Empirical Research on Culture, Media, and the Arts* 30, nos. 1–2:19–33.

———. 2003. *After Adorno*. New York: Cambridge University Press.

———. 2004. "Musical Practice and Social Structure: The Sociology of Music and Its Toolkit." In *Empirical Musicology: Aims, Methods, Prospects*, ed. Eric Clark and Nicholas Cook, 35–56. Oxford: Oxford University Press.

de Santos, Martin. 2009. "Fact-Totems and the Statistical Imagination: The Public Life of a Statistic in Argentina 2001." *Sociological Theory* 27, no. 4:466–89.

Diego, Jacobo A. 1983. "El teatro: El gauchesco y el sainete." In *Buenos Aires: Historia de cuatro siglos*, ed. José Luis Romero, 2:356–75. Buenos Aires: Abril.

Dillon, César, and Juan Sala. 1997. *Teatro Doria-Teatro Marconi*. Vol. 1 of *El teatro musical en Buenos Aires*. Buenos Aires: Ediciones de arte Gaglianone.

———. 1999. *Teatro Coliseo*. Vol. 2 of *El teatro musical en Buenos Aires*. Buenos Aires: Ediciones de arte Gaglianone.

Dilthey, Wilhelm. 1988. *Selected Works*. Vol. 1, *Introduction to the Human Sciences*. Princeton, NJ: Princeton University Press.

DiMaggio, Paul. 1982a. "Cultural Entrepreneurship in Nineteenth Century Boston: Pt. 1, The Creation of an Organizational Base for High Culture in America." *Media, Culture and Society* 4:33–50.

———. 1982b. "Cultural Entrepreneurship in Nineteenth Century Boston: Pt. 2, The Classification and Framing of American Art." *Media, Culture and Society* 4:303–22.

———. 1987. "Classification in Art." *American Sociological Review* 52, no. 4:440–55.

———. 1992. "Cultural Boundaries and Structural Change: The Extension of the High Culture Model to Theater, Opera and the Dance, 1900–1940." In *Cultivating Differences: Symbolic Boundaries and the Making of Inequality*, ed. Michèle Lamont and Marcel Fournieur, 21–57. Chicago: University of Chicago Press.

———. 1994. Introduction to "Meaning and Measurement in the Sociology of Culture," ed. Paul DiMaggio. Special issue, *Poetics* 22, no. 4:263–67.

Douglas, Mary. 1966. *Purity and Danger*. London: Routledge.

Douglas, Mary, and Baron Isherwood. 1979. *The World of Goods: Toward an Anthropology of Consumption*. New York: Basic.

Dowd, Timothy. 2004. "Concentration and Diversity Revisited: Production Logics and the U.S. Mainstream Recording Market, 1940 to 1990." *Social Forces* 82, no. 4:1411–55.

Dowd, Timothy, Kathleen Liddle, Kim Lupo, and Anne Borden. 2002. "Organizing the Musical Canon: The Repertoires of Major U.S. Symphony Orchestras, 1842 to 1969." *Poetics: Journal of Empirical Research on Culture, Media, and the Arts* 30, nos. 1–2:35–61.

Duneier, Mitchell. 1999. *Sidewalk*. New York: Farrar, Straus and Giroux.

Durkheim, Emile. 1965. *The Elementary Forms of Religious Life*. New York: Free Press.

Durkheim, Emile, and Marcel Mauss. 1963. *Primitive Classification*. Chicago: University of Chicago Press.

Echevarría, Néstor. 1979. *El arte lírico en la Argentina*. Buenos Aires: Imprima.

Eco, Umberto. 1979. *Lector in fábula*. Barcelona: Lumen.

———. 1984. *Carnival!* Approaches to Semiotics no. 64. New York: Mouton/de Gruyter.

———. 1991. "Los límites de la interpretación." *Revista de Occidente* 118:12–29.

———. 1994. *Apocalypse Postponed*. Bloomington: Indiana University Press.

———. 1978/1994. *The Civilizing Process: Sociogenetic and Psychogenetic Investigations*. London: Wiley-Blackwell.

Elias, Norbert, and Eric Dunning. 1986. *Quest for Excitement: Sport and Leisure in the Civilizing Process*. London: Blackwell.

Estudio de población judía en ciudad de Buenos Aires y 24 partidos del Gran Buenos Aires. 2004. Buenos Aires: JOINT.

Evans, David T. 2005. "Speaking Over and Above the Plot: Aural Fixation, Scopophillia, Opera and the Gay Sensibility." *Theory, Culture and Society* 22, no. 2:99–119.

Eyerman, Ron, and Andrew Jamison. 1998. *Music and Social Movements: Mobilizing Traditions in the Twentieth Century*. Cambridge: Cambridge University Press.

Faulkner, Robert. 1983. *Music on Demand*. New Brunswick, NJ: Transaction.

Featherstone, Mike. 1992. "The Heroic Life and Everyday Life." *Theory, Culture and Society* 9, no. 2:159–82.

Feijoo, María del Carmen. 1993. "Los gasoleros: Estrategias de consumo de los NUPO." In *Cuesta abajo*, ed. Alberto Minujin and Eduardo Bustelo, 229–52. Buenos Aires: Losada.

———. 1995. "Los gasoleros." *CIAS Revista del Centro de Investigación y Acción Social* 2:174–92.

Fine, Gary Alan. 1992. "The Culture of Production: Aesthetic Choices and Constraints in Culinary Work." *American Journal of Sociology* 97, no. 5:1268–94.

———. 1998. *Morel Tales: The Culture of Mushrooming*. Cambridge, MA: Harvard University Press.

———. 2003. "Crafting Authenticity: The Validation of Identity in Self-Taught Art." *Theory and Society* 32, no. 1:153–80.

———. 2004. *Everyday Genius: Self-Taught Art and the Culture of Authenticity*. Chicago: University of Chicago Press.

Fish, Stanley. 1982. *Is There a Text in This Class?* Cambridge, MA: Harvard University Press.

Fonarow, Wendy. 2006. *Empire of Dirt: The Aesthetics and Rituals of British Indie Music*. Middlebury, CT: Wesleyan University Press.

Foucault, Michel. 1972. *The Archaeology of Knowledge*. New York: Pantheon.

———. 1978. *An Introduction*. Vol. 1 of *The History of Sexuality*. New York: Pantheon.

———. 1979. *Discipline and Punish: The Birth of the Prison*. New York: Vintage.

———. 1988. *The Care of the Self*. Vol. 3 of *The History of Sexuality*. New York: Vintage.

———. 2003. *Society Must Be Defended*. London: Picador.

Freud, Sigmund. 1920/2003. *Beyond the Pleasure Principle*. New York: Penguin.

———. 1930/2005. *Civilization and Its Discontents*. New York: Norton.

———. 1959. *Group Psychology and the Analysis of the Ego*. New York: Norton.

Friedson, Elliot. 2005. *Professional Dominance: The Social Structure of Medical Care*. Vancouver: University of British Columbia Press.

Frith, Simon. 1981. *Sound Effects*. New York: Pantheon.

Fulcher, Jane. 1987. *The Nation's Image: French Grand Opera as Politics and Politicized Art*. New York: Cambridge University Press.

Gallo, Ezequiel. 1984. *La pampa gringa*. Buenos Aires: Sudamericana.

Gamson, Joshua. 1994. *Claims to Fame: Celebrity in Contemporary America*. Berkeley and Los Angeles: University of California Press.

Gans, Herbert. 1974/1999. *High Culture and Popular Culture: An Analysis and Evaluation of Taste*. Rev. ed. New York: Basic.

———. 1992. Preface to *Cultivating Differences: Symbolic Boundaries and the Making of Inequality*, ed. Michèle Lamont and Marcel Fournieur, vii–xv. Chicago: University of Chicago Press.

García Canclini. 1979. *La producción simbólica*. Buenos Aires: Siglo XXI.

———. 1987. *Culturas híbridas*. Buenos Aires: Sudamericana.

Garfinkel, Harold. 1964. "Studies of the Routine Grounds of Everyday Activities." *Social Problems* 11:225–50.

Garriga, José. 2007. *Haciendo amigos a las piñas: Violencia y redes sociales de una hinchada del fútbol*. Buenos Aires: Prometeo.

Gayol, Sandra. 1999. "Conversaciones y desafios en los cafés de Buenos Aires (1870–1910)." In *Historias de la vida privada en la Argentina*, ed. Fernando Devoto and Marta Madero, 2:156–82. Buenos Aires: Taurus.

Geertz, Clifford. 1973. *The Interpretation of Cultures*. New York: Basic.

———. 1983. *Local Knowledge: Further Essays in Interpretive Anthropology*. New York: Basic.

Gerhard, Anselm. 1998. *The Urbanization of Opera*. Chicago: University of Chicago Press.

Giddens, Anthony. 1992. *The Transformation of Intimacy*. Stanford, CA: Stanford University Press.

Gilroy, Paul. 1993. *The Black Atlantic: Modernity and Double Consciousness*. Cambridge, MA: Harvard University Press.

Ginzburg, Carlo. 1981. *The Cheese and the Worms: The Cosmos of a Sixteenth-Century Miller*. Baltimore: Johns Hopkins University Press.

———. 1986/1989. *Clues, Myths, and the Historical Method*. Translated by John Tedeschi and Anne C. Tedeschi. Baltimore: Johns Hopkins University Press.

———. 1990. "Indicios: Raíces de un paradigma de inferencias indiciales." In *Mitos, emblemas, indicios: Morfología e historia*, 138–75. Barcelona: Gedisa.

Gitlin, Todd. 1991. "The Movie of the Week." In *Rethinking Popular Culture: Contemporary Perspectives in Cultural Studies*, ed. Chandra Mukerji and Michael Schudson, 335–55. Berkeley and Los Angeles: University of California Press.

Goffman, Erving. 1959. *The Presentation of Self in Everyday Life*. New York: Doubleday Anchor.

———. 1961. *Asylums: Essays on the Social Situation of Mental Patients and Other Inmates*. New York: Doubleday Anchor.

———. 1963. *Stigma: Notes on the Management of Spoiled Identity*. Englewood Cliffs, NJ: Prentice-Hall.

———. 1974. *Frame Analysis: An Essay on the Organization of Experience*. New York: Harper & Row.

Goode, William J. 1959. "The Theoretical Importance of Love." *American Sociological Review* 24, no. 1:38–47.

Gordillo, Gastón. 2003. *Landscape of Devils*. Durham, NC: Duke University Press.

Gorelik, Adrián. 1998. *La grilla y el parque*. Buenos Aires: Quilmes.

Gramsci, Antonio. 1951. "Letteratura e vita nazionale." In *I quaderni*, 127–41. Torino: Riuniti.

Grazian, David. 2003. *Blue Chicago: The Search for Authenticity in Urban Blues Clubs*. Chicago: University of Chicago Press.

———. 2004. "The Production of Popular Music as a Confidence Game: The Case of the Chicago Blues." *Qualitative Sociology* 27, no. 2:137–58.

———. 2007. *On the Make: The Hustle of Urban Nightlife*. Chicago: University of Chicago Press.

Grigon, Claude, and Jean Claude Passeron. 1989. *Le savant et le populaire*. Paris: Seuil.

Grindstaff, Laura. 2002. *The Money Shot: Trash, Class, and the Making of TV Talk Shows*. Chicago: University of Chicago Press.

Griswold, Wendy. 1987a. "The Fabrication of Meaning: Literary Interpretation in the United States, Great Britain, and the West Indies." *American Journal of Sociology* 92, no. 1:1077–1117.

———. 1987b. "A Methodological Framework for the Sociology of Culture." *Sociological Methodology* 17:1–35.

———. 1994. *Culture and Societies in a Changing World*. London: Routledge.

Groos, Arthur, and Roger Parker. 1988. *Reading Opera*. Princeton, NJ: Princeton University Press.

Gutierrez, Leandro, and Luis Alberto Romero. 1995. *Sectores populares: Cultura y política*. Buenos Aires: Sudamericana.

Habermas, Jurgen. 1969. *The Structural Transformation of the Public Sphere*. Cambridge, MA: MIT Press.

———. 1984. "Modernidad: Un proyecto incompleto." *Punto de vista* 21:14–28.

Halbwachs, Maurice. 1925/1952. *Les cadres sociaux de la mémoire*. Paris: Presses Universitaires de France.

Hall, Stuart. 1980. *Culture, Media, Languages*. London: Hutchinson.

Halle, David. 1993. *Inside Culture: Art and Class in the American Home*. Chicago: University of Chicago Press.

Halperín Donghi, Tulio. 1987. "Para que la imigración? Ideología y política inmigratoria en la Argentina (1810–1914)." In *El espejo de la historia*. Buenos Aires: Sudamericana.

Hanser, Amy. 2006. "Sales Floor Trajectories: Distinction and Service in Postsocialist China." *Ethnography* 7, no. 4:461–91.

Harper, Douglas. 1987. *Working Knowledge: Skill and Community in a Small Shop*. Chicago: University of Chicago Press.

Harrington, C. L., and D. D. Bielby. 1995. *Soap Fans: Pursuing Pleasure and Making Meaning in Everyday Life*. Philadelphia: Temple University Press.

Hebdige, Dick. 1979. *Subculture: The Meaning of Style*. New York: Methuen.

Heimer, Carol, and Arthur Stinchcombe. 1980. "Love and Irrationality: It's Got to Be Rational to Love You Because It Makes Me So Happy." *Social Science Information* 19, nos. 4/5:697–754.

Heinich, Nathalie. 2001. *La sociologie de l'art*. Paris: La Découverte.

Hennion, Antoine. 1993. *La passion musicale*. Paris: Metaille.

———. 1997. "Baroque and Rock: Music, Mediators and Musical Taste." *Poetics: Journal of Empirical Research on Culture, Media, and the Arts* 24, no. 6:415–35.

———. 2001. "Music Lovers: Taste as Performance." *Theory, Culture and Society* 18, no. 5:1–22.

———. 2007. "The Things That Hold Us Together: Taste and Sociology." *Cultural Sociology* 1, no. 1:97–114.

Hennion, Antoine, and Joël-Marie Fauquet. 2001. "Authority as Performance: The Love of Bach in Nineteenth-Century France." *Poetics* 29, no. 1:75–88.

Hennion, Antoine, and Emilie Gomart. 1999. "A Sociology of Attachment: Music

Amateurs, Drug Users." In *Actor Network Theory and After*, ed. John Law and John Hassard, 220–47. Oxford: Blackwell.

Hennion, Antoine, Sophie Maisonneuve, and Emilie Gomart. 2000. *Figures de l'amateur*. Paris: La Documentation Francaise.

Heritage, John, and David Greatbatch. 1986. "Generating Applause: A Study of Rhetoric and Response at Party Political Conferences." *American Journal of Sociology* 92, no. 1:110–57.

Hirsch, Paul. 1972. "Processing Fads and Fashions." *American Journal of Sociology* 77, no. 4:639–59.

———. 2000. "Cultural Industries Revisited." *Organization Science* 11, no. 3:356–61.

Hirschkind, Charles. 2001. "The Ethics of Listening: Cassette-Sermon Audition in Contemporary Cairo." *American Ethnologist* 28, no. 3:623–49.

Hobsbawm, Eric, and Terence Ranger, eds. 1983. *The Invention of Tradition*. New York: Cambridge University Press.

Hochschild, Arlene. 1983. *The Managed Heart*. Berkeley and Los Angeles: University of California Press.

Hodge, Julius. 1979. "The Construction of the Teatro Colón." *The Americas* 36, no. 2:235–55.

Hoggart, Richard. 1957. *The Uses of Literacy*. New York: Oxford University Press.

Hornby, Nick. 1992. *Fever Pitch*. London: Penguin.

———. 2003. *Songbook*. London: Riverhead Trade.

Hourcade, Eduardo. 1999. "La pampa gringa, invención de una sociabilidad europea en el desierto." In *Historias de la vida privada en la Argentina*, ed. Fernando Devoto and Marta Madero, vol. 3. Buenos Aires: Taurus.

Hutcheon, Linda, and Michael Hutcheon. 2000. *Bodily Charm: Living Opera*. Lincoln: University of Nebraska Press.

Huyssen, Andreas. 1990. *After the Great Divide*. Bloomington: Indiana University Press.

Illouz, Eva. 2003. *Oprah Winfrey and the Glamour of Misery: An Essay on Popular Culture*. New York: Columbia University Press.

———. 2007. *Cold Intimacies: The Making of Emotional Capitalism*. London: Polity.

Ingarden, Roman. 1977/1989. "Concreción y reconstrucción." *Estética de la recepción*, ed. Rainier Warning. Madrid: Visor.

Iser, Wolfgang. 1978. *The Act of Reading: A Theory of Aesthetic Response*. Baltimore: University of Maryland Press.

James, Daniel. 1988. *Resistance and Integration: Peronism and the Argentine Working Class, 1946–1976*. New York: Cambridge University Press.

Jameson, Frederic. 1986. "Third-World Literature in the Era of Multinational Capitalism." *Social Text* 15:65–88.

Jarratt, Kent. 1999. "Opera on the Couch: A Psychotherapist Listens to Opera." *Opera News* 64, no. 3 (September): 1–5.

Jauss, Hans Robert. 1982. *Toward an Aesthetic of Reception*. Minneapolis: University of Minnesota Press.

Jay, Martin. 2005. *Songs of Experience*. Berkeley and Los Angeles: University of California Press.

Jenkins, Henry. 1992. *Textual Poachers: Television Fans and Participatory Culture*. New York: Routledge.

Jepperson, Ronald, and Anne Swidler. 1994. "What Properties of Culture Should We Measure?" *Poetics: Journal of Empirical Research on Culture, Media, and the Arts* 22, no. 4:212–33.

Jindra, Michael. 1994. "Star Trek Fandom as a Religious Phenomenon." *Sociology of Religion* 55, no. 1:27–51.

Joas, Hans. 2000. *The Genesis of Values*. Chicago: University of Chicago Press.

———. 2007. *Do We Need Religion? On the Experience of Self-Transcendence*. Boulder, CO: Paradigm.

Johnson, James H. 1995. *Listening in Paris: A Cultural History*. Berkeley and Los Angeles: University of California Press.

Johnson, Victoria. 2007. "What Is Organizational Imprinting? Cultural Entrepreneurship in the Founding of the Paris Opera." *American Journal of Sociology* 113, no. 1:97–127.

———. 2008. *Backstage at the Revolution: How the Royal Paris Opera Survived the End of the Old Regime*. Chicago: University of Chicago Press.

Johnson, Victoria, Jane Fulcher, and Thomas Ertman. 2007. *Opera and Society in Italy and France from Monteverdi to Bourdieu*. Cambridge: Cambridge University Press.

Kamerman, Jack, and Rossana Martorella. 1983. *Performers and Performances*. South Handley: Bergin & Garvey.

Katz, Jack. 1988. *Seductions of Crime*. New York: Basic.

———. 1999. *How Emotions Work*. Berkeley and Los Angeles: University of California Press.

Katz, Jack, and Thomas Csordas. 2003. "Phenomenological Ethnography in Sociology and Anthropology." *Ethnography* 4, no. 3:275–88.

Kaufman, Jason. 2004. "Endogenous Explanation in the Sociology of Culture." *Annual Review of Sociology* 30:335–57.

Kerman, Joseph. 1956/1988. *Opera as Drama*. Rev. ed. Berkeley and Los Angeles: University of California Press.

Kilgannion, Corey. 2008. "Cameras Show If Surf Is Good, but Surfers Are Getting in Way." *New York Times*, January 27.

Klosterman, Chuck. 2004. *Killing Yourself to Live: 85% of a True Story*. New York: Scribner.

Koestenbaum, Wayne. 1993. *The Queen's Throat: Opera, Homosexuality, and the Mystery of Desire*. New York: Poseidon.

Laclau, Ernesto. 1991. *New Reflections on the Revolution of Our Time*. London: Verso.

Lahire, Bernard. 2003. "From the Habitus to an Individual Heritage of Dispositions: Towards a Sociology at the Level of the Individual." *Poetics: Journal of Empirical Research on Culture, Media, and the Arts* 31, no. 5:329–55.

Lakoff, Andrew. 2006. *Pharmaceutical Reason*. New York: Cambridge University Press.

Lamont, Michèle. 1992. *Money, Morals, and Manners: The Culture of the French and the American Upper-Middle Class*. Chicago: University of Chicago Press.

———. 2000. *The Dignity of Working Men: Morality and the Boundaries of Race, Class, and Immigration*. Cambridge, MA: Harvard University Press.

Lamont, Michèle, and Marcel Fournieur, eds. 1992. *Cultivating Differences: Symbolic Boundaries and the Making of Inequality*. Chicago: University of Chicago Press.

Lamont, Michèle, and Annette Lareau. 1988. "Cultural Capital: Allusions, Gaps and Glissandos in Recent Theoretical Developments." *Sociological Theory* 6, no. 2:153–68.

Lamont, Michèle, and Virag Molnar. 2002. "The Study of Boundaries in the Social Sciences." *Annual Review of Sociology* 28:167–95.

Landi, Oscar. 1988. *Reconstrucciones*. Buenos Aires: Puntosur.

Lareau, Annette. 2003. *Unequal Childhoods: Class, Race, and Family Life*. Berkeley and Los Angeles: University of California Press.

Latour, Bruno. 2005. *Reassembling the Social: An Introduction to Actor-Network-Theory*. New York: Oxford University Press.

Leigh Scott, Katherine. 2009. "The Star and the Stalker." *Opera News* 74, no. 2 (August): 1–10.

Lena, Jennifer. 2004. "Meaning and Membership: Samples in Rap Music, 1979 to 1995." *Poetics: Journal of Empirical Research on Culture, Media, and the Arts* 32, nos. 3–4:297–310.

Levin, David. 1994. Introduction to *Opera through Other Eyes*, ed. David Levin, 1–18. Stanford, CA: Stanford University Press.

Levine, Donald. 1997. "Social Theory as a Vocation: Engaging with Future Challenges." *Perspectives* 19, no. 2:1–8.

Levine, Lawrence. 1988. *Highbrow and Lowbrow*. Cambridge, MA: Harvard University Press.

Lindenberger, Herbert. 1984. *Opera: The Extravagant Art*. Ithaca, NY: Cornell University Press.

———. 1998. *Opera in History: From Monteverdi to Cage*. Stanford, CA: Stanford University Press.

Lindholm, Charles. 1988. "Lovers and Leaders: An Analysis of Psychological and Sociological Models of Charisma." *Social Science Information* 27, no. 1:13–45.

———. 1998. "Love and Structure." *Theory, Culture and Society* 15, no. 3:243–63.

Liut, Martín. 2002. "El renacimiento de la opera." *La Nación*, April 7.

———. 2003. "Crece la opera off." *La Nación*, August 8.

———. 2004. "Locos por la opera." *La Nación*, May 23.

Lizardo, Omar. 2005. "Can Cultural Capital Theory Be Reconsidered in the Light of World Polity Institutionalism? Evidence from Spain." *Poetics: Journal of Empirical Research on Culture, Media, and the Arts* 33, no. 2:81–100.

———. 2006. "How Cultural Tastes Shape Personal Networks." *American Sociological Review* 71, no. 5:778–807.

Long, Elizabeth. 1986. "Women, Reading and Cultural Authority: Some Implications of the Audience Perspective in Cultural Studies." *American Quarterly* 38, no. 4:591–612.

Lopes, Paul. 1992. "Innovation and Diversity in the Popular Music Industry, 1969–1990." *American Sociological Review* 56, no. 1:56–71.

———. 2002. *The Rise of a Jazz Art World*. Cambridge: Cambridge University Press.

———. 2006. "Culture and Stigma: Popular Culture and the Case of the Comic Book." *Sociological Forum* 21, no. 3:387–414.

Lukatis, Ingrid. 1989. "Church Meeting and Pilgrimage in Germany." *Social Compass* 36, no. 2:201–18.

Luna, Félix. 1998. *Cultura y población desde la independencia hasta el centenario (1810–1916)*. Buenos Aires: Planeta.

Mahler, Matthew. 2008. "Sociologizing the Subject/Object Divide: Toward a Socioanalytic Understanding of Passions." *Perspectives: Newsletter of the ASA Theory Section* 30, no. 3:5–11.

Marcus, George E. 1995. "Ethnography in/of the World System: The Emergence of Multi-Sited Ethnography." *Annual Review of Anthropology* 24:95–117.

Marcuse, Herbert. 1955. *Eros and Civilization*. Boston: Beacon.

Mark, Noah. 1998. "Birds of a Feather Sing Together." *Social Forces* 77, no. 2:453–85.

Marsalis, Wynton. 1988. "Music; What Jazz Is—and Isn't." *New York Times*, July 31.

Marx, Karl. 1846/1978. *The German Ideology*. In *The Marx-Engels Reader* (2nd ed.), ed. Robert C. Tucker, 146–200. New York: Norton.

———. 1852/1978. *The 18th Brumaire of Louis Bonaparte*. In *The Marx-Engels Reader* (2nd ed.), ed. Robert C. Tucker, 594–617. New York: Norton.

"Más allá de cualquier dificultad." *La nación*, May 17, 2007.

Massey, Douglas S. 1998. "Why Does Immigration Occur? A Theoretical Synthesis." In *The Handbook of International Migration*, ed. Charles Hirschman et al., 34–52. New York: Sage.

Matamoro, Blas. 1972. *El Teatro Colón*. Buenos Aires: CEAL.

Mauss, Marcel. 1950/1990. *The Gift*. New York: Norton.

McCleary, Kristen L. 2002. "Culture Commerce: An Urban History of Theater in Buenos Aires 1880–1920." Ph.D. diss., University of California, Los Angeles.

McCormick, Lisa. 2009. "Higher, Faster, Louder: Representations of the International Music Competition." *Cultural Sociology* 3, no. 1:5–30.

Melick, Jennifer. 2003. "The Discreet Charm of the Berliozoisie." *Opera News* 68, no. 6 (December) 1–3.

Menger, Pierre. 1999. "Artistic Labor Markets and Careers." *Annual Review of Sociology* 25:541–74.

———. 2001. "Artists as Workers: Theoretical and Methodological Challenges." *Poetics: Journal of Empirical Research on Culture, Media, and the Arts* 28, no. 4:241–54.

Minujin, Alberto. 1995. *Cuesta abajo*. Buenos Aires: Unicef/Losada.

Mitchell, Emily. 1998. "Standing Room Only." *Opera News* 63, no. 6 (December): 1–8.

Molotch, Harvey. 2003. *Where Stuff Comes From: How Toasters, Toilets, Cars, Computers and Many Other Things Come to Be As They Are*. New York: Routledge.

Monjeau, Federico. 1999. "El siglo del tango." In *Argentina en el siglo XX*, ed. Carlos Altamirano, 251–56. Buenos Aires: Ariel.

Moya, José C. 1998. *Cousins and Strangers*. Berkeley and Los Angeles: University of California Press.

Mujica Láinez, Manuel. 1979. *El Gran Teatro*. Buenos Aires: Sudamericana.

———. 1983. "Mis memoria del Teatro Colón." In *Vida y gloria del Teatro Colón*, 1–9. Buenos Aires: Cosmogonias.

Mukarovsky, Jan. 1978. *Structure, Sign, and Function: Selected Essays*. Translated and edited by John Burbank and Peter Steiner. New Haven, CT: Yale University Press.

Myerhoff, Barbara, and Sally F. Moore, eds. 1975. *Symbol and Politics in Communal Ideology*. Ithaca, NY: Cornell University Press.

Nietzsche, Friedrich. 1888/1976. "The Case of Wagner." In *The Birth of Tragedy*, trans. Walter Kaufmann. New York: Random House.

———. 1895/1967. "Nietzsche contra Wagner." In *The Portable Nietzsche*, ed. Walter Kaufmann, 661–83. New York: Penguin.

O'Connor, Erin. 2005. "Embodied Knowledge: The Experience of Meaning and the Struggle towards Proficiency in Glassblowing." *Ethnography* 6, no. 2:183–204.

"Le ofrecieron a Ruckauf un papel en la ópera-ballet Edipo Rey." *El Día*, October 30, 2000.

Olick, Jeffrey, and Daniel Levy. 1997. "Collective Memory and Cultural Constraint: Holocaust Myth and Rationality in German Politics." *American Sociological Review* 62, no. 6:921–36.

Osterrieth, Anne. 1989. "Medieval Pilgrimage: Society and Individual Quest." *Social Compass* 36, no. 2:145–57.

Pace, Enzo. 1989. "Pilgrimage as Spiritual Journey." *Social Compass* 36, no. 2:229–44.

Palomino, Pablo. 2007. "Tango, samba y amor." *Apuntes de investigación del CECYP*, no. 12:71–101.

Parkin, Frank. 1984. "El cierre social como exclusión." In *Marxismo y teoría de clases: Una critica burguesa*. Madrid: Espasa Calpe.

Parks, Tim. 2002. *A Season with Verona: Travels around Italy in Search of Illusions, National Character and Goals*. London: Arcade.

Pasolini, Ricardo O. 1999. "La ópera y el circo en el Buenos Aires de fin de siglo: Consumos teatrales y lenguajes sociales." In *Historias de la vida privada en la Argentina*, ed. Fernando Devoto and Marta Madero, 2:228–73. Buenos Aires: Taurus.

Pearson, R. E. 2007. "Bachies, Bardies, Trekkies and Sherlockians." In *Fandom: Identities and Communities in a Mediated World*, ed. J. Gray, C. L. Harrington, and C. Sandvoss, 98–109. New York: New York University Press.

Peirce, Charles Sanders. 1980. *Perspective on Peirce: Critical Essays on Charles Sanders Peirce*. Edited by Richard J. Bernstein. New Haven, CT: Yale University Press.

Perlman, Marc. 2004. "Golden Ears and Meter Readers: The Contest for Epistemic Authority in Audiophilia." *Social Studies of Science* 34, no. 5:783–807.

Peterson, Richard A. 1997. *Creating Country Music: Fabricating Authenticity*. Chicago: University of Chicago Press.

Peterson, Richard A., and N. Anand. 2004. "The Production of Culture Perspective." *Annual Review of Sociology* 30:311–34.

Peterson, Richard A., and David G. Berger. 1975. "Cycles in Symbol Production." *American Sociological Review* 40, no. 2:158–73.

———. 1996. "Measuring Industry Concentration, Diversity and Innovation in Popular Music." *American Sociological Review* 61, no. 1:175–78.

Peterson, Richard A., and Roger Kern. 1996. "Changing Highbrow Taste: From Snob to Omnivore." *American Sociological Review* 61, no. 5:900–907.

Peterson, Richard A., and Albert Simkus. 1992. "How Musical Tastes Mark Occupational Status Groups." In *Cultivating Differences: Symbolic Boundaries and the Making of Inequality*, ed. Michèle Lamont and Marcel Fournieur, 152–86. Chicago: University of Chicago Press.

Plan estratégico de cultura de la ciudad de Buenos Aires. 2006. Buenos Aires: Gobierno de la Ciudad Autónoma de Buenos Aires.

Plattner, Stuart. 1996. *High Art Down Home*. Chicago: University of Chicago Press.

Plotkin, Mariano Ben. 2001. *Freud in the Pampas: The Emergence and Development of a Psychoanalytic Culture in Argentina*. Stanford, CA: Stanford University Press.

———. 2003. *Argentina on the Couch: Psychiatry, State and Society, 1880 to the Present*. Albuquerque: University of New Mexico Press.

Poizat, Michel, 1992. *The Angel's Cry: Beyond the Pleasure Principle in Opera*. Ithaca, NY: Cornell University Press.

Pollini, Margarita. 2002. *Palco, cazuela y paraíso*. Buenos Aires: Sudamericana.

Prieto, Adolfo. 1988. *El discurso criollista en la formación de la Argentina moderna*. Buenos Aires: Sudamericana.

Pujol, Sergio. 1989. *Las canciones del inmigrante*. Buenos Aires: Almagesto.

Radway, Janice. 1984. *Reading the Romance: Women, Patriarchy and Popular Literature*. Chapel Hill: University of North Carolina Press.

Rinesi, Eduardo. 1994. *Buenos Aires salvaje*. Buenos Aires: Armas de la crítica.

Robbins, Bruce, ed. 1992. *Intellectuals: Aesthetics, Politics, Academics*. Minneapolis: University of Minnesota Press.

Robinson, Paul. 1986. *Opera and Ideas: From Mozart to Strauss*. Stanford, CA: Stanford University Press.

———. 2002. *Opera, Sex, and Other Vital Matters*. Chicago: University of Chicago Press.

Roffman, Alejandro, and Luis Alberto Romero. 1973. *Sistema socioeconomico y estructura regional*. Buenos Aires: Amorrortu.

Roland, Ellen. 1991. *Opera in Seventeen Century Venice*. Berkeley and Los Angeles: University of California Press.

Romero, José Luis, ed. 1983. *Buenos Aires: Historia de cuatro siglos*. 2 vols. Buenos Aires: Abril.

Rosselli, John. 1984. *The Opera Industry in Italy from Cimarosa to Verdi*. New York: Cambridge University Press.

———. 1990. "The Opera Business and the Italian Immigrant Community in Latin America, 1820–1930: The Example of Buenos Aires." *Past and Present* 127, no. 1:155–82.

Rossman, Gabriel. 2004. "Elites, Masses, and Media Blacklists: The Dixie Chicks Controversy." *Social Forces* 83, no. 1:61–78.

Rotella, Carlo. 2002. *Good with Their Hands: Boxers, Bluesmen and Other Characters from the Rust Belt*. Berkeley and Los Angeles: University of California Press.

Rother, Larry. "An Argentine Institution Sees Hope Amid Chaos." *New York Times*, November 23, 2005.

Rubinich, Lucas. 1992. *Tomar la cultura del pueblo: Bajar la cultura al pueblo*. Buenos Aires: GECUSO.

———. 2001. "Algunos significados de la palabra gorila." *Apuntes del investigación del CECYP*, no. 7:67–83.

Said, Edward. 1996. *Representations of the Intellectual: The 1993 Reith Lectures*. New York: Vintage.

Salas, Horacio. 1996. *La Argentina del centenario*. Buenos Aires: Planeta.

Salessi, Jorge. 2000. *Médicos, maleantes y maricas*. Buenos Aires: Beatriz Viterbo.

Sanders, Clinton. 1990. *Customizing the Body: The Art and Culture of Tattooing*. Philadelphia: Temple University Press.

Sanguinetti, Horacio. 2002. *Opera y sociedad en Argentina*. Buenos Aires: Gaglianone.

Santoro, Marco. 2000. "Alla Scala: Cambiamento istituzionale e trasformazioni sociali dell'opera italiana tra otto e novecento." *Polis* 2:255–76.

Sarfatti-Larson, Magali. 1993. *Behind the Postmodern Facade*. Berkeley and Los Angeles: University of California Press.

Sarlo, Beatriz. 1988. *Una modernidad periférica: Buenos Aires 1920 y 1930*. Buenos Aires: Nueva Visión.

———. 1991. *La imaginación técnica: Sueños modernos de la cultura argentina*. Buenos Aires: Nueva Visión.

———. 1993. *Borges: A Writer on the Edge*. Edited by John King. London: Verso.

———. 1998. *La máquina cultural: Maestras, traductores y vanguardistas*. Buenos Aires: Ariel.

Schechner, Richard. 1985. *Between Theatre and Anthropology*. Philadelphia: University of Pennsylvania Press.

Schepper-Hughes, Nancy. 1993. *Death without Weeping: The Violence of Everyday Life in Brazil*. Berkeley and Los Angeles: University of California Press.

Schimmel, Kimberly S., C. Lee Harrington, and Denise D. Bielby. 2007. "Keep Your Fans to Yourself: The Disjuncture between Sport Studies' and Pop Culture Studies' Perspectives on Fandom." *Sport in Society* 10, no. 4:580–600.

Schutz, Alfred. 1967. *Phenomenology of the Social World*. Evanston, IL: Northwestern University Press.

Schwartz, Barry. 1996. "Memory as a Cultural System." *American Sociological Review* 61, no. 5:908–27.

Scobie, James. 1974. *Buenos Aires: Plaza to Suburb, 1870–1910*. New York: Oxford University Press.

Scobie, James, and Aurora Ravina de Luzzi. 1983. "El centro, los barrios y el suburbio." In *Buenos Aires: Historia de cuatro siglos*, ed. José Luis Romero, 1:167–88. Buenos Aires: Abril.

Seidman, Steven. 1991. *Romantic Longings: Love in America, 1830–1980*. New York: Routledge.

Semán, Pablo. 2006. *Bajo continuo: Exploraciones descentradas sobre cultura popular*. Buenos Aires: Gorla.

Sennett, Richard. 1977. *The Fall of Public Man*. New York: Knopf.

———. 2008. *The Craftsman*. New Haven, CT: Yale University Press.

Sewell, William. 1992. "A Theory of Structure: Duality, Agency and Transformation." *American Journal of Sociology* 98, no. 1:1–29.

———. 1997. "Geertz, Cultural Systems, and History: From Synchrony to Transformation." *Representations* 59, no. 1:35–55.

Sforza, Nora. 1990. "La edad dorada del Colón y la búsqueda de prestigio social." *Todo es historia* 242:64–73.

Sherman, Rachel. 2005. "Producing the Superior Self: Strategic Comparison and Symbolic Boundaries in Luxury Service Work." *Ethnography* 6, no. 2:131–58.

Shrum, Wesley. 1996. *Fringe and Fortune: The Role of Critics in High and Popular Art.* Princeton, NJ: Princeton University Press.

Sigal, Silvia. 2006. *La Plaza de Mayo.* Buenos Aires: Siglo XXI.

Simmel, Georg. 1911. *Philosophische Kultur.* Leipzig: Kröner.

———. 1916. "Die Krisis der Kultur." *Frankfurter Zeitung*, February 13.

———. 1950. *The Sociology of Georg Simmel.* Edited by Kurt H. Wolff. New York: Free Press.

———. 1955. *Conflict and the Web of Group Affiliations.* New York: Free Press.

———. 1958. "The Adventure." In *Simmel on Culture*, ed. David Frisby and Mike Featherstone, 221–32. London: Sage.

———. 1972. *On Individuality and Social Forms.* Chicago: University of Chicago Press.

Sollis, Todd B. 2006. "First Steps." *Opera News* 71, no. 6 (December): 1–3.

Stamatov, Peter. 2002. "Interpretative Activism and the Political Uses of Verdi's Operas in the 1840s." *American Sociological Review* 67, no. 3:345–66.

Stinchcombe, Arthur L. 1965. "Social Structure and Organizations." In *Handbook of Organizations*, ed. James G. March, 142–93. New York: Rand McNally.

Storey, James. 2006. "Investing Opera as Art in 19th Century Manchester." *International Journal of Cultural Studies* 9, no. 4:435–56.

Subercaseaux, Bernando. 1986. *El debate internacional sobre políticas culturales.* Santiago de Chile: CENECA.

Sudnow, William. 1993. *Ways of the Hand.* Cambridge, MA: MIT Press.

Sumption, J. 1975. *Pilgrimage: An Image of Medieval Religion.* London: Faber.

Sutcliffe, Tom. 2001. *The Faber Book of Opera.* New York: Faber & Faber.

Swidler, Anne. 2001. *Talk of Love.* Berkeley and Los Angeles: University of California Press.

Tacchi, Jo. 2003. "Nostalgia and Radio Sound." In *The Auditory Culture Reader*, ed. Michael Bull and L. Back, 281–95. Oxford: Berg.

Taussig, Michael. 1992. *Mimesis and Alterity.* London: Routledge.

Taylor, Charles. 1989. *Sources of the Self: The Making of the Modern Identity.* Cambridge, MA: Harvard University Press.

———. 1992. *The Ethics of Authenticity.* Cambridge, MA: Harvard University Press.

Thornton, Sarah. 1996. *Club Cultures: Music, Media, and Subcultural Capital.* Hanover, NH: University Press of New England.

Tilly, Charles. 1998. "The Trouble with Stories." In *Teaching for the 21st Century*, ed. Ronald Aminzade and Bernice Pescosolido, 256–71. Thousand Oaks, CA: Pine Forge.

Torche, Florencia. 2007. "Social Status and Cultural Consumption: The Case of Reading in Chile." *Poetics: Journal of Empirical Research on Culture, Media, and the Arts* 35, nos. 2–3:70–92.

Torres, Héctor A. 1993. *El mapa social de Buenos Aires (1940–1990).* Serie Difusión, 3. Buenos Aires: ScyT.

———. 1998. "Procesos recientes de fragmentación socioespacial en Buenos Aires: La suburbanización de las élites." Seminario de Investigación Urbana "El nuevo milenio y lo urbano," Instituto de Investigaciones Gino Germani, University of Buenos Aires, November.

———. 2001. "Cambios socioterritoriales en Buenos Aires durante la década de 1990." *EURE* (Pontificia Universidad Católica de Chile) 27, no. 80:33–56.

Towse, Ruth. 1993. *Singers in the Marketplace: The Economics of the Singing Profession.* Oxford: Clarendon.

Turkle, Sherry. 1975. "Symbol and Festival in the French Student Uprising." In *Symbol and Politics in Communal Ideology.*, ed. Sally F. Moore and Barbara Myerhoff, 68–101. Ithaca, NY: Cornell University Press.

Turner, Victor. 1967. *The Forest of Symbols: Aspects of Ndembu Ritual.* Ithaca, NY: Cornell University Press.

———. 1974. *Dramas, Fields and Metaphors: Symbolic Action in Human Society.* Ithaca, NY: Cornell University Press.

———. 1977. *The Ritual Process: Structure and Anti-Structure.* Ithaca, NY: Cornell University Press.

Van Eijck, Keo. 2001. "Social Differentiation in Musical Taste Patterns." *Social Forces* 79, no. 2:1163–85.

Van Gennep, Arnold. 1961. *The Rites of Passage.* Chicago: University of Chicago Press.

Veblen, Thorstein. 1899/1979. *The Theory of the Leisure Class.* New York: Penguin.

Verón, Eliseo. 1999. *La semiosis social.* Barcelona: Gedisa.

Vila, Pablo, and Pablo Semán. 1999. "Rock chabón e identidad juvenil." In *Los noventa: Política, sociedad y cultura en América Latina y Argentina de fin siglo*, ed. Daniel Filmus, 225–58. Buenos Aires: FLACSO/EUDEBA.

Villarreal, Juan. 1996. *La exclusion social en Argentina.* Buenos Aires: Norma.

Wacquant, Loïc. 2003. *Body and Soul: Notebooks of an Apprentice Boxer.* New York: Oxford University Press.

———. 2005. "Carnal Connections: On Embodiment, Apprenticeship, and Membership." *Qualitative Sociology* 28, no. 4:445–71.

Wagner Pacifici, Robin, and Barry Schwartz. 1991. "The Vietnam Veterans Memorial: Commemorating a Difficult Past." *American Journal of Sociology* 97, no. 2:376–420.

Wallman, Margarita. 1976. *Balcones del cielo.* Buenos Aires: Emecé.

Walzer, Michael. 1990. *The Company of Critics: Social Criticism and Political Commitment in the 20th Century.* New York: Basic.

———. 1965. *The Revolution of the Saints: A Study in the Origins of Radical Politics.* Cambridge, MA: Harvard University Press.

Warning, Rainier, ed. 1989. *Estética de la recepción.* Madrid: Visor.

Weber, Marianne. 1975. *Max Weber: A Biography.* New York: Wiley.

Weber, Max. 1905/1930. *The Protestant Ethic and the Spirit of Capitalism.* London: Unwin Hyman.

———. 1946a. "Class, Status, Party." In *From Max Weber: Essays in Sociology*, trans. and ed. H. H. Gerth and C. Wright Mills, 189–95. New York: Oxford University Press.

———. 1946b. "The Sociology of Charismatic Authority." In *From Max Weber: Essays in Sociology*, trans. and ed. H. H. Gerth and C. Wright Mills, 245–42. New York: Oxford University Press.

———. 1978. *Economy and Society: An Outline of Interpretive Sociology.* Edited by Guenther Roth and Claus Wittich. 2 vols. Berkeley and Los Angeles: University of California Press.

———. 1997. *Sociología de la religión.* Madrid: Istmo.

Weber, William. 1976. *Music and the Middle Class: The Social Structure of Concert Life in London, Paris and Vienna.* London: Holmes & Meier.

———. 2001. "From Miscellany to Homogeneity in Concert Programming." *Poetics: Journal of Empirical Research on Culture, Media, and the Arts* 29, no. 2:125–34.

White, Harrison, and Cynthia White. 1965. *Canvases and Careers.* New York: Wiley.

Widick, Richard. 2003. "Flesh and the Free Market: (On Taking Bourdieu to the Options Exchange)." *Theory and Society* 32, no. 5:679–723.

Williams, Raymond. 1977. *Marxism and Literature.* New York: Oxford University Press.

Willis, Paul. 1978. *Profane Culture.* London: Routledge.

Wolff, Jane. 1983. *Aesthetics and the Sociology of Art.* London: Allen & Unwin.

Wolk, Douglas. 2007. *Reading Comics: How Graphic Novels Work and What They Mean.* New York: Da Capo.

Wortman, Ana, ed. 2003. *Pensar las clases medias: Consumos culturales y estilos de vida urbanos en la Argentina de los noventa.* Buenos Aires: La Crujía.

Zapponi, Elena. 2007. "La individualización contemporánea de la noción de amor a Dios." *Apuntes de investigación del CECYP,* no. 12:103–30.

Zavisca, Jane. 2005. "The Status of Cultural Omnivorism: A Case Study of Reading in Russia." *Social Forces* 84, no. 2:1233–55.

Zelizer, Viviana. 2005. *The Purchase of Intimacy.* Princeton, NJ: Princeton University Press.

Zerubavel, Eviatar. 1996. "Social Memories: Steps to a Sociology of the Past." *Qualitative Sociology* 19, no. 3:283–99.

Zolberg, Vera. 1990. *Constructing a Sociology of the Arts.* New York: Cambridge University Press.

Zorbaugh, Harvey Warren. 1929. *The Gold Coast and the Slum.* Chicago: University of Chicago Press.

INDEX